SPIRALGUIDE

Travel With Someone You Trust®

Contents

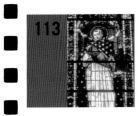

Original text by Teresa Fisher and Tim Jepson
Revised and updated by Apostrophe S

Edited, designed and produced by AA Publishing, a trading name
of AA Media Limited, whose registered office is Fanum House,
Basing View, Basingstoke, Hampshire RG21 4EA.
Registered number 06112600.

Published in the United States by AAA Publishing,
1000 AAA Drive, Heathrow, Florida 32746-5063.
Published in the United Kingdom by AA Publishing.

ISBN: 978-1-59508-426-2

Cover design and binding style by permission of AA Publishing
Color separation by AA Digital Department
Printed and bound in China by Leo Paper Products

A04190
Maps in this title produced from mapping © MAIRDUMONT/Falk
Verlag 2011
Transport map © Communicarta Ltd, UK
(except pp180–181 & 202)

The Magazine

A great holiday is more than just lying on a beach or shopping till you drop – to really get the most from your trip you need to know what makes the place tick. The Magazine provides an entertaining overview to some of the social, cultural and natural elements that make up the unique character of this engaging city.

Who's Who
OF THE MEDICI

Few cities are as closely linked to one family as Florence is to the Medici, the powerful dynasty who ruled the city almost continuously for over three centuries and whose generous patronage of the arts contributed to the city's Renaissance revival. Everywhere you go in Florence, the Medici name crops up.

Lorenzo de Medici with the Sasseti family

Giovanni di Bicci – The Banker

The prosperity of the Medici was largely due to Giovanni di Bicci (1360–1429), the founder of the family. He established the Medici Bank in Florence and, thanks to his shrewd business acumen, it soon became the most profitable bank in Europe. Once he'd landed the Pope's bank account, the family's fortune was secured.

Cosimo il Vecchio (the Elder) – Patron of the Arts

It was with Giovanni's son, Cosimo (1389–1464), that the "Medici rule" really began. Pope Pius II called him "King in everything but name" and the city's governing body, the Signoria, bestowed upon him the title Pater Patriae (Father of the Country). Even so, he kept a low profile, rejecting Filippo Brunelleschi's designs for the family palace (➤ 104–105) as too ostentatious and settling for a more discreet symbol of Medici power from which to govern the city.

THE MEDICI COAT OF ARMS

Throughout the city you'll notice the ubiquitous Medici coat of arms: a cluster of red balls on a gold background. Some say it signifies the shield of the legendary knight Averardo, a descendant of the family; others claim they are medicinal pills, recalling the family's possible origins as doctors *(medici);* or perhaps pawnbroker's coins, a symbol of their financial background.

Cosimo inherited his father's financial nous, and increased the family fortune tenfold, but he is best remembered for his ardent support of the arts and humanism during the flowering of the Renaissance in Florence. Keen to build churches, palazzi and libraries that would last a thousand years like the buildings of ancient Rome, Cosimo commissioned the city's finest architects to construct scores of buildings (including the churches of San Marco and San Lorenzo) and appointed some of the greatest artists of the day to adorn them.

He died leaving a peaceful, wealthy city – "the new Rome". He was succeeded by his sickly son, Piero the Gouty (1416–69), who died soon afterwards, leaving Cosimo's grandson, Lorenzo to assume power.

Lorenzo il Magnifico – Poet and Humanist

Lorenzo (1449–92), a humanist and a great poet, was devoted to literary pursuits as well as to affairs of state and promoted the study of Dante, Boccaccio and Petrarch.

His rule was not uneventful: Pope Sixtus IV withdrew the papal account from the Medici

Cosimo de Medici

Detail from a portrait of Lorenzo de Medici "The Magnificent" by Giorgio Vasari

Bank, causing near bankruptcy; then there was the Pazzi conspiracy of 1478 – an attempt by the rival Pazzi family to assassinate Lorenzo and bring about the downfall of the Medici. Following Sixtus's death, Lorenzo befriended the new Pope Innocent VIII, and his son, Giovanni de Medici, was made Cardinal. When, three weeks after Giovanni's consecration, Lorenzo died, the Pope declared, "The peace of Italy is now at an end".

He was right. Two years later, in 1494, Charles VIII of France invaded Italy and Lorenzo's eldest son, Piero, surrendered the city. The citizens instantly drove him out for not having resisted the French King effectively, and, swayed by the persuasive oratory of Dominican monk Girolamo

Savonarola (➤ 70), they formed a republic. (Savonarola was later condemned to death for heresy and burned at the stake in Piazza della Signoria (➤ 60–61).)

Giovanni De Medici – The First Medici Pope

In 1512, the Medici forced their way back into the city, led by Cardinal Giovanni (1475–1521), and the disillusioned Florentines welcomed them back. From then on, the Medici were determined to maintain power, using force if necessary. In 1513, Giovanni was crowned Pope Leo X. He continued to rule Florence from Rome.

Alessandro – A Dissolute and Tyrannical Leader

On Leo X's death, Alessandro (1510–37) took control of the city's government, guided by Pope Clement VII (Giulio de Medici, grandson of Lorenzo the Magnificent, and supposed father of Alessandro) in Rome. Under him the Florentine state became a duchy, but Alessandro proved a corrupt, despotic duke. He was murdered by his cousin, Lorenzaccio.

Cosimo I – A Forceful Ruler

Cosimo I (1519–74) succeeded Alessandro, and immediately set about destroying all opposition: he publicly executed the leaders of exiled republican armies in Piazza della Signoria, and asserted Florentine authority with brute force by attacking the other major cities of Tuscany. Siena lost half its population during one such stampede and, to this day, many Sienese still refuse to set foot in Florence.

Unlike his predecessors, Cosimo I didn't patronize the arts for art's sake, but rather for self-glorification. He did, however, commission Vasari to build magnificent new offices to house his administration *(uffizi)*, and he established a highly effective government machine. Just as well, as his descendants, who nominally ruled Florence for another six generations, preferred the high life to state affairs. Yet nobody ever challenged them. After all, they were the Medici – the all-powerful, invincible dynasty of Florence. When Anna Maria Ludovica, the last in the line, died in 1743, the entire city grieved.

Cosimo I in the Piazza della Signoria

FLORENCE ON A PLATE
The city's food and wine

Whether it's an ice-cream, a picnic bought from a market, or a meal outdoors on a summer evening, eating out in Florence can be every bit as memorable as admiring the city's paintings and sculptures.

A typical Tuscan meal begins with *antipasti* or *bruschetta* (can be spread with olive, anchovy, tomato or chicken liver paste). First courses *(primi piatti)* might include classic Tuscan soups, such as *zuppa di ceci* (chickpea soup) or *ribollita* (a vegetable soup with beans and Tuscan black cabbage, thickened with yesterday's bread). The most traditional pasta dish is *pappardelle con la lepre* (wide noodles with a bolognese-style sauce made with hare). Whatever else you eat here, the chances are beans will feature – notably white cannellini beans: not for nothing do other Italians nickname Tuscans *mangiafagioli* – bean-eaters.

Hearty Carnivores

For *secondi* (the main course), no trip to Florence would be complete without the celebrated *bistecca alla fiorentina* – an enormous steak from Italy's finest beef cattle, the Tuscan Chianina breed. Other popular meat dishes include *arista alla fiorentina* (pork loin with rosemary), named after the Greek *aristos*, meaning "very good", and game – especially *cinghiale* (wild boar) – in season. Many older Tuscan meat dishes are based on

offal, a tradition dating back to ancient times when the patricians ate the meat and the poor got the leftovers. Specialities include *trippa alla fiorentina* (tripe in a rich tomato sauce), *lampredotto* (pork intestines) and *fegatelli* (pork liver sautéed in wine). Once a dying breed, the small street stalls *(trippai)* selling these products are now thriving, as Florentines rediscover their culinary roots.

The Tuscan New Wave

Once upon a time, the only wine you'd find in a Florentine restaurant would have been thin, watery Chianti, produced in the hills south of the city and presented in a distinctive straw-covered flask. Look hard enough today and you'll still find the flasks and as many different types of Chianti as there are paintings in the Uffizi. Some Chianti is still little more than

---

SLOW FOOD

The Slow Food movement began in Turin in 1986, when fast-food giant McDonald's unveiled plans to open its first Italian outlet in Rome. A Torinese journalist, Carlo Petrini, and a group of friends, issued a joke manifesto entitled "Slow Food", which they felt was the opposite of McDonald's implied gastronomic philosophy. What began as a joke spread across Italy, and then worldwide, carrying a message that emphasized the need for superlative ingredients, locally sourced; the humane rearing of animals; the preservation of traditional foodstuffs; and the need for conviviality and pleasure in the business of buying and eating food. Trattorias in Florence embraced by Slow Food include Nerbone (in the Mercato Centrale); Gozzi Sergio (Piazza San Lorenzo 8r); Del Bricco (Via San Niccolò 8r); Del Fagioli (Corso Tintori 47r); and Cibrèo (Via dei Macci 122r).

passable, but much has improved out of sight (bottles with the Gallo Nero, or Black Cockerel, mark are usually a reliable choice). However, most Florentine restaurants now offer Tuscan wines from a huge range of producers, including big names such as Vino Nobile di Montepulciano and Brunello and Rosso di Montalcino, plus new-wave "Super Tuscans", where traditional Italian grape varieties such as Sangiovese (Chianti's staple grape) are mixed with French varietals such as Merlot and Cabernet Sauvignon. But be warned: many of these wines do not come cheap.

A Wafer from Perfection

At the end of meal – or simply when the fancy takes you – do what the Florentines do and have an ice-cream *(un gelato)* instead of an ordinary pudding. In the celebrated Vivoli *gelateria* (Via Isole delle Stinche 7r), Florence has long had one of Italy's best ice-cream parlours. Lately, however, it has been challenged by a new kid on the block, Grom (Via del Campanile, at the corner with Via delle Oche), where one of the house specials – the Crema di Grom, made with organic eggs, biscuits and Valrhona Ecuadorian chocolate – is already a classic.

> A Tuscan market is a joy, but this teeming emporium will stop you in your tracks

Extend your research by trying Carabé (Via Ricasoli 60r), whose Sicilian owners are third-generation ice-cream makers, or Perchè No! (Via dei Tavolini 19r), which has been serving classic vanilla, chocolate and pistachio, among other flavours, for longer than anyone can remember.

Biggest and Best

Markets lend heart and character to most cities, and Florence is no exception, but the Tuscan capital has more of a market than most. Why? Because in the Mercato Centrale, built in 1874, it has the largest covered food hall in Europe. A Tuscan market is a joy at the best of times but this teeming emporium will stop you in your tracks. A fantastic and flamboyant medley of colour and activity, it is crammed with fruit, vegetables, bread, meat, pasta, olive oil and seasonal specialities such as figs, truffles, wild boar, cherries and plump porcini mushrooms. If this market is too much, or too busy, visit the Mercato di Sant'Ambrogio, a neighbourhood market not far from Santa Croce in Piazza Lorenzo Ghiberti (Monday–Friday 7–2).

The Mercato Centrale, its stalls brimming with fresh and other produce, is where locals shop

THE ART OF
Fashion

Milan may be the home of Italian high fashion, but over the years Florence has spawned or nurtured three of the country's biggest and best-known designer names – Gucci, Pucci and Ferragamo.

It isn't just that Florence inspires designers, it is interesting that many of the clothes designed in Milan and elsewhere are actually manufactured in Florence and neighbouring Prato – 75 per cent of all "Made in Italy" textiles, to be precise. Florence also has one of Europe's leading fashion shows, Pitti Moda, and if you want to browse designer stores, then Via de' Tornabuoni and Via della Vigna Nuova contain just about every name you can think of, from Armani and Prada to Versace and Dolce e Gabbana.

Gucci

The key name in these streets, though, is still Gucci, for it was in Florence that Guccio Gucci (1881–1953) founded the firm three generations ago. Guccio had developed his taste for beauty and elegance while working as a lift attendant in London's Savoy Hotel at the beginning of the 20th century. In 1921, he opened a small workshop selling a range of luggage and saddlery – hence the trademark bit and stirrups, derived from the company's humble origins.

Guccio Gucci and his wife

Around the 1950s and 60s, Gucci classics such as the bag with the bamboo handle, the moccasin with the metal bit and the flowered Flora silk scarf were created. The company also adopted the GG logo, taken from the initials of its founder, as an ornamental motif for handbags, accessories and luggage made in Gucci's distinctive tan-coloured canvas and honey-cured leather.

More recently, Gucci went through a tricky period of family infighting, but was restored to health during the tenure of New York designer Tom Ford, and is now one of the fashion world's most powerful global brands.

**Dresses by Emilio Pucci modelled
on the rooftop of the Palazzi Pucci**

Emilio Pucci in 1959 surrounded by his flamboyant designs

Jet-set Darling

The fashion career of Marchese Emilio Pucci (1914–92), the aristocratic Florentine fighter-pilot and war hero turned designer turned politician, began by chance. In 1948, a fashion designer captured him on film on the ski slopes of St Moritz wearing a stylish, sleek-fitting outfit that he'd designed himself. From that day on, ski clothing changed forever and a new fashion empire was born.

Pucci was best known for his opulent colours, supple fabrics and extravagant prints. He dyed silks (using age-old techniques) in rich hues and designed unmistakable patterns using combinations of bright and pastel colours and geometric shapes on silk jersey. There was a time when a Pucci printed dress cost more than its equivalent weight in gold, and no fashionable celebrity or jet-setter boarded a plane without at least one packed in her suitcase. Soon Pucci prints were everywhere – on shoes, handbags, luggage, pyjamas, lingerie – the Apollo 15 crew even carried a Pucci-designed flag to the moon. His designs remain every bit as popular today, and his empire is now directed by his daughter (▶ 133).

Shoemaker to the Stars

Salvatore Ferragamo (1899–1960) learnt his trade as a young boy, making shoes for the people of his village in southern Italy. Aged 15, he emigrated to America and opened a custom-made shoe store in Hollywood. Before long he was crafting shoes for Hollywood stars and would go on to design for the likes of Greta Garbo, Marilyn Monroe and Audrey Hepburn.

On returning to Italy in 1927, Ferragamo chose Florence as a place to settle, playing a pivotal role in the international fashion and the history of shoemaking. His studies of the foot's anatomy and lasts (the wooden forms used to mould the leather of the shoes) led to the invention of the Ferragamo method, a revolutionary technique in the art of shoemaking. In the absence of quality leather during the war years, he experimented with new materials ranging from the legendary cork wedge (created for Judy Garland, patented in 1936 and immediately imitated throughout the world) to uppers in raffia, rope or candy wrapper cellophane.

His family still administers his fashion empire from the original flagship store in Via de' Tornabuoni (which also houses a shoe museum), producing accessories and clothing to accompany the trademark shoes.

Salvatore Ferragamo's store on Via de' Tornabuoni

ARTISTIC PIONEERS
The men who changed history

The Renaissance did not happen overnight, nor did it take place only in Florence, but the Tuscan capital was its crucible, and several of the city's artists were prime movers in the greatest upheaval in Western art.

To understand how Florence's artists changed painting, it's necessary to know what paintings looked like before they took up their brushes. For the most part this is easy, because most paintings looked the same – they depicted religious subjects (usually saints or the Madonna and Child) and looked more or less like Byzantine icons (flat, stylized and lacking in depth, detail or emotion).

The Genius of Giotto
Come the dramatic social changes in the Italy of the 13th century, with increasing wealth and a rise in trade (textiles and banking in particular),

Above: Detail of the *Annunciation* by Leonardo da Vinci, on display in the Uffizi Gallery

such paintings, which had prevailed for hundreds of years, began to look old-fashioned. A new artistic language was needed. But new approaches often need genius, and in Giotto di Bondone, Florentine art found one.

Much about Giotto's life is a mystery, including the place and date of his birth (probably Florence, in 1266). What is beyond doubt is the fact that his iconoclastic approach, along with the work of contemporaries such as Cimabue and Pietro Cavallini, swept away convention, as he filled paintings with narrative incident, emotion, buildings, spatial depth, realistic figures and more. Much of his work is outside Tuscany, in Padua and Assisi, but glimpses of his genius can be seen in Florence in the *Maestà* in the Uffizi and the Bardi and Peruzzi chapels in Santa Croce.

All in Perspective

Many artists developed Giotto's ideas, but at the beginning of the 15th century, one of the fundamentals of painting – perspective – was still not fully understood. Today, its principles seem obvious, learned by school children. To see and use these principles for the first time, however, required genius. That genius was Masaccio (1401–28), whose light burned brightly but briefly – he died aged just 27. His most exalted works are the frescoes in the Cappella Brancacci (➤ 148), paintings so startling that even the Michelangelo came here to make sketches. But one of the earliest, and most dramatic examples of the "new" art of perspective comes in Masaccio's fresco of *La Trinità* (1427) in Santa Maria Novella (➤ 118). On its unveiling, stunned Florentines queued for days to see the painting, unable to believe that what appeared to be a three-dimensional space had been created on a solid wall.

The Trinity by Tommaso Masaccio, in Santa Maria Novella

MARVELS OF MARBLE AND BRONZE
A Florentine Quartet

Florence's surfeit of paintings can obscure the fact that the city also boasts some of the world's greatest works of sculpture. Here are four of the best:

Michelangelo's *David*

The world's most famous sculpture was commissioned in 1501 to symbolize the virtues of the Florentine republic and its freedom from foreign and papal domination. The single block of marble – thin, and riddled with cracks – had been quarried 40 years earlier, and previously defeated many other artists, including Leonardo da Vinci. It took six years to complete and was initially displayed with gilded hair and a skirt of copper leaves, both lost or removed during the statue's tumultuous history. Note the over-large head and hands, designed to emphasize the monumentality of what was always intended to be an outdoor statue viewed from below.

Cellini's *Perseus*

Benvenuto Cellini (1500–71) was a dissolute and swashbuckling figure: multi-talented – he was among the finest goldsmiths of any era – a braggart, bully and self-confessed murderer who was forced to flee countless cities for innumerable crimes (including, at one point, stealing the Pope's jewels). *Perseus* (1545), in the Loggia dei Lanza (formerly the Loggia della Signoria, is his masterpiece. During its casting – which many thought would be impossible – Cellini stoked the furnaces so high that his house caught fire. As the inferno raged, and the bronze threatened to cool too soon, he threw all available metal (including cutlery and the family pewter) into the mix. Two days later, when the bronze had cooled, the figure was revealed complete save for three toes, which were added later.

The Rape of the Sabine Women

Cellini's *Perseus* would overshadow most sculptures, but not its companion in the Loggia dei Lanza, *The Rape of the Sabine Women* (1583) by the French-born sculptor Giambologna (1529–1608). Carved

Clockwise: *David; The Rape of the Sabine Women; Mary Magdalene; Perseus*

from one of the largest blocks of marble ever seen in Florence, the work conveys extraordinary movement and energy, Giambologna having extracted three intricately entwined figures in a violent spiral motion from the stone's awkward shape. The sculptor had no ambition other than to create a study of an old man, young man and young woman. The sculpture's present name was coined later.

Mary Magdalene

The life of Donatello (*c*.1386–1466) lacked the soap-opera drama of Cellini or Michelangelo, but his sculpture was every bit as innovative and touched with technical and artistic genius. His figure of *St George* (for Orsanmichele) features the first rigorous use of perspective in Western art, but the figure of *Mary Magdalene*, created in 1455 (and now in the Museo dell'Opera del Duomo), is even more revolutionary; almost modern and expressionist in its unsettling realism. Carved from a block of poplar, it shows a withered Mary after her 30 years' atonement in the wilderness, covered only by her hair, her form emaciated but filled with extraordinary spiritual power.

PLEASURE DOMES
How the other half lived

Wealthy families such as the Medici could display their immense riches in the shape of paintings and sculptures, but a vast palace – the bigger the better – made a more powerful statement.

One of the first, the Palazzo Medici-Riccardi (1444; ➤ 104–105), was built for the Medici by Michelozzo, who championed the use of rustication – building with vast, rough-hewn blocks of stone – to unite, as he put it, "an appearance of solidity and strength with the light and shade so essential to beauty under the glare of an Italian sun." The style would influence palaces across the city and beyond for a century. But Michelozzo was being disingenuous. The reason rustication was so popular was that palaces for the likes of the Medici had to be as much fortresses in times of trouble as places to live.

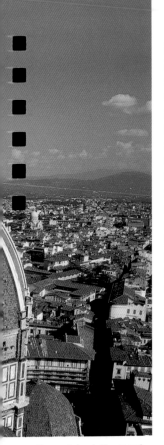

Florence's iconic Duomo and the red-tiled roofs of the city

Classical Order

Giovanni Rucellai was a merchant grown wealthy on *oricello*, Florence's famous red dye, from which his family took its name. In 1446 he commissioned Leon Battista Alberti to build him a palace. Alberti was a man with firm ideas about what constituted good architecture, and the Medici's penchant for rustication was not among them. Only the house of a tyrant can look like a fortress, he wrote. Instead, his palace was the first in the city to make use of the old Classical orders (Doric, Ionic and Corinthian), which are woven into a delightful facade that contains the Rucellai family emblem (Fortune's sail) entwined with trios of Medici rings, an allusion to the marriage of Rucellai's son to a granddaughter of Cosimo de Medici.

Size is All

The type of palace Alberti abhorred is exemplified by the nearby Palazzo Strozzi (► 127), a colossal memorial in stone to banker Filippo Strozzi, once called the "first man of Italy" and the head of the city's anti-Medici faction. He bought and demolished a dozen townhouses to make way for the palace, designed by Giuliano da Sangallo. Building continued for almost half a century until 1536, incorporating both rustication and a more classically inspired cornice. It was the last of almost a hundred palaces built in the city during the 15th and 16th centuries.

The Medici – Again

Not the last ever, however, for the Medici emerged again to create an even larger palace in the overblown shape of the Palazzo Pitti (► 142–147). The building was begun on a more modest scale in 1457 by Luca Pitti, a wealthy banker. Pitti died in 1472, and by 1549 his family had fallen on such hard times that it was forced to sell out – to Cosimo de Medici. By the time Cosimo, or more precisely his wife, had finished with the palace, it was three times its original size, and would be the Medici's home until the dynasty's demise almost 200 years later.

VINTAGE RETAIL

One of the joys of exploring Florence's streets is stumbling across the city's little-known traditional shops, from centuries-old pharmacies to historic gems selling everything from fine silk to marbled paper. Here are the best, in order of the year they were established.

1561 Farmacia SS Annunziata (▶ 111) has beautiful old wood cabinets stocked with natural skin, hair and other products in its elegant signature black-and-white packaging. Many are made to recipes that are unchanged in almost 500 years. *Via dei Servi 80r.*

1612 Officina Profumo-Farmaceutica di Santa Maria Novella (▶ 126) is the most famous pharmacy in Italy, and one of the oldest in the world. Many products are made to original recipes devised by Santa Maria's Novella's monks. *Via della Scala 16.*

1720 Filistrucchi specializes in the finest human-hair wigs, masks, make-up, beards and other props for private and commercial use in film, theatre and television. Numerous worldwide stars are discreet clients. *Via Giuseppe Verdi 9.*

1786 Antico Setificio Fiorentino supplies exquisite silks still made on original looms and according to traditional Florentine techniques. By appointment Monday to Friday 9–1 and 2–5 (tel: 055 213861). *Via Lorenzo Bartolini 4.*

1865 Giulio Giannini & Figlio (▶ 156) specializes in Florence's traditional marbled paper, all in Giannini's distinctive patterns. It comes in sheets or covers books, journals, frames, bookplates and other stationery. *Piazza de' Pitti 37r.*

1857 Sbigoli Terrecotte offers a vivid collection of beautiful hand-painted Tuscan terracotta and other ceramics. Buy anything from a mug to a ceramic-topped table. *Via Sant'Egidio 4r.*

1889 Gino Campani Cornici is typical of Florence's many tiny, specialized artisans' workshops, selling handmade picture frames in numerous styles. Custom frames can be made up in about a week. *Via dei Servi 22r.*

1895 Castorina (➤ 156) is one of many workshops in the Oltrarno district, and offers mouldings and carved wood objects, with a vast choice of wood, finish, inlay and pattern. *Via di Santo Spirito 13–15r.*

1918 Bronzista Baldini has hundreds of objects in bronze, many handmade to original 16th-century designs – anything from swans, angels and cherubs to flowers, dolphins and towel racks. Designs can be made to order. *Via Palazzuolo 101–103r.*

1919 Madova may only sell gloves, but what gloves: sumptuous leather, classic styles, every colour under the sun, and linings of silk, lambswool or cashmere. *Via de' Guiciardini 1r.*

1931 Del Moro is the only place to go in Florence if you want the finest hats, made on traditional wooden moulds in the best velvet, wool, leather, felt or straw. *Lungarno delle Grazie 18.*

1954 Fonte dei Dolci (➤ 110) is the Florentines' first port of call for sweets, chocolates, biscuits and other confectionary (plus Tuscan savouries), all beautifully presented and packaged. *Via Nazionale 120–122r.*

Officina Profumo-Farmaceutica di Santa Maria Novella

THE POET'S PATH

Dante Alighieri, Italy's greatest medieval poet, hailed from Florence, and loved, lived and wrote in the city before he was banished from his birthplace to die in exile.

Dante's Beloved

Dante Alighieri was born in Florence into a minor noble family in 1265, and baptized in the Battistero as Durante – later contracted to Dante. Just a few streets away, he is said to have sat on the Sasso di Dante (Dante's Stone, between Via dello Studio and Via Proconsolo) and watched the construction of the cathedral. At the end of Via dello Studio is the Palazzo Salviati, birthplace of Beatrice Portinari, Dante's lifelong muse, who he described as, "not of mortal man but of God." The palace courtyard contains the Nicchia di Dante (Dante's Niche), from which he spied on his beloved as a child. Close by, in Via Dante Alighieri – no one knows exactly where – is the original house of Dante's birth. The Casa di Dante (► 72–73) is a reconstruction of a house in the vicinity where he lived.

Love Lost

Sadly for Dante, Beatrice had been promised to another, and at 17 she married Simone de' Bardi. Seven years later she was dead. Dante had been betrothed (aged 12) to Gemma Donati, whom he probably married in the church of Santa Margheria de' Cerchi on Via Santa Margherita. The porch features the Donati family crest, and the interior contains several tombs of the Portinari – for this was the parish church of Beatrice's family. Dante's own parish church, San Martino del Vescovo, is nearby.

Dante Aligheri and The Divine Comedy by Domenico Michelino (left); Museo Casa di Dante

Path to Exile

Dante was educated, not in Florence, but in Bologna and Padua and he went on to pursue a political and military career. No politician of the time could escape Florence's factions, and in particular the split between the White and Black Guelphs, the city's ruling party. In 1289 Dante fought for Florence against the Ghibelline faction of the city of Arezzo. In 1302 Dante's White Guelph sympathies, and the triumph of the Blacks, saw him exiled from the city. He never returned, spending the years before he died (in Ravenna in 1321) wandering Italy and writing the epic on which his fame is based, *La Divina Commedia,* or *The Divine Comedy*.

The Bitter End

From the time Dante was exiled he signed himself "Dante Alighieri, a Florentine by birth but not by character," reserving some of the most vitriolic passages in *The Divine Comedy* for Florence, a city of "self-made men and fast-got gain" – and Florentines, who he famously described as *"avara, invidiosa e superba"* – mean, envious and proud. And so Dante was lost to Florence, but not, 700 years later, to those who can still find echoes of the poet in the city's ancient streets.

ENLIGHTENED
Florence
The Ground-Breaking Years

Florence is best known for the Renaissance, which saw the transformation of Western art, the birth of modern science and the development of political thought.

Birth of a City

Florence would not have existed but for the Etruscans, the pre-Roman race that dominated much of central Italy and who founded Fiesole, in the hills above the present city. They were eventually overcome by the Romans, who set up a camp by the Arno from which they hounded the Etruscans into submission. In 59BC, Julius Caesar's agrarian law provided land to retired army veterans, including the area around the camp, creating the conditions for Florence's more permanent establishment and early growth. By the nineth century Florence was part of the massive Holy Roman Empire and ruled by the Margraves. The first city-state, or *comune*, was formed in the early 12th century and the foundations of the modern city began to immerge.

The Flowering Renaissance

Prospering trade brought a strong banking system to medieval Florence with wealthy bankers emerging as the new patrons of the arts. The stage was set for the Renaissance or rebirth, a cultural movement that burgeoned in the city. With the emergence of two great artists, Leonardo da Vinci (1452–1519) and Michelangelo (1475–1564), these combinations were truly dynamic. It was not only in the field of art that Leonardo brought the city into the limelight, he also instigated exploration into engineering and science.

Scientific Revolution

From the 15th century the development of science gathered momentum. Leonardo was producing drawings relating to anatomy and nature; he

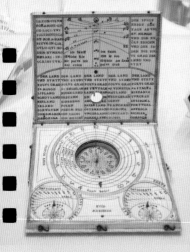

was conducting experiments and creating aerodynamic plans, even producing innovative designs for flying machines. Moving into the 16th century, one man dominated the scientific scene. Often regarded as "the father of science", Galileo Galilei (1564–1642) had strong links with Florence and had the patronage of Florentine bankers and the Medicis. His revolutionary study of mechanics and astronomy, and his improvement to the telescope, are among the most significant scientific developments in history.

Top left and top right: Instruments from the Museo di Storia della Scienza
Above: Michelangelo's *Pieta* in the Museo dell'Opera del Duomo, Florence

Political Thought

If art and science feature strongly in the ascendancy of Florence, then its contribution to politics was also dominant. Another key name of the Renaissance was Niccolò Machiavelli (1469–1527) whose masterpiece *The Prince*, an analytical work linking political science and reason with the study of human nature, set a precedent for political thought for generations. Florence may have later lost its dominance in Europe but these early pioneers left their mark, not only in Italy but also throughout the world. Florence may now be seen as a shrine to beautiful art and a jewel basking in its Renaissance glory but the latest politician to breathe new life into the city, mayor Matteo Renzi, brings with him a host of reforms he intends to implement (► 34).

THE PAST AS PAGEANT
Florence's festive year

The Tuscan capital offers several colourful events with their roots in the city's rich history, as well as a full calendar of artistic, cultural and other festivals.

Florence wastes no time when it comes to festivals. As early as New Year's Day it is into its stride, when the Sfilata dei Canottieri sees a regatta of traditional boats on the River Arno. In April, the Diladdarno is three weeks of music, exhibitions and street events that celebrate the history of Oltrarno. But fairs and events take place across the city year-round – contact tourist offices or visit www.firenzeturismo.it for full details.

Easter Explosion

Florence's major religious festival is the Scoppio del Carro, literally the "Explosion of the Cart", which takes place on Easter Sunday, commemorating a legend from the time of the Crusades about the lighting of a holy flame. A team of six white oxen hauls a cart from the Porta a Prato, one of the city's medieval gates, to Piazza del Duomo, the catch being that the cart is filled with fireworks. During the midday Mass, a "dove" flies down a wire from the high altar and ignites the cart's load.

The Big Match

Religion is also the pretext for the most colourful of Florence's festivals, the Calcio Storico, a soccer tournament. Piazza Santa Croce hosts the first game on 24 June, the feast day of St John the Baptist, the city's patron saint. But this is no ordinary game: the teams wear medieval costume; each team contains countless players; and rules are conspicuous by their absence. The result is mayhem. The event commemorates a game that took place during a siege of the city in 1530. Four teams take part, representing Florence's medieval quarters – Santa Croce, San Giovanni, Santo Spirito and Santa Maria Novella. The victors win a calf, which is roasted and shared by the teams and inhabitants of the winning quarter.

Culture and Crickets

The Maggio Musicale (www.maggiofiorentino.com), one of Europe's most prestigious musical festivals, takes place at venues around the city between late April and early June. Also more restrained is the charming Festa della Rificolona (7 September), a procession of children bearing lanterns to Piazza della Santissima Annunziata to mark the Virgin's birthday. Equally charming is the Festa del Grillo (first Sunday after Ascension) in Cascine Park, when amid the many stalls, people sell cages containing crickets, which are bought and then released – perhaps a throwback to the tradition by which men serenaded their lovers by leaving crickets to "sing" on their doorsteps.

The opening ceremony for the Calcio Storico in Piazza della Signoria

THE PAST PRESERVED
Restoring a city

Time does not stand still for works of art, and Florence's vast cultural patrimony means that the city is engaged in a constant battle to safeguard its thousands of paintings and sculptures.

Piazza Santa Croce after the floods in 1966

Restoration is a never-ending task in Florence. As the cradle of the Renaissance, the city now shoulders a huge responsibility – to preserve its artistic heritage. Consequently, it is one of the leading centres for art restoration, with projects large and small almost constantly underway, from major buildings and works of art to the tiny workshops of Santo Spirito and Santa Croce, where craftsmen lovingly repair their many treasures.

Wake of the Flood

Restoration has always been a fact of Florentine life, but never was it more important than in the wake of the infamous flood of 1966, when the Arno burst its banks after 40 days of continuous rain, including 50cm (19.7 inches) in the two days before the disaster. Around 500,000 tonnes of mud and water crashed through the city in the first, lethal wave, killing 35 people and destroying homes. In places the water rose 6m (20 feet) above street level, filling cellars – including those of the Uffizi.

Restoration experts at the time estimated it would take 20 years for all the damaged treasures to be restored, but nearly 40 years later about a third are still undergoing repair. The institution hardest hit by the flood was the low-lying National Library, with 1.5 million volumes damaged (a million beyond repair). Until this time, not a great deal was known about paper restoration but as a direct consequence of the disaster the world's top experts hurriedly pooled their know-how and devised new drying methods, chemical treatments and rebinding techniques.

Golden Boy

Restoration techniques continue to evolve in Florence, and in 2008 laser technology helped clean and reveal secrets hidden for years as Donatello's bronze statue of *David* (➤ 64), created in the 1440s, received its first facelift in more than a century. With a laser normally used for treating the eye condition glaucoma, restorers at the Bargello have not only removed layers of wax, oils and pigment – added in the 18th century by the Uffizi to make the statue darker to match other sculptures

Restoring a painting after flood damage

in its collection – but also revealed that Donatello added gold leaf to the statue to highlight the figure's clothing. The laser penetrated the layers of grime and the surviving gold leaf without causing any damage.

Chequered Past

The restoration of an even more famous statue, Michelangelo's *David*, in 2004, was not quite as straightforward. The statue has had a long and turbulent history. As early as 1527, someone threw a bench out of the window of the Palazzo Vecchio, breaking his left arm in three places. In 1544, his left shoulder fell off, killing a peasant who had come to pay his respects to Cosimo I. And for centuries, until 1873, when it was taken to the Accademia, the statue had resided outside in Piazza della Signoria, at the full mercy of the elements. Even after being taken to the Accademia, it was kept wrapped up for nine years while the classical tribune, built to house the figure, was completed. When eventually revealed, the statue was covered in mould. The final straw came in 1992, when a madman smashed the left foot with a hammer. In 2004, a controversial restoration saw abrasive powders used to remove some of the grime, though critics say the cleaning was over-harsh and damaged the figure.

NOT JUST A STAGE SET
Florence Moving On

Subject to contrary belief, Florence is no longer just about the past. If you study the city a little closer you will see that it is slowly developing a progressive, innovative side to its personality.

Looking to the Future

It's possible to think that Florence is set in a Renaissance time warp. Thousands of tourists come every year to soak up the atmosphere of historic buildings, immerse themselves in art galleries, gaze at monumental statues and eat traditional Florentine food. However, although that is still very much the essence of Florence, there are signs that the city has started to embrace the 21st century and is moving with the times.

Modern Face of Shopping and Nightlife

While Florence has a large number of artisan workshops and family businesses, these now have to compete with contemporary stores. Outlet designer shopping is big business, and visitors can now find cosmopolitan restaurants serving international cuisine alongside traditional trattorias. Hip trendy bars are popular, particularly in the Oltrarno district, where fashion guru Roberto Cavalli has invested in Florence's nightlife.

City Infrastructure

Behind the changing face of Florence is a dynamic young mayor Matteo Renzi, who came to office in 2009. Among his campaign pledges, those already implemented include the removal of graffiti, improved safety in Cascine Park, improved public toilet facilities, WiFi points in strategic places and a pedestrian-only Piazza del Duomo. Florence is proud of its heritage; but it wants to be seen as a destination for both cultural and contemporary Italian life.

Above: Roberto Cavalli's shop is on Via de'Tornabuoni in Florence

Finding Your Feet

First Two Hours

Don't be daunted by the prospect of getting to Florence or finding your way around once you're there. The public transport systems are easy to use and there is an excellent road and rail network.

Arriving by Air

Galileo Galilei Airport, Pisa

The main airport for Florence and Tuscany is at **Pisa** (80km/50 miles west of Florence). In addition to scheduled services (including Alitalia, British Airways and Lufthansa), it also handles a number of charter and low-cost companies.

- For further **airport information**, tel: 050 849111 (switchboard), 050 849300 (flight information, daily 8am–10pm; www.pisa-airport.com. Tourist information, tel: 050 849300; www.pisaturismo.it

There are three principal ways to reach Florence from here:
By train A train runs direct to Florence from the airport's own rail station five times a day between 6:40am and 10:20pm. Alternatively, a shuttle runs every 30 to 40 minutes (journey time is five minutes) from outside the airport to Pisa's main rail station, Pisa Centrale. Here you can pick up fast trains to Florence's main station, Santa Maria Novella (www.grandistazioni. it). Journey time to Florence is about an hour. Remember to validate your ticket (► box opposite).
By car It costs less to rent a car for the day and leave it in Florence than it does to take a taxi. There are several **car-rental desks** at the airport including Avis (tel: 050 42028) and Europcar (tel: 050 41081). Pisa Airport is located beside the main A11 Florence–Pisa *autostrada* (motorway). The journey takes around one hour. See Driving, ► 37–38.
By bus Terravision (tel: 050 26080; www.terravision.eu) offers 13 buses daily to Florence Santa Maria Novella station. Buses meet incoming flights from 8:40am to 00:20am. Tickets cost €10 (€16 return). Journey time is 70 minutes. Tickets can be bought at the Terravision desk in Arrivals, online or at several outlets in Florence, including the Hotel Reservation Desk near platform 16 at Santa Maria Novella station. Buses leave from in front of the station for Pisa airport from 3:35am to 7:10pm.

Amerigo Vespucci Airport, Florence

Sometimes referred to by its old name of **Peretola**, this small airport is located just 4km (2.5 miles) northwest of Florence on the plain between Florence and Sesto Fiorentino. It has seen a steady increase recently in both regional and international flights: carriers include Meridiana, Lufthansa and Air France.

- For more **airport information**, tel 055 306 1300, www.aeroporto.firenze.it). For flight information, tel: 055 315874, 055 306 1702 or 055 306 1705 from 6am to midnight.
By car All the **major car-rental firms** have offices here, including Hertz (tel: 055 307370), Sixt (tel: 055 309790), Avis (tel: 055 315588) and Thrifty–Italy by Car (tel: 055 300413) but, considering the short distance involved, you may prefer to take public transport into the centre.
By "Fly by Bus" Bus companies ATAF and SITA run **regular shuttle services** called *Vola in bus* to and from the main bus station or Autostazione Sita, immediately west of Santa Maria Novella station, with departures every 30 minutes from 6am to 8:30pm (then hourly to 11:30). Return buses to

the airport run half-hourly from 5:30am to 8pm, then hourly until 11pm. Look for the light-blue SITA buses immediately outside Arrivals. Tickets (€4.50) are sold on board; the journey takes around 20 minutes. For further information, contact ATAF (tel: 800 424 500; www.ataf.net).

By taxi This is the **most expensive option**. A taxi to the city centre takes 15 minutes or so. Expect to pay about €20, plus possible surcharges for baggage, travelling on Sundays, etc. The rate will be indicated on the meter. There is a **taxi rank outside Arrivals**. For further information contact Radio Taxi Firenze (tel: 055 4242, 055 4390, 055 4499, 055 4798).

Guglielmo Marconi Airport, Bologna

This sizeable airport, 105km (65 miles) northeast of Florence, caters for both **scheduled services** (Alitalia, Air France, BA, Lufthansa, etc) and **charter airlines**.

■ For further **airport information** (flight information 5am to midnight, tel: 051 647 9615;www.bologna-airport.it). For tourist information, tel: 051 647 2113; www.bolognaturismo.info

There are two main ways to reach Florence from Bologna:

By train Frequent, fast trains (two or three an hour) run from **Bologna Centrale railway station** straight to Florence and the journey takes just over one hour. (An "Aerobus" shuttle service (tel: 051 290290; www.atc.bo.it) ferries passengers from the airport to the train station roughly every 20 minutes from 6am to midnight and takes about 20 minutes.) Tickets cost €5 and can be purchased on the bus.

By car You'll find the usual car-rental booths inside **Terminal A** (Arrivals) including Europcar (tel: 051 647 2111), Avis (tel: 051 647 2032) and Maggiore (tel: 051 647 2007).

Arriving by Train

Santa Maria Novella Railway Station

Florence is one of the **main arrival points** for trains from Europe, with direct rail links with Paris, Frankfurt and other major European cities. The station lies right at the heart of the city (tel: 055 235 2595; www.trenitalia.it or www.grandistazione.it).

Rail Travel

When using Italian railways, always remember to validate your train ticket by stamping it in one of the yellow-coloured machines located at the entrance to most platforms. Otherwise the ticket controller on the train may charge you a heavy fine.

Getting Around

Florence is a very compact city, centred around its majestic Duomo (▶ 88–94) in Piazza del Duomo. The best way to see the sights is on foot – indeed, a large part of the city centre, from the Duomo southwards to the Uffizi (▶ 52–59), is pedestrianized.

Driving

Driving in Florence is not easy. Much of the centre is **closed to traffic** and there is a complex one-way system. **Parking** is also extremely difficult in the city centre.

Public Transport

Florence's bus service is relatively foolproof and you can pick up **timetables and maps** for the local bus services from the tourist information offices (► 39) or any ATAF ticket office, such as the one outside Santa Maria Novella train station.

■ Environmentally friendly **electric minibuses** called A, B, C and D ply the main tourist routes. For further information, contact ATAF (Terminal Piazza Stazione, tel: 800 424500, www.ataf.net, open daily 7:15am–7:45pm).

Electric Minibuses

Bus A   Starts at Santa Maria Novella station and heads southwards into the old centre (past Palazzo Strozzi, Orsanmichele, Piazza della Repubblica), then out to the northeast quarters of town to Beccaria.

Bus B   Runs a circular route more or less along the north bank of the Arno from Vittorio Veneto to Piave and back.

Bus C   Runs from Piazza San Marco through the eastern quarters of the city, past Santa Croce, across the river and ends at Santa Maria Sopararno near the Ponte Vecchio.

Bus D   Starts at Santa Maria Novella station and heads south of the river past the church of Santa Maria del Carmine, Santo Spirito and Palazzo Pitti continuing eastwards to Ferruci.

■ Buy tickets from newsstands, tobacconists and bars displaying the bus company sign, or at the ATAF booth on Piazza Stazione. Remember to **stamp tickets** in the small orange franking machines on the bus when you start your journey.

■ A **single ticket** (valid for 70 minutes) costs €1.20 or €2 if bought on board; one valid for 24 hours costs €5 (unlimited buses within the time limit).

■ A *multiplo* gives you four 70-minute tickets for €4.50. A *three-day* (The Giorno) costs €12 and gives you three days' unlimited travel on all buses and trains in the Florence district.

■ An electronic Carta Agile can be purchased for €10 or €20 and offers ten or 20 70-minute tickets. It can be used for one or more people and must be swiped as many times as there are passengers.

■ The Passepartour (€22 adults, €15 for under-5s) offers unlimited travel on ATAF routs for 24 hours, plus the open-top Firenze City Sightseeing Bus.

Taxis

■ **Official taxis** are usually white and can be hired from **official ranks** at the station, Piazza di Santa Maria Novella, Piazza di San Marco, Piazza della Repubblica, Porta Romana and Via Pellicceria.

■ They are not a cheap mode of transport and you must be prepared to pay **supplements** for baggage placed in the boot (€0.62 per item), for journeys between 10pm and 6am (starting fare is €5.70), for travel on Sundays (starting fare is €4.48) and public holidays and for journeys to and from the airport. Generally speaking, when you get into a taxi the meter will be set at €2.64 (plus extra charges mentioned above), then the cost of your journey will be around €0.82 per kilometre travelled, and €0.10 for each 117m (127.5 yards) or 16 seconds stationary.

■ Also beware...if you **phone for a taxi** (radio taxis tel: 055 4390, 055 4798, or 055 4242), the meter starts to run from the moment you book it, *not* the moment it picks you up.

■ Taxi drivers are generally **honest** and all taxis should have a meter. If the driver pleads that it's broken, agree a price before you start.

Useful Websites

- For **general information** try the following:
  www.firenzeturismo.it
  www.enit.it
  www.aboutflorence.com
  www.fionline.it
  www.firenze.net

- For train travel information try the state railways website at
  www.trenitalia.it
- For information on museums, art and history try
  www.museionline.it
  www.commune.fi.it
  www.uffizi.firenze.it

City Centre Tourist Information Offices

A visit to one of Florence's four tourist information offices is a good first port of call for maps and information on what's on. Ask for an up-to-date list of opening hours for all main museums and galleries and for a copy of their annual **Avvenimenti** (Events) booklet for details of temporary exhibitions and festivals (or visit www.firenzeturismo.it).

Main Office
⊞ 196 A3 ✉ Via Cavour 1r
☎ 055 290832 or 055 290833
⊙ Mon–Sat 8:30–6:30,
Sun 8:30–1:30

West City Centre
⊞ 194 C2 ✉ Manzoni 16
☎ 055 23320
⊙ Mon–Fri 9–1

Train Station Office
⊞ 195 D3 ✉ Piazza Stazione 4a
☎ 055 212245
⊙ Mon–Sat 9–7, Sun 8:30–2

East City Centre
⊞ 200 C4 ✉ Borgo Santa Croce
29r ☎ 055 234 0444
⊙ Mon–Sat 9–7, Sun 9–2
(Nov–Mar Mon–Sat closes 5pm)

Street Addresses

- Don't be put off by Florence's **dual address system**. Each street has a double set of numbers: a black or blue number indicates a hotel or private residence, while a red number denotes a shop, restaurant or business.
- Throughout **Spiral Florence** you'll notice that some addresses have the **letter 'r'** after the street number. This stands for **rosso** (red) and therefore distinguishes it from a residential address.

City Tours

There are a number of excellent organized sightseeing tours around the city, the best include:

- Associazione Guide Turistiche Fiorentine (Via Giuseppe Verdi 10, tel: 347 737 8374; www.guidesinflorence.it): this organization offers **academic tours** of Florence and Fiesole (▶ 179–181).
- Walking Tours of Florence (Via Sassetti 1, tel: 055 264 5033; www.italy.artviva.com): **fun itineraries** with such themes as "Beautiful Views of Florence" and "Highlights of the Uffizi".
- Florence by Bike (Via Zanobi 91r–120r/122r, tel: 055 488992; www.florencebybike.it): see the city at a **sedate pace**. Also rents bicycles.
- The Accidental Tourist (Via Roma 647, San Donato in Collina, tel: 055 699376; www.accidentaltourist.com): **cycling and walking** in Tuscany.

Admission Charges

The cost of admission for places of interest is indicated by price categories:
Inexpensive under €4   **Moderate** €4–€6.50   **Expensive** over €6.50

Accommodation

Florence has a wide range of accommodation, but suffers from a shortage of good hotels in the mid-range price bracket. Prices are generally higher than elsewhere in Italy, and you'll need to book well in advance for much of the year. Where you stay is not a vital factor, although the city's least expensive hotels are mostly in the least appealing or least convenient locations.

Grading

The Italian State Tourist Office grades all Italian hotels from one-star (the lowest category) to five-star (luxury). The old *pensione* classification, which referred to a simple hotel or set of rooms, no longer exists, but you may still see one-star hotels calling themselves a *pensione*.

The grading criteria are complicated. Generally one-star hotels are budget options, and often have shared bathrooms or a handful of rooms with private bathrooms; two-star hotels have private bathrooms; and rooms in three-star hotels usually have telephones and televisions. Four-star hotels represent a jump in price and quality, while the rare five-star hotels are a class apart.

Location

In Florence, the main concentrations of one- and two-star hotels are in the streets east of the station – Via Faenza, Via Nazionale and Via Fiume – and the far less convenient streets around Piazza della Libertà on the northeast edge of the city centre. You'll need to take a bus or taxi if you're staying in the latter. The former are far more convenient, but – as in most cities – the railway station district is relatively unappealing (but rarely dangerous).

Noise can be a problem in Florence, even in smart hotels, and it can be worth asking for a room at the back of a hotel or looking onto a central courtyard or garden. Some hotels have double-glazing, but on hot nights – unless there's air-conditioning – you'll probably need to open windows.

Prices

- Prices for every room in a hotel are set by law and must be displayed in the reception area and in each room. Prices can vary within a hotel, so ask to see a variety of rooms if you're not happy with your own.
- Prices should include all taxes, but **watch out for surcharges**, especially overpriced breakfasts *(prima colazione)*, which may or may not be included in the room rate: where it's optional, it's invariably cheaper and more fun to have breakfast in a bar. Good buffet-style breakfasts are becoming more widespread, but a Florentine hotel "breakfast" generally means little more than a bread roll, jam and coffee.
- Hotels may also add surcharges for air-conditioning and garage facilities, if appropriate. Laundry, drinks from mini-bars and phone calls from rooms invariably incur high tariffs.

Booking

- Book all hotels in advance year-round, for Florence doesn't have a low season to speak of – though the quietest months are November, January and February. Easter and June to September are always busy.
- Reservations should be made by phone and followed by a faxed or email confirmation. It is also an idea to reconfirm bookings a couple of days before arrival. A double with twin beds is *una doppia*, and if there's a double bed, *una matrimoniale*. A single is *una singola*.
- Hoteliers are obliged to register guests, so on checking in you have to hand over your passport. It's returned within a few hours, or on the day

of departure. Check-out times range from around 10am to noon, but you should be able to leave luggage at reception for collection later in the day.

■ For information on bed and breakfast options, contact AB&AB (tel: 055 654 0860; www.abba-firenze.it).

■ For late bookings, or further information, contact the Consorzio Florence, Viale Volta 72 (tel: 055 553941 or toll-free in Italy 800 866 022; www.promhotels.it).

Accommodation Prices
Prices are for a double room with private bathroom
€ under €150   €€ €150–€200   €€€ over €200

Alessandra €
Noise is unlikely to be a problem at this two-star hotel on a peaceful back street running from Santa Trìnita (► 129) towards the Ponte Vecchio. The 28 rooms are spacious and some have nice touches such as wooden floors, but only around half have private bathrooms (those with shared bathrooms are cheaper): about the same proportion have TVs and air-conditioning.

➕ 199 E5 ✉ Borgo SS Apostoli 17 ☎ 055 283438; www.hotelalessandra.com

Bellettini €
Like the similarly priced Casci, the Bellettini stands out in its two-star class. The 27 rooms are plain but clean, though half have TVs, and all have telephones and air-conditioning. The atmosphere is welcoming, the breakfasts more generous than in many hotels, and the location – in a small street west of the Cappelle Medicee (► 95–97) – central and convenient.

➕ 195 E2 ✉ Via de' Conti 7 ☎ 055 213561; www.hotelbellettini.com

Brunelleschi €€
The four-star, 96-room Brunelleschi has an excellent central position in a quiet back street between the Duomo and Piazza della Signoria. A wonderful conversion of an historic site, it was designed by Italo Gamberini, and is built round a Byzantine chapel and the fifth-century Torre della Pagliazza, one of the city's oldest-known structures. It even contains a small museum devoted to some of the archaeological treasures unearthed during construction. Rooms and communal areas combine a modern and pared-down look with features that have been retained or copied from the original buildings.

➕ 195 F1 ✉ Via dei Calzaiuoli–Piazza Santa Elisabetta 3 ☎ 055 27370; www.hotelbrunelleschi.it

Casci €
The Casci is one of the best two-star hotels in Florence, thanks to its position (just north of Piazza del Duomo), the warm welcome of its multilingual family owners, a good buffet breakfast, the fair prices, and the range of clean rooms, all of which are decorated in a pleasant, modern style. All 25 rooms have TVs and only a handful look onto the busy Via Cavour (but these have efficient double-glazing). The frescoed main salon makes a delightful place for breakfast. There is free internet access in the hotel lobby where coffee and drinks are available.

➕ 196 B3 ✉ Via Cavour 13 ☎ 055 211686; www.hotelcasci.com

Helvetia & Bristol €€€
The 18th-century Helvetia & Bristol may have rivals for the title of "best hotel in Florence", but none can really compete with the historic pedigree and panache of this elegant five-star retreat. It is located between Via de' Tornabuoni and Piazza Strozzi in the west of the city centre, and its past guests

have included Pirandello, Stravinsky, De Chirico and Bertrand Russell. The decor of the communal areas, 34 rooms and 18 suites is mostly old-world and elegant – antiques, rich fabrics and period paintings – but the facilities and standards of service are modern and efficient. A first choice if money is no object.

✚ 195 D1 ✉ Via dei Pescioni 2
☎ 055 287814; www.royaldemeure.com

Hermitage €€

You need to book early to have any chance of securing one of the 27 intimate rooms at this charming three-star hotel. It owes its popularity to the amiable service, the good facilities (several bathrooms have Jacuzzis), and a superb position almost overlooking the Ponte Vecchio. Not all rooms have river or bridge views, however, and those that do can be relatively noisy, despite double-glazing: if this is a concern, request courtyard rooms. In summer, you can take breakfast on the delightful roof terrace.

✚ 199 E5 ✉ Vicolo Marzio 1-Piazza del Pesce ☎ 055 287216;
www.hermitagehotel.com

JK Place €€

This small, ultra-chic townhouse hotel is Florence's first boutique hotel, with 20 elegant rooms, decorated with antique furnishings and contemporary art. Home comforts include a log fire, home-made cakes, a profusion of fresh flowers and breakfast in bed. There is also a library and a roof terrace for balmy summer evenings, with exceptional views. The JK Lounge is a new sophisticated bar and restaurant, its chic pink room is particularly striking for a pre-dinner drink.

✚ 195 D2 ✉ Piazza Santa Maria Novella 7
☎ 055 264 5181; www.jkplace.com

Loggiato dei Serviti €€

Although this hotel isn't the best-located of Florence's three-star hotels – you'll have a longish walk to most sights – there are few complaints about its tremendous sense of style and good taste. The 38 rooms and four suites vary in size and individual decoration, but all have a largely serene and minimal look – a nod to the building's original 16th-century role as a Servite monastery – that is lightened by fine fabrics and the occasional painting and antique. Choose between rooms that look over Brunelleschi's piazza or the gardens of the Accademia delle Belle Arti to the rear.

✚ 196 C3 ✉ Piazza SS Annunziata 3 ☎ 055 289592; www.loggiatodeiservitihotel.com

Morandi alla Crocetta €€

This three-star gem bears the cultivated stamp of its ex-pat owner, Kathleen Doyle, who has lived in Florence since she was 12. Her charm and good taste pervade the hotel's 12 rooms, all of which – while individually decorated – boast antiques, attractive fabrics, period prints and paintings, and colourful rugs laid over polished wooden floors. The nicest room features fragments of fresco from a converted chapel from the monastery that once occupied the site. Via Laura lies east of Piazza della Santissima Annunziata, so the hotel doesn't have a terribly convenient location, but such is its appeal that you'll still have to book well in advance to secure one of its rooms.

✚ 196 C3 ✉ Via Laura 50 ☎ 055 234 4747; www.hotelmorandi.it

Westin Excelsior €€€

Dominating Piazza Ognissanti overlooking the River Arno, this hotel is a showpiece in its own right, housed in a stunning Renaissance palace. Frescoes, coffered ceilings and marble blend perfectly with modern technical innovations and high standards of service and comfort. A feature is the roof garden where you will find the hotel's restaurant and bar, ORVM, a glass edifice with breathtaking views from the outside terrace.

✚ 194 B1 ✉ Piazza Ognissanti 3 ☎ 055 27151; www.westinflorence.com

Food and Drink

Eating and drinking in Florence can be every bit as memorable as the city's museums and galleries. Restaurants run the gamut, from Michelin-starred gastronomic temples to one-roomed trattorias with simple cooking and rudimentary decor. There's also a broad range of cafes and bars.

Places to Eat

The differences between types of restaurant in Florence is becoming increasingly blurred. Once, a restaurant *(una ristorante)* was smart and expensive, a *trattoria* was simple and cheap, an *osteria* even simpler and cheaper, and a *pizzeria* a no-frills place to fill up on pizza and little more. These days, the old-style trattoria – typically with red-checked tablecloths and wicker-covered bottles of Chianti – is fast disappearing, to be replaced by a more modern type of eating place (often called an *osteria*) with young attitudes to style and cuisine. The term *ristorante* can now be applied to most eating establishments, and pizzerias now often serve a range of pastas, salads and other main courses. The chief thing to remember is that price and appearance are no guarantee of quality.

Other terms you may come across are *enoteca*, which means wine bar, and usually indicates a place to buy wine by the glass or bottle and the chance to eat a limited selection of light meals or snacks. A *fiaschetteria* or *vinaio* is similar, but often much simpler; these were once found all over Florence – today, they're a dying breed. The same cannot be said of the *gelateria*, or ice-cream parlour, a mainstay of just about every Italian town or city.

Eating Hours

- Bars open from 7am or earlier to serve **breakfast** *(la colazione* or *la prima colazione)* which generally consists of coffee (cappuccino or caffè latte) and a plain or filled sweet croissant *(una brioche)*.
- **Lunch** *(il pranzo)* starts around 12:30 and finishes at about 2, although most restaurants stay open a little later.
- **Dinner** *(la cena)* begins at about 8, although many restaurants open before this to cater for tourists used to dining earlier.
- Bars that are busy in the day usually close at around 8 or 9pm, but there are plenty of **late bars** or bars such as Rex (► 82) that are aimed more at the nocturnal visitor.

Meals

- Italian meals start with *antipasti*, which are followed by a first course, or *il primo*, of pasta, soup or rice. The main or second course *(il secondo)* is the meat or fish course, and is accompanied by vegetables *(contorni)* or salad *(insalata)*, which are usually served separately. Fruit *(frutta)* or cheese *(formaggio)* are often served as an alternative to *dolce* (pudding). For more information on Tuscan specialities ► 10–13.
- Most meals are accompanied by bread *(pane)* and mineral water *(acqua minerale)*, for which you pay extra. Ask for mineral water fizzy *(gassata)* or still *(non gassata)*.
- Meals are followed by grappa, a bitter digestif such as *amaro*, an espresso coffee *(un caffè)*, or an infusion such as camomile – note that Italians never drink cappuccino after dinner.
- You are not obliged to wade through every course – at lunch or in less expensive restaurants it is perfectly acceptable to have a pasta and salad and little more. More expensive and popular restaurants, however, may take a dim view of such an approach, especially at dinner.

Cafes and Snacks

■ In cafes and bars it always **costs less to stand at the bar** – prices for bar service and for sitting down *(terrazza* and *tavola)* should be listed by law somewhere in the bar. If you choose to order at the bar, the procedure is to pay for what you want first at the separate cash desk *(la cassa)* and then take your chit *(lo scontrino)* to the bar and repeat your order. You cannot pay at the bar. If service seems slow, a coin placed on the bar as a tip with your *scontrino* often works wonders.

■ If you sit down, then a waiter will take your order. It's very bad form to pay at *la cassa* and then try to sit down – the owner or waiter will soon appear to move you on if you try. If you do pay to sit down, however, you can sit for almost as long as you wish having made a single purchase.

■ Cafes and bars are excellent sources of sandwiches *(tramezzini),* filled rolls *(panini)* and – sometimes – light meals. Also look out for small shops or bakeries selling pizza by the slice *(pizza al taglio).*

Set Menus

■ Try to avoid restaurants that seem full of foreigners – they'll invariably be overpriced and sub-standard – and restaurants that offer *un menù turistico* (a tourist menu). Such menus may appear good value and provide you with the security of knowing what you'll pay – but portions are often small, wine (if offered) poor, the food quality third-rate, and the dishes unimaginative (usually a pasta with simple tomato sauce and plain grilled meat with a salad or single side dish).

■ In smarter restaurants, *un menù degustazione* or *menù gastronomico* is one that offers several tasters of the restaurant's signature dishes, and can be a good way of approaching a meal if you can't decide what to eat from the à la carte menu.

Paying

■ The **bill** in Italian is *il conto* – at the end of meal ask for *"il conto, per favore"* (the bill, please). This should come as a formal itemized receipt – if it appears on a scrawled piece of paper the restaurateur is breaking the law and you are within you rights to demand a proper bill *(una ricevuta).*

■ Until recently, virtually all eating places included a **cover charge** known as *pane e coperto* (bread and cover), something the authorities are trying to discourage – if included, it is not optional.

■ Some bills may include service *(servizio):* if they don't, **tip at your discretion**. Round up to the nearest €2–€5 in pizzerias, *enotecas* and other less expensive places; otherwise tip 10 to 15 per cent of the total bill.

Etiquette and Smoking

■ Your fellow visitors may not dress up, but Florentines generally make an effort sartorially when dining out – "smart casual" is good enough for most places, though you should be more elegant in top restaurants such as the Enoteca Pinchiorri (➤ 77) or Alle Murate (➤ 76). Men should wear a jacket and tie for the former.

■ Smoking is now banned in all enclosed public places, including bars, cafes and restaurants.

Restaurant Prices

Expect to pay per person for a meal, excluding drinks and service

€ under €20   €€ €20–€45   €€€ over €45

Shopping

Florence is excellent for shopping. Across the city you'll find a wide variety of shops selling mouth-watering food and wine, exquisite designer clothes, wonderful shoes and leatherware, fine jewellery, sumptuous fabrics, artisan items such as marbled paper, and a host of paintings, prints and antiques.

Specialist Shops

■ Florence is a relatively affluent city, and its chief strengths for shoppers are **luxury goods**, especially leather and high-quality shoes and clothes. The main **designer stores** group in the west of the city on Via de' Tornabuoni and its surrounding streets, notably Via della Vigna Nuova. Shops selling **leather** are widespread, but workshops and mid-market stores centre on the Santa Croce district. **Jewellers** are found primarily on and around the Ponte Vecchio, their home since the 16th century, though you'll find jewellers on most busy city streets. The same goes for **artisans' workshops** and craft shops, though there are concentrations in the Oltrarno, especially on and just off Via Maggio, as well as streets like Via della Porcellana in the west of the city. Here you can buy everything from furniture to marble paper, a Florentine speciality.

■ Via Maggio and its adjacent streets are also home to many of Florence's main **antique shops** and commercial **art galleries**, though such shops are also dotted elsewhere across the city centre.

■ The centre is also where you'll find most of the main **bookshops**, **kitchen** and **household goods** shops – another area in which Italy excels – and **department stores**, of which Coin and Rinascente are best (▶ 80 and 133).

■ **Food** and **wine** are good buys, but check import restrictions on meat and other products if you wish to take purchases home: safe items include pasta, wine, olive oils, most cheeses and specialities such as the spicy Panforte cake of Siena. You can buy good produce in most neighbourhood food stores *(alimentari),* but for the best gourmet and other provisions, head for the superlative **Mercato Centrale** near San Lorenzo (▶ 111).

Markets

■ Outside the Mercato, the streets around **San Lorenzo** are filled with a general market, a good place for inexpensive clothes, bags and souvenirs.

■ Other less well-known markets include **Sant'Ambrogio** (▶ 81), a food market northeast of Santa Croce, and the small flea market, or Mercato delle Pulci, near by in **Piazza dei Ciompi** (▶ 81).

■ Florence's biggest weekly market is held in the **Parco delle Casine** near the River Arno to the west of the city centre every Tuesday (8–1): few visitors come here, and prices for goods of all descriptions are highly competitive.

Opening Times

Opening times for most stores are Tuesday to Saturday from about 8 or 9 to 1 and 3:30/4 to 8. Most close on Monday morning or one other half-day a week, but increasingly, Florence's shops are moving to all-day opening *(orario continuato),* which means Tuesday to Saturday from 9 or 10 to 7:30 or 8. Department stores also open on Sunday.

Credit Cards

Credit cards are accepted in most large shops, but cash is still preferred in small stores: check before making purchases. Non-European Union visitors can take advantage of tax-free shopping on some goods: many shops belong to the Tax-Free Shopping System and will guide you through the procedures.

Entertainment

Florence offers a broad spectrum of entertainment, from world-class orchestras and music festivals to funky bars and huge dance clubs. Most of the cultural entertainment is easily accessible to visitors, although most theatre and cinema presentations are in Italian. The city also hosts several major festivals, most notably the Maggio Musicale, one of Italy's leading classical music festivals.

Information

- The best sources of information are the city's various visitor centres (➤ 39), which generally carry full lists, pamphlets and posters of forthcoming concerts and other cultural events.
- Alternatively, consult the listings section of Florence and Tuscany's main daily newspaper, *La Nazione*, or the monthly *Firenze Spettacolo*, a detailed and dedicated listings magazine. It contains a section in English, but the layout is such that you should be able to understand the listings even if you don't speak Italian. Also try online newspapers such as www.florencenewspaper.it
- The *Guida Gay Italia* and the national monthly gay magazine, *Babilonia* (available from newsagents), provide helpful information for gay travellers. A useful website for information on gay venues and events around the city is www.gay.it/pinklily.

Tickets

Events tickets can be obtained from individual box offices or through **Box Office**, the central ticket agency, with outlets at Via Alamanni 39 (tel: 055 210804; www.boxofficetoscana.it or www.boxol.it, Mon–Fri 9:30–7, Sat 9:30–2).

Festivals

The key festivals in Florence are detailed below, but there are also many more events, information on which can be obtained from visitor centres.

The year opens with the **Sfilata dei Canottieri**, a regatta of traditional boats on the River Arno on New Year's Day (1 January). From mid-March to early April is **Diladdarno**, three weeks of music and events celebrating the traditions of the Oltrarno district. Holy Week (preceding Easter) sees special services and processions held in churches across Florence. The **Scoppio del Carro**, or "Explosion of the Cart", concludes the Easter Sunday ceremonies (➤ 30). May and June see the **Maggio Musicale** arts and music festival, while on 24 June Florence celebrates **St John's Day**, with a parade and fireworks display around Piazza le Michelangelo.

The **Festa del Grillo**, or "Festival of the Cricket", is held on Candlemas, (usually in June). It involves a large market, but traditionally revolved around the sale of crickets in small cages, released for good luck. The most vivid of the city's festivals is the **Calcio Storico (Calcio in Costume)**, three fast, violent soccer games played in medieval dress, on the day after the Feast of St John (see above): other dates are picked from a hat on Easter Sunday. The Virgin Mary's birthday is marked by the **Festa delle Rificolone** (7 September), with street parties, floats and a procession of children bearing coloured lanterns to Piazza della Santissima Annunziata.

Admission Prices

Inexpensive under €3   **Moderate** €3–€6.50   **Expensive** over €6.50

Eastern Florence

Getting Your Bearings

This district represents the very heart of Florence. Here you will find some of the city's finest buildings; its main square and the showcase of its power and might – Piazza della Signoria; and the masterpieces of some of the world's greatest painters in the internationally renowned Uffizi Gallery.

Above left: Neptune Fountain, Piazza della Signoria

Further east, you'll find Santa Croce, Florence's pantheon and one of its most remarkable churches. The surrounding neighbourhood provides a rare glimpse of workaday Florence – an area few tourists penetrate, with lively local markets, tiny workshops and simple homes.

This eastern area also embraces the city's medieval kernel, from the maze of tiny alleyways and hidden lanes of Dante's neighbourhood north of Piazza della Signoria to such imposing civic buildings as the Palazzo Vecchio and the Bargello – once the prison, but now one of Italy's leading sculpture museums. All around are grand buildings, reminders of Florence's prime, when it was among the richest and most celebrated cities in Christendom.

You'll also find the largest selection of shops, bars and restaurants here. By night, this is the liveliest part of town and, with most of its streets pedestrianized and many of the buildings illuminated, the perfect venue for an after-dinner stroll.

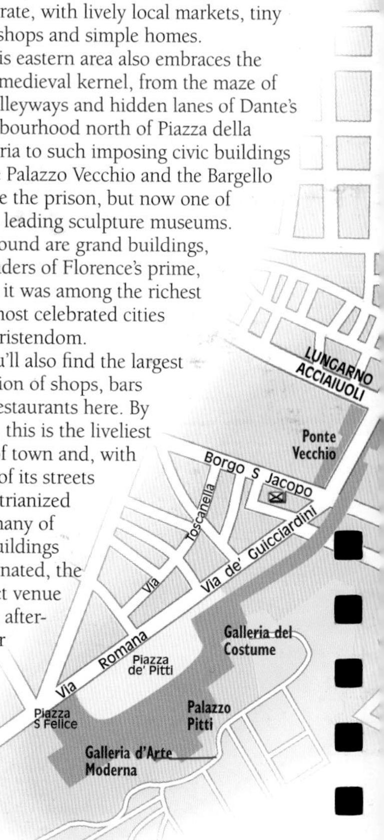
LUNGARNO ACCIAIUOLI
Ponte Vecchio
Borgo S Jacopo
Toscanella
Via de' Guicciardini
Via
Via Romana
Piazza de' Pitti
Galleria del Costume
Piazza S Felice
Palazzo Pitti
Galleria d'Arte Moderna

At Your Leisure

- **5** Museo di Storia della Scienza ➤ 70
- **6** Palazzo Vecchio ➤ 70
- **7** Loggia dei Lanzi ➤ 71
- **8** Orsanmichele ➤ 72
- **9** Casa di Dante ➤ 72
- **10** Badia Fiorentina ➤ 73
- **11** Bar Vivoli Gelateria ➤ 73
- **12** Casa Buonarroti ➤ 74
- **13** Museo dell'Opera di Santa Croce and Cappella dei Pazzi ➤ 74
- **14** Museo Horne ➤ 75

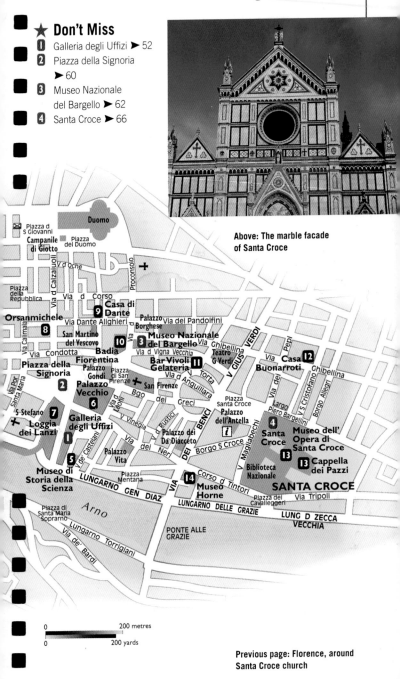

★ Don't Miss

Above: The marble facade of Santa Croce

Piazza d S Giovanni

Duomo

Campanile di Giotto

Piazza del Duomo

V d'Oche

Proconsolo

V d Calzaiuoli

Via d Corso

Piazza della Repubblica

Casa di Dante

9

Via d Corso

Orsanmichele

Via Dante Alighieri

Palazzo Borghese

Via dei Pandolfini

8

San Martino del Vescovo

10

3 Museo Nazionale del Bargello

Via Ghibellina Teatro G Verdi

V GIUS VERDI

Pepi

Via

Casa Buonarroti

12

Via Condotta

Badia Fiorentina

Via d Vigna Vecchia

Chibellina

Piazza della Signoria

Via Por Santa Maria

Palazzo Gondi

Piazza di San Firenze

Bar Vivoli Gelateria **11**

Via d Torta

V S Cristofano

Borgo Allegri

2

Palazzo Vecchio

6

San Firenze

Via d Anguillara

Piazza Santa Croce

Largo Piero Bargellini

S Stefano **7**

Loggia dei Lanzi

Galleria degli Uffizi

1

V Vinegia

Via d Lamberti

Bgo dei Greci

Via d Rustici

Palazzo dell'Antella

VIA DEI BENCI

4 Santa Croce

Museo dell' Opera di Santa Croce

5

Palazzo Vita

Via de' Castellani

Palazzo dei Da Diaccetto

Via del Neri

Borgo S Croce

Magliabechi

13

13 Cappella dei Pazzi

Museo di Storia della Scienza

LUNGARNO GEN DIAZ

Piazza Mentana

Corso d Tintori

VIA

14 Museo Horne

Biblioteca Nazionale

SANTA CROCE

Piazza di Santa Maria Soprarno

Arno

LUNGARNO DELLE GRAZIE

Piazza dei Cavalleggeri

Via Tripoli

LUNG D ZECCA VECCHIA

Lungarno Torrigiani

Via de' Bardi

PONTE ALLE GRAZIE

| 0 | 200 metres |
| 0 | 200 yards |

Previous page: Florence, around Santa Croce church

In Two Days

If you're not quite sure where to begin your travels, this itinerary recommends a practical and enjoyable two-day tour of Eastern Florence, taking in some of the best places to see using the Getting Your Bearings map on the previous page. For more information see the main entries.

Day One

Morning
The **❶ Galleria degli Uffizi** (Uffizi Gallery, ➤ 52–59) is on every visitor's must-see list. Make sure you pre-book or arrive really early (preferably well before the doors open at 8:15am) to avoid the worst of the queue.

Lunch
Enjoy a light lunch at Cantinetta dei Verrazzano (➤ 79) or at Caffè

Italiano, just off **❷ Piazza della Signoria** (➤ 60–61). Complete your lunch break with a coffee on one of the cafe terraces in the piazza and marvel at the mass of statuary in front of you and in the **❼ Loggia dei Lanzi** (left, ➤ 71–72).

Afternoon
It's easy to spend a couple of hours inside **❻ Palazzo Vecchio** (➤ 70–71, pictured above) – the imposing former town hall and home of the Medici family – in Piazza della Signoria. Remember to book in advance if you want to visit the secret passageways.

Evening
Join the immaculately preened locals on their evening ritual *passeggiata* (stroll), window-shopping and people-watching in boutique-lined Via dei Calzaiuoli and Via Roma. Then round off the evening with dinner at Cibrèo (➤ 77).

Day Two

Morning
Spend a couple of hours admiring the dazzling collection of Renaissance statuary and bronzes at the **3 Museo Nazionale del Bargello** (➤ 62–65; exhibits above and below), one of Italy's most important museums. Treat yourself to a mid-morning ice cream at **11 Bar Vivoli** (➤ 73), reputedly the finest *gelateria* in Italy. The various chocolate flavours, including bitter, white and chocolate orange, are particularly delicious. Stay with the sculptural theme at **12 Casa Buonarroti** (➤ 74). Here you can see some of Michelangelo's sketches and his earliest known work.

Lunch
Depending on your budget, you can splash out at Cibrèo (➤ 77), one of Florence's best restaurants or have a snack at Caffè Cibrèo (➤ 78) nearby.

Afternoon
Make your way to Piazza di Santa Croce. Visit the impressive Gothic church of **4 Santa Croce** (➤ 66–69) to see the tombs of many famous Florentines, including Michelangelo, Machiavelli and Galileo. Be sure to visit the **13 Museo dell'Opera di Santa Croce** and the Cappella dei Pazzi (➤ 74) in the two cloisters alongside the church. Afterwards, spend some time in the cloisters, one of the most tranquil spots in Florence. Stroll back to the city centre along the banks of the Arno, stopping en route at the **5 Museo di Storia della Scienza** (➤ 70), a museum dedicated to the history of science and housed in one of the city's oldest buildings.

Evening
Stop at one of the riverside cafes beyond the **Ponte Vecchio** (➤ 122), for an early evening aperitif. Then try out some of the regional specialities at the tiny Buca dell'Orafo (➤ 124).

❶ Galleria degli Uffizi

The Uffizi is a gallery of superlatives: it is one of the greatest art galleries in the world; one of the oldest (inaugurated by Francesco I de Medici in 1581); and the most visited museum in Italy. Other galleries may have more works of art, but what makes the Uffizi's 1,800-strong collection so remarkable is that almost every single painting and sculpture is noteworthy.

The gallery was originally designed to house the administrative offices (*uffizi*) of the Grand Duchy of Tuscany, and the matching pair of handsome arcaded buildings is considered Giorgio Vasari's finest architectural work. The lower floors incorporated a secretariat, the city archives, a church, a theatre and the Mint, while the third-floor corridors, lit by huge glass windows, were lined with antique sculptures and paintings from the Medici villas, along with scientific instruments, arms and other objets d'art. In 1737, Anna Maria Ludovica, sister of Gian Gastone, the last Medici Grand Duke, bequeathed the Uffizi and the entire art collection to the city.

Early Days
Many people think of the Uffizi primarily as a gallery of paintings, but, for a long time after its opening, visitors came mainly to see the splendid collection of Hellenistic and Roman sculptures. In the 19th century these ancient statues were a must for all those on the Grand Tour (an extensive journey round the premier cultural sites in Europe). Edward Gibbon made 12 tours of the gallery before looking at a single painting, and Percy Bysshe Shelley ignored them altogether. John Ruskin's enthusiasm for the Renaissance paintings here, however, encouraged a new breed of visitor to the Uffizi – artists who copied the Renaissance style, giving birth to the Pre-Raphaelite movement. The statuary is still on display – in the vestibule at the top of the stairs, in Room 1 (often closed to the public) and in the main corridors.

Getting In
Rule one: be patient! The Uffizi receives over 1.5 million visitors a year and, for security reasons, only 660 people are allowed in at any one time. There are three clearly marked entrances – one for individuals, one for groups and one for pre-booked visitors

Right: Detail of the head of the Madonna by Fra Filippo Lippi

(► Inside Info, page 59). Each usually has long queues, so make sure you're standing in the right one.

To minimize queuing time, arrive very early (queuing sometimes starts at 7am) or in the late afternoon. The busiest times are weekends, Tuesdays and at lunch-time (between 11am and 3pm). Winter (November–March) is marginally quieter than the summer season. Allow at least half a day for your visit. Be prepared to queue for a couple of hours and reckon on spending at least three hours inside. After that, sensory overload sets in and you'll be ready to visit the bar and lovely rooftop terrace.

Finding Your Way Around

The gallery is located on the third floor: 45 rooms spanning European art from the 13th to the 18th century. The glittering collection of Florentine Renaissance paintings attracts the most attention, but there are many other fine works from elsewhere in Italy (Siena and Venice in particular), Holland, Germany and Spain. Paintings that have been restored are marked with a round red label.

Above: The galleries of the Uffizi and the Corridoio Vasariano fringe the Arno

The museum is very well laid out, with all the rooms arranged by school and in chronological order. Florentine and Tuscan Gothic and Early Renaissance paintings take up most of the East Corridor (rooms 1–15). A short South Corridor (with diverting views of the Arno) connects to the West Corridor, which is devoted to 16th-century Italian paintings (High Renaissance and Mannerism) and works by non-Italian artists, among them Dürer, Rubens, Van Dyck, Rembrandt and Goya. The entrance to the Corridoio Vasariano (see panel, below) is located here, as is a small cafe-bar.

Room 2

This is one of the most fascinating rooms of the entire collection. Here you will find three Gothic altarpieces depicting the **Maestà** (the *Madonna Enthroned*) by Giovanni Cimabue (*c.*1285), Duccio di Buoninsegna (*c.*1285) and Giotto di Bondone (*c.*1310). Each one makes progressive strides towards naturalism and control of perspective, especially Giotto's Madonna (in the centre), whom he portrays as a real woman. Her breasts and knees show through her clothes, her hair can be seen under her veil and her cheeks and lips are pink. By contrast, Cimabue's solemn Madonna (on the right) does not have such realistic features. Duccio's

CORRIDOIO VASARIANO

In 1565, Francesco I commissioned Giorgio Vasari to build an elevated walkway linking the Uffizi with the Palazzo Pitti (► 142–147), so the Medici and their entourage could walk from one to the other without mixing with the hoi polloi. The resulting "corridor" is 1km (0.5 miles) in length and supported on brackets, it crosses the Ponte Vecchio, skirting the Mannelli Tower and the church of San Felicita en route to the Palazzo Pitti. It is lined with a collection of artists' self-portraits. It is well worth trying to join one of the occasional tours (maximum 30 people, minimum ten).

Madonna (on the left) shows the development of the Sienese School, with its great attention to decorative detail and to the alternating use of colour. However, Duccio's Madonna is even less realistic than Cimabue's. Notice how the throne in Giotto's work is firmly on the ground, while angels and saints gather round – even *behind* the throne. This marks the beginning of a major artistic revolution – the use of perspective to provide depth and realism, which was to develop in Florence over the next 200 years.

Below: Looking alongside the Uffizi towards the Ponte Vecchio

Room 3

Simone Martini and Lippo Memmi's lyrical *Annunciation* (1333) and Ambrogio Lorenzetti's *Presentation of Jesus in the Temple* (1342) demonstrate the flowering of 14th-century Sienese painting. The Lorenzetti painting is another example of early experimentation with techniques of perspective.

Rooms 6–7

Gentile da Fabriano's Gothic *Adoration of the Magi* (1423) in Room 6 and Domenico Veneziano's early Renaissance **altar panel with Santa Lucia dei Magnoli** (1445) in Room 7 are further striking and much-loved examples of the development of perspective. Veneziano

Piero della Francesca's diptych portraying *The Duke and Duchess of Urbino*

followed the rules of linear perspective (formulated by Filippo Brunelleschi) in his work to create architectural space. Note also the halos, which appear as transparent circles of gold, painted with depth and perspective, rather than as flat gold discs.

The **diptych of *The Duke and Duchess of Urbino*** (*c.*1465) by Piero della Francesca (in Room 7) is among the best-known portraits in the Uffizi. The Duke wanted to be portrayed faithfully, warts, wrinkles and all, but he always insisted on being depicted in profile to hide his war wound – a disfigurement caused by a sword blow. The town in the Duchess's portrait is Gubbio in Umbria, where she died giving birth to her ninth child and first son. The portrait was painted posthumously.

Room 8

The *Madonna and Child with Two Angels* (*c.*1465) in Room 8 is a masterpiece of warmth and humanity. It was painted by the monk Filippo Lippi, who ran away with a nun – the model for this painting.

Rooms 10–14

These four small rooms, containing Botticelli's most celebrated works, are the museum's most popular. His paintings have an innocent, idealistic quality about them, unlike the work of his contemporaries, who were focusing on perspective, proportion and anatomy. In *Primavera* (*c.*1481), for example, he depicts a perfect forest in springtime – where all the fruit is ripe and all the flowers are in full bloom. Venus and her assistant Cupid are in the centre; on the right is Zephyr, the west wind who joins Flora to give life to Spring (in the floral dress). On the left are the three Graces and Mercury, who's working hard to keep the clouds away from the forest.

Botticelli's *Birth of Venus* (1485) was the last of his mythological paintings and the first "pagan" nude of the Renaissance. By painting Venus instead of Mary, Botticelli expressed his fascination with classical mythology, in common with many Renaissance artists. It is probably the most celebrated painting in the gallery, yet, like so many of the famous works of art here, it still has the power to overwhelm despite its overexposure on calendars and greetings cards.

LA TRIBUNA

The Medici kept their finest treasures in the Tribune (Room 18), a small octagonal room designed to represent the cosmos: the red walls symbolized Fire; the weathervane Air; the mosaic floor of *pietre dure* Earth; and the cupola, with its mother-of-pearl lining, was the heavenly vault. At the time of writing La Tribuna was closed for restoration and is due to reopen in June 2011 when the public will be able to view only from the entrance to preserve the room's delicate furnishings.

Room 15

It is often said that Botticelli brings the 15th century to a close, while the genius of Leonardo da Vinci introduces the 16th, and this room certainly demonstrates that passage from "antique" to "modern". Look for the **Baptism of Christ** (*c.*1470) by Andrea del Verrocchio, Leonardo's teacher. Leonardo helped out by painting the angel in blue (on the left). When Verrocchio saw his work outclassed by his young protégé, he vowed he would never paint again. Alongside is Leonardo's unfinished **Adoration of the Magi** (1481).

Room 25

The **Doni Tondo** (*c.*1505), a circular portrayal of the Holy Family commissioned by Agnolo Doni on the occasion of his marriage to Maddalena Strozzi, is the earliest confirmed painting by Michelangelo. It is striking for its vibrant colours and the unusual, twisted pose of the Virgin. Notice the attention to anatomical detail. A sculptor at heart, Michelangelo was so interested in studying the human body that he attended dissections in order to understand its structure better.

Room of the Niobe, built to house a Roman copy of *Niobe and her Children*

Room 28

Venus of Urbino (1538) by Titian (Tiziano Vecellio) is considered one of the most beautiful nudes ever painted, and

was famously described by poet Lord Byron as "the definitive Venus". The model was possibly Eleanora Gonzaga, wife of Francesco Maria della Rovere, who is portrayed with her clothes on in the painting alongside, together with the same dog.

Rooms 41–45

The final rooms of the Uffizi contain important 17th- and 18th-century **European artworks** including works by Rubens and Canaletto (Room 42), Goya (Room 45), and two Rembrandt **self-portraits** (Room 44).

TAKING A BREAK

The Uffizi has an excellent cafe in the West Corridor (towards the end of the numbered sequence of rooms) and terrace. Alternatively, walk out into the Piazza della Signoria and visit **Caffè Rivoire** (➤ 79).

🚉 200 A5 ✉ Piazzale degli Uffizi 6 ☎ 055 238 8651 (055 294883 or www.tickitaly.com for advance booking); www.uffizi.firenze.it
🕐 Tue–Sun 8:15–6:50. Closed 1 Jan, 1 May and 25 Dec. Last tickets 45 mins before closing 🚌 23 and B 💶 Expensive

This sensual nude by Titian was purchased by the Duke of Urbino – hence its name *The Venus of Urbino*

Madonna of the Goldfinch by Raphael in Room 26

GALLERIA DEGLI UFFIZI: INSIDE INFO

Top tips If you are able to plan your visit, book a ticket by credit card (tel: 055 294883 – five days in advance; or online at www.weekendafirenze.com for the Uffizi and eight other galleries at least 24 hours in advance). Pre-booked tickets specify an entrance time, but you can stay in the gallery as long as you like, and will cut down dramatically on time spent waiting to get in. You pay a small fee and pick up the tickets at the gallery when you visit.

- If you have come especially to see a **favourite painting**, check at the information desk to ensure that it is on display *before* paying the entry fee.
- The **cafe-bar and rooftop terrace** in the West Corridor (beyond Room 45) is a good place to escape the crowded galleries.

In more depth Art **aficionados** will probably want to visit the Uffizi at least twice. Concentrate your first visit on the **Florentine Renaissance** (rooms 1–15) and save the **High Renaissance** and **Mannerism** in Florence (rooms 16–29) for a second visit.

Hidden gems The *Madonna of the Magnificat* (rooms 10–14), notable as one of Botticelli's earliest religious paintings, is every bit as beautiful as the more famous *Primavera* and *The Birth of Venus* but is often overlooked in the clamour to see the more celebrated paintings.

- In Room 26, look for Raphael's *Madonna of the Goldfinch* (*c*.1506), an exceptionally tender painting portraying the Virgin Mary with babies Jesus and John the Baptist caressing a small bird.

2 Piazza della Signoria

Piazza della Signoria is Florence's most famous square. With its daily hubbub of visitors and locals, handsome palazzi, sophisticated cafe terraces and dazzling collection of buildings and statuary, it is also where the city's heart beats loudest.

For centuries the square has been at the centre of Florentine affairs and it was here that Roman Florentia was founded. In the Middle Ages, the land was owned by the Ghibellines (a group of feudal lords who claimed to represent imperial power) but they were eventually defeated by the Guelphs (a rival feudal faction who supported the autonomy of *Comuni* or consular magistracy). The Guelphs destroyed all the Ghibelline houses, decreed that nothing was to be built where the traitors' buildings had once stood, and consequently created the magnificent square as a symbol of their power.

The piazza is dominated by the **Palazzo Vecchio** (➤ 70–71), built at the end of the 13th century. Among the works inside is a bronze *Judith and Holofernes* by Donatello, symbolizing liberty. The bell in the campanile was rung to summon citizens to the square for *parlamenti* (public meetings). In front of the palace, a series of patriotic sculptures graces the *arringhiera* (oration terrace), where orators once stood to "harangue" the citizens. The works include *Marzocco* (a lion with its paw on the coat of arms of the city), named after Mars, god of war and ancient protector of Florence (the original is in the Bargello, ➤ 62–65), and a copy of Michelangelo's *David*, a work regarded as the embodiment of Republican triumph and placed here, rather than in its planned location near the Duomo. Near by is the **Loggia dei Lanzi** (➤ 71–72), which shelters some of Florence's finest sculptures.

Among the other statues in the square is the awkward fountain of *Neptune* by Bartolommeo Ammannati, which symbolizes Cosimo I's naval victories. Nicknamed *Il Biancone* (the Big White One), the work was much criticized by contemporaries, provoking the harsh exclamation (attributed to Michelangelo) "Ammannati, Ammannati, what lovely marble you have ruined!" Cosimo himself is depicted on horseback near the centre of the square (➤ 9).

Palazzo Vecchio towers over the Piazza della Signoria

Above: The statue of *Hercules and Cacus* in the piazza

TAKING A BREAK

An especially pleasant way to admire the square is to sit on the terrace of the classy **Caffè Rivoire** (➤ 79), sipping a cup of its celebrated hot chocolate.

➕ 199 F5   ✉ Piazza della Signoria   🚌 23 and B

PIAZZA DELLA SIGNORIA: INSIDE INFO

Top tip Allow at least **half an hour to admire** the unique collection of buildings and statuary here. Then take time to **people-watch** and to soak up the atmosphere of the busy square.

One to miss Baccio Bandinelli's ungainly statue *Hercules and Cacus* (alongside the copy of Michelangelo's *David*) was described by Benvenuto Cellini as an "old sack full of melons".

Hidden gem Look out for the ravishing **bronze water nymphs** adorning the Neptune Fountain (beside the Palazzo Vecchio).

❸ Museo Nazionale del Bargello

The Bargello houses one of Italy's most important collections of sculpture, with celebrated works by Michelangelo, Giambologna and Donatello among others. It is also the oldest surviving civic building in Florence.

The fortress-like structure has had many incarnations. It was originally constructed in 1255 as the headquarters of the Capitano del Popolo (a post holding supreme authority in the government), then briefly became the home of the *Podestà* (chief magistrate). From the 16th century until 1859, the Medici turned it into the residence of the Bargello (head of police), a torture chamber and the city gaol. Finally, in 1865, after renovation, it became one of the first National Museums of Italy. The building's design, with its mighty battlemented facade and skinny 12th-century tower (which possibly predates the original structure), was so popular that it was used as a model for the grand Palazzo Vecchio (➤ 70–71).

The Courtyard
The museum occupies three floors, centred around a porticoed courtyard with a well and an elegant external stairway decorated with ancient terracotta plaques and coats of arms. Until 1786 this was the scene of executions, and those sentenced to death would spend their last night in the chapel on the first floor. Following execution, their bodies were hung from the windows. It was also customary to paint effigies of condemned men on the wall facing Via della Vigna Vecchia. Evidently, Andrea del Castagno became so good at this that he earned himself the unfortunate nickname "Andrea of the Hanged Men".

Detail from the *Carrand Triptych* by Giovanni di Francesco

Sculptural Highlights
The first room of the museum, dedicated to Michelangelo and his contemporaries, is one of the finest. Michelangelo's best-known sculpture here is his **Bacchus** (1496–97), a witty

interpretation of the god of wine and enjoyment, portrayed in an unsteady, drunken pose. Alongside is a more conventional *Bacchus* by Sansovino (Andrea Contucci).

Other works by Michelangelo include the highly innovative **Pitti Tondo** (c.1504), in which the Madonna's head comes out of the circular frame, adding life and movement to the figures. Michelangelo also used the technique of *non-finito*, whereby some of the marble is smoothed to reflect the light, whereas other parts are left rough and "unfinished", lending depth.

He used this technique again in **Brutus** (1540), the only bust he ever sculpted, to give the face a strong, masculine expression. It is thought that the bust was inspired by an event that occurred three years previously when Lorenzino (known as Lorenzaccio) de Medici was killed by Duke Alessandro, his cousin and a tyrannical ruler of Florence.

Other noteworthy sculptures in the room include a large bronze bust of **Cosimo I** (1548) by Benvenuto Cellini and Giambologna's famous bronze of **Mercury** (1564). You'll find further Giambologna sculptures, including

A PRISONER

Bernardo Baroncelli was one of the Bargello's most notorious prisoners. He was executed here in 1478 for his part in the Pazzi conspiracy – the failed attempt to assassinate Lorenzo the Magnificent – and his body was hung from a window as a warning to other anti-Medici conspirators.

The Turkey and an aviary of other bronze birds (made for the animal grotto at the Medicis' Villa di Castello), on the first-floor loggia.

Adjoining the loggia, the Salone del Consiglio Generale (General Council Hall) contains a host of works by Donatello. In the centre of the room is the **Marzocco lion**, the symbol of Florence that once sat in Piazza della Signoria. To its left stands Donatello's early marble sculpture of *David* (1408–12), remarkable for its attention to detail – originally there was even a strip of leather running from David's right hand to the body of the sling resting on the giant's head. Here too you'll find Donatello's later sculpture of *St George* (1416–20) and his most celebrated bronze – yet another *David* (1440), the first free-standing nude statue by a Western artist since antiquity. If you compare the bronze David with the earlier marble sculpture, it is hard to believe that they are the work of the same artist. Unlike his earlier work, the bronze, inspired by the sculptures of classical Rome, was designed to be viewed from all sides. This was a novel concept in the 15th century, as until then sculptures had been used solely to decorate architecture and the figures' backs were usually against a wall or in a niche.

Finally, look out for Brunelleschi's and Lorenzo Ghiberti's trial bronze panels depicting Abraham about to sacrifice Isaac, their entries to the competition held in 1401 for the commission to create Florence's Battistero doors (➤ 92–93).

If you are short of time, skip the remaining rooms on the first floor and make your way to the colourful, enamelled **terracottas of the della Robbia family** on the second floor. You'll notice similar terracottas on many public buildings throughout the city. Also on this floor is the most important collection of small **Renaissance bronzes** in Italy, comprising animals, statuettes and bells, among other objects, with pieces by Giambologna and Cellini (➤ Inside Info panel, opposite).

Glazed terracotta bust of a woman by Luca della Robbia

TAKING A BREAK

Da Pennello (Via Dante Alighieri 4r, tel: 055 294848, Tue–Sat noon–3, 7–10), an *osteria* renowned for its superb *antipasti* buffet, is excellent for a meal.

➕ 196 B1 ✉ Via del Proconsolo 4 ☎ 055 238 8606. Advance tickets 055 294883 🕐 Tue–Sun 8:15–1:50 (opens later in summer but times vary). Last ticket sold 40 mins before closing; closed 1st, 3rd and 5th Sun and 2nd and 4th Mon of the month and some public hols 🚌 14, 23 and A 💵 Moderate

Right: *Il Pescatore* by Vincenzo Gemito is on display in the Bargello's courtyard

MUSEO NAZIONALE DEL BARGELLO: INSIDE INFO

Top tips You may have to **queue** to get into the museum. Note that last **admission** is at 1:10pm and the staff ask all visitors to leave the museum shortly afterwards.
■ Ideally, allow yourself **a couple of hours** once inside the museum.

Must-sees *Bacchus* by Michelangelo (ground floor).
■ *Mercury* by Giambologna (ground floor).
■ Donatello's bronze, free-standing *David* (first floor).

Ones to miss Don't spend time in the small first-floor exhibition rooms or the Arms and Armour Collection (second floor), unless this is your particular interest.

Hidden gems Look for the medieval **Madonna sculptures** in the Sala del Trecento on the ground floor.
■ Make time to see Giambologna's delightful bronze birds on the first-floor loggia – they are easily neglected en route to Donatello's more famous statues in the General Council Hall.
■ On the second floor, look for *Lady with a Posy*, which is attributed to Andrea del Verrocchio.

4 Santa Croce

Together with the Duomo (➤ 88–92) and Santa Maria Novella (➤ 118–121), the mighty Gothic Franciscan church of Santa Croce was one of three churches funded by the Comune (the city government) as symbols of civic pride. At the time of its construction (c.1294), it was one of the largest churches in the Christian world, reflecting the then immense popularity of Franciscan preaching. The white-, green- and pink-striped marble neo-Gothic facade was added between 1853 and 1863, and the campanile was added in 1847.

Florentine Pantheon

On first impression, Santa Croce's architectural austerity, open timber roof (typical of all Franciscan churches), gloomy lighting and huge proportions give it the feel of a large barn. On closer inspection – with its numerous tombs, funerary monuments and nearly 300 tombstones – it resembles more a cemetery or a museum of religious sculpture. For this is the city pantheon, where the most illustrious Florentines are either buried or remembered, together with wealthy local dignitaries, who paid vast sums of money to be buried alongside them.

The first monument along the right aisle is the **tomb of Michelangelo**, a cumbersome work by Giorgio Vasari incorporating a bust of the great artist and allegorical figures representing Painting (left), Sculpture (centre) and Architecture (right). Michelangelo died in Rome in 1564 and was buried here a few days later. He had previously chosen the spot but, unfortunately, never finished the

Santa Croce's imposing facade draws attention from other buildings

The soaring interior of the Cappella dei Pazzi

Pietà (➤ 103) he'd intended for his tomb – it would have been a more moving memorial.

Other monuments and tombs worth viewing (all in the right aisle beyond Michelangelo's tomb) include those of the philosopher Niccolò Machiavelli (d.1527); composer Gioacchino Antonio Rossini (d.1868); scholar and humanist Leonardo Bruni (d.1444), whose effigy holds a copy of his masterwork, *History of Florence*; and Dante, perhaps the greatest poet of all time, who died in exile in Ravenna, where he was buried.

For centuries, Florentines tried to get Dante's body back and in the 16th century Michelangelo promised to sculpt a magnificent tomb for him. When his tomb in Ravenna was

GALILEO GALILEI

In the left-hand aisle stands one of the most imposing monuments in the church. It is devoted to scientist Galileo Galilei (1564–1642). His body was kept out of sight, beyond the sacristy, for 100 years after his death. The reason? His popularization of the Copernican view of the universe, with the sun at its centre, brought him into conflict with the Church; he was condemned by the Inquisition and denied burial on consecrated ground.

eventually opened it was empty except for a casket containing a parchment scroll written by two monks. It explained how they'd removed his remains for safe keeping lest he be taken back to the city that had once so cruelly banished him.

Treasured Art

At one time the walls of Santa Croce were completely decorated with frescoes by Giotto and his pupils. But, in the 16th century, Cosimo I instructed Vasari to plaster them over while "rearranging" the church. Nevertheless, some magnificent Trecento frescoes have been preserved in the transept, providing a fascinating opportunity to compare the masterworks of Giotto with those of his successors.

The frescoes in the Cappella Peruzzi and Cappella Bardi (to the right of the sanctuary) were painted by Giotto towards the end of his life. Unfortunately, he painted them on dry plaster rather than on more durable wet plaster and, having badly deteriorated, they were covered in whitewash for many years. Eventually restored in 1959, these fragmentary, pastel-hued frescoes count among some of his finest works. The Cappella Bardi shows **scenes from the life of St Francis** (*c.*1317) and the Cappella Peruzzi depicts **scenes from the life of St John the Divine** (right wall) and **the life of St John the Baptist** (left wall), painted between 1320 and 1325. The frescoes are notable for their sense of pictorial space, naturalism and narrative drama, especially those in the Cappella Bardi. See how Giotto conveys the feelings of **St Francis** (above the arch) as he receives the stigmata.

The move towards realism marked a decisive break with the artistic traditions of the preceding century, and the start of the modern era in painting. You can see just how revolutionary Giotto's work was if you compare his frescoes

The cloisters and Cappella Pazzi, on the south side of Santa Croce

with the 13th-century altarpiece here, which also illustrates scenes from the life of St Francis.

The frescoes in the Cappella Baroncelli portraying **scenes from the life of the Virgin** (in the right transept) were once thought to be by Giotto, but they have since been attributed to his pupil Taddeo Gaddi. The scene in which the angels announce the birth of Christ to the shepherds is considered the earliest night scene ever painted in fresco (1338). The Cappella Castellani in the south transept has some later, more decorative frescoes by Taddeo's son, Agnolo, while, in the left transept, the second Cappella Bardi contains a wooden crucifix by Donatello, which was scathingly dismissed by Filippo Brunelleschi as resembling "a peasant on a cross".

Detail of the vaulted ceiling of Cappella Peruzzi, with a series of frescoes by Giotto

Next to the church (to the right as you face the facade), housed in two cloisters, you will find the Museo dell'Opera di Santa Croce and the Cappella dei Pazzi (➤ 74–75).

TAKING A BREAK

Almost alongside Santa Croce (to the left as you face the facade), **Baldovino** (➤ 77) serves a good selection of inexpensive pizzas, light meals or full lunches and dinners.

➕ 200 C5 ✉ Piazza Santa Croce ☎ 055 246 6105; www.santacroce.firenze.it 🕐 Church: Mon–Sat 9:30–5:30, Sun 8–1 for worship only, 1–5:30 for tourist visits. Masses weekdays 8am, 9am, 6pm, Sat 6pm, Sun and public holidays 8am, 9:30am, 11am, noon, 6pm. Closed some public hols 🚌 14, 23 and C 💰 Moderate (plus Cappella dei Pazzi and Museo dell'Opera di Santa Croce)

SANTA CROCE: INSIDE INFO

Top tip Have some **loose change** handy to illuminate Giotto's frescoes and to listen to the polyglot phone commentary.

One to miss The sacristy contains a largely unremarkable collection of reliquaries, missals and vestments from different centuries.

Hidden gems The marble **pulpit** by Benedetto da Maiano is notable for the five intricately sculpted scenes from the life of St Francis.
■ Look for Donatello's relief, the *Annunciation*, in the right aisle. This superb work in gilded *pietra serena* is one of the finest reliefs of the early Florentine Renaissance.

In more depth To see more treasures rescued from the church when it was flooded in 1966, visit the Museo dell'Opera di Santa Croce and the Cappella dei Pazzi (➤ 74–75).

At Your Leisure

5 Museo di Storia della Scienza

In one of the city's oldest buildings, the restored Museum of the History of Science is a must for anyone interested in Tuscan-born scientist and mathematician to the Medici court, Galileo Galilei (1564–1642), or the development of science.

During the 16th century, the Florentines strove to foster scientific knowledge and the collection contains over 5,000 instruments, appliances and mathematical tools, offering insights into such disciplines as chemistry, electricity, magnetics, surgery and gynaecology.

🕐 Jun–Sep Mon, Wed–Fri 9:30–5, Tue and Sat 9:30–1; Oct–May Mon, Wed–Sat 9:30–5, Tue 9:30–1. Closed some public hols. Last tickets 30 mins before closing 🚌 23 🎫 Moderate

6 Palazzo Vecchio

The Old Palace, with its solid, rusticated facade, crenellated roof and bell tower 94m (308 feet) high, is outstanding among monuments of Florentine civic architecture and a symbol of the Republic's authority. Constructed between 1298 and 1302 as the Palazzo della Signoria, the residence of the *Signoria* (government), it then became the ducal palace of the Medicis. During Florence's brief spell as capital of Italy (1865–71), it was the seat of the National Parliament. Today it houses the city council and the Children's Museum of Florence (► panel, page 75).

Once inside, be sure to see the vast Salone dei Cinquecento (Hall of the Five Hundred), created to house the new general parliament and later decorated

Ghirlandaio frescos in Palazzo Vecchio

Several rooms are devoted to Galileo; exhibits include two of his original telescopes, his middle finger (cut from his dead body), various instruments, and the broken lens with which he discovered the satellites of Jupiter (rooms 4–5). Other highlights include the Florentine globes, and the massive armillary sphere (Room 7) used to illustrate the motion of planets and stars.

🗺 200 A4 ✉ Piazza dei Giudici 1
☎ 055 293493; 055 265311; www.imss.fi.it

SAVONAROLA

The martyred religious leader Girolamo Savonarola spent his last days imprisoned in the Palazzo Vecchio. In 1497, he had staged his hugely popular "Bonfire of Vanities" (the burning of books, fancy clothes and works of art) in the square below. Just one year later, the tide of opinion had turned and he was burned at the stake for attempting to bring morality and virtue to Florence.

by Cosimo I with frescoes and sculptures recalling the history of Florence and the Medicis. Don't miss Michelangelo's magnificent marble group representing Victory, intended for the tomb of Pope Julius II; also, the ornate, windowless study adjoining the hall, used by Cosimo's son, Francesco I, for his collections of coins, glass and semi-precious stones.

The Medici suite of rooms, each dedicated to the glorification of a different family member, corresponds to the Apartment of the Elements on the next floor, where the rooms are each dedicated to a different god, prompting Giorgio Vasari's famous comparison: "The rooms above…are where the origins of the celestial gods dwell in painting…together with the great virtues his Majesty sets in the creatures down here who, leaving a great mark among mortals…are

The inner courtyard of the Palazzo Vecchio, decorated with frescoes to celebrate Francesco I's marriage to Joanna of Austria

terrestrial gods." The rooftop views from the top-floor loggia, and from the luxury apartments of Eleanor of Toledo (wife of Cosimo I de Medici), are divine.

🔁 200 B5 ✉ Piazza della Signoria ☎ 055 276 8224. Phone to book a place on a secret passageway tour ⏰ Fri–Wed 9–7, Thu and public holidays 9–2. Closed some public holidays. Last tickets one hour before closing 🚍 23 and B 💶 Moderate; combined ticket with Cappella Brancacci: expensive

7 Loggia dei Lanzi

The loggia was conceived in 1382 as a stage for all the most important ceremonies held in Florence – an architecturally innovative structure with round arches and classical proportions, looking towards Renaissance ideals at a time when pointed Gothic arches were

still very much in vogue. Originally called the Loggia della Signoria, it was renamed after Cosimo I's bodyguards, the Lanzi or "Lancers".

The loggia was later turned into a splendid open-air museum, with ancient Greek and Roman, as well as Renaissance, figures. One of the finest is Giambologna's fluid *Rape of the Sabine Women* (1583), carved from a single block of flawed marble (▶ 21). The most famous is the bronze statue of *Perseus* (1554) by Benvenuto Cellini (▶ 21) while, in the centre, one of the oldest, *Menelaus Supporting the Body of Patroclus*, is a Roman copy of the Greek original, dated 400BC.

🔲 199 F5 ✉ Piazza della Signoria
🚌 23 and B 🎫 Free

8 Orsanmichele

A church with a difference – Orsanmichele was built in 1337 as a grain market. Inside you can still see grain shoots and, to the left of the main entrance, above the doorway leading up to the grain stores, a carving of an overflowing bushel. The market was built on the site of a monastic garden, hence the name, derived from Orto di San Michele (Garden of St Michael). Soon after its completion it was converted into a

Carvings on the exterior wall niches at Orsanmichele depict members of the guilds at work

A fleur-de-lys decorates Orsanmichele

church, although grain was stored on the upper floors until 1569.

Start your visit by walking round the building's exterior. You'll notice 14 niches, each containing a statue of the patron saint of a guild and, beneath them, sculptures illustrating the guild's type of work. The statues are mostly copies; some of the originals are conserved in the museum inside the building. The interior is most unusual – square with two parallel naves of equal importance – and contains a beautiful jewel-encrusted tabernacle (1349–59) by Andrea Orcagna.

🔲 195 E1 ✉ Via dell'Arte della Lana, corner of Via dei Calzaluoi ☎ 055 284944 🕐 Tue–Sun 10–5, Museum Mon 10–5 🚌 A 🎫 Free

9 Casa di Dante

Although the medieval poet Dante Alighieri lived near here, this house is a reconstruction dating from 1911. Despite this, the small museum successfully manages to evoke Dante's life and times.

Ethereal frescoes grace the ceiling of the Badia Fiorentina

Several rooms are devoted to 13th-century Florence, with models and plans showing the development of the city, Dante's role as a Guelph, his exile from Florence in 1309 because of his sympathies with the White Guelphs when the Black Guelphs became dominant, and his works, including *The Divine Comedy*.

Up the road is the unadorned Church of Santa Margherita, where Dante met Beatrice Portinari, who inspired his poetry, and where he married Gemma Donati. Beatrice and Gemma are buried here. The church is also called the Chiesa di Dante, as it was at the heart of the poet's social, political and spiritual life.

➕ 196 B1 ✉ Via Santa Margherita 1 ☎ 055 219416; www.museocasadidante.it ⏲ Apr–Sep daily 10–6; Oct–Mar Tue–Sun 10–5 🚌 14, 23 and A 💶 Inexpensive

⑩ Badia Fiorentina

The Badia Fiorentina is the oldest monastery in Florence, founded in 978 by the mother of Marquis Ugo of Tuscany. The monks here enhanced the area's reputation as an important centre of book production with their papermaking, illuminating and book-binding. Ugo, nicknamed the "Great Baron", was a popular figure in medieval Florence and would organize readings of Dante's work in the church. A Mass is still celebrated in his honour on 21 December.

The monastery has been restructured several times, and over the years the church has been rotated 180 degrees. Its pièce de résistance is a magnificent altarpiece showing *The Virgin Appearing to St Bernard* (1485) by Filippino Lippi, and there are excellent views of the hexagonal campanile from the fresco-clad cloisters.

➕ 200 B5 ✉ Via del Proconsolo, entrance on Via Dante Alighieri ☎ No phone ⏲ Church has restricted and varying opening hours; consult tourist office for details 🚌 14, 23 and A 💶 Free

⑪ Bar Vivoli Gelateria

It is generally accepted that the Florentines make some of the best ice-cream in the world and this *gelateria*, in a hidden alleyway at the heart of the Santa Croce district, is

Battle of the Centaurs was carved by Michelangelo in his youth

reputed to produce the best in town. Be prepared to queue for the rich and creamy concoctions, which include all the favourites together with such unusual flavours as fig, meringue, pear, chestnut and zabaglione.

➕ 200 C5 ✉ Via Isola delle Stinche 7r
☎ 055 292334 🕒 Tue–Sun 7:30am–midnight
🚌 14 and A

🔢 Casa Buonarroti

This is the former home of artist and sculptor Michelangelo Buonarroti (commonly known by just his first name). However, you will be disappointed if you come expecting every room to be crammed with his works, though two of his masterpieces have become the symbols of the

museum: the serene *Madonna of the Steps*, carved when he was just 15 or 16 years old and thought to be his earliest work; and the more complex *Battle of the Centaurs*.

The museum also has over 200 Michelangelo drawings, the world's largest collection. For reasons of conservation, however, just a small selection is on view at any one time. According to Giorgio Vasari, just before he died in 1564 Michelangelo burned "a great number of drawings, sketches, and cartoons made by his hand so that no one would see the labours he endured and the ways he tested his genius, and lest he should appear less than perfect".

Other highlights include a model of *David* in a wooden cart, showing how the statue was transported from Piazza della Signoria to the Accademia (▶ 98–99), and a gallery of paintings depicting Michelangelo meeting with various popes and sovereigns. The rest of the museum provides a rare glimpse inside a 16th-century palazzo, complete with period furnishings.

➕ 201 D5 ✉ Via Ghibellina 70 ☎ 055 241752; www.casabuonarotti.it 🕒 Wed–Mon 9:30–2. Guided visits by reservation. Last ticket 30 mins before closing. Closed some public hols 🚌 14 and A 💰 Expensive

🔢 Museo dell'Opera di Santa Croce and Cappella dei Pazzi

Adjoining Santa Croce (▶ 66–69) are the old monastic buildings of the church housing the Museo dell'Opera di Santa Croce and the Cappella dei Pazzi. The refectory (part of the museum) houses such radiant frescoes as Taddeo Gaddi's *Tree of the Cross* and *Last Supper*, removed from the church to reveal earlier works and, most famous of all, Giovanni Cimabue's celebrated *Crucifix*, devastated by the 1966 flood (▶ 32–33).

The star attraction, however, is the Cappella dei Pazzi, one of the purest works of Renaissance architecture in Florence. Commissioned by the Pazzi family, arch-rivals of the Medici, and designed by Brunelleschi between 1442 and 1446, it is striking in its simplicity: plain grey and white stone walls, with perfectly proportioned arches, domes, scallops, arcading and one small stained-glass window. The painted terracotta *tondi* depicting the Apostles are by Luca della Robbia; the Evangelists in the pendentives by Brunelleschi; the main altar, the frieze of cherubs, and *Agnus Dei* are by Donatello. A doorway leads back to the cloisters, a peaceful corner and an ideal place to rest awhile.

🚹 201 D4 ⊠ Piazza di Santa Croce 16
☎ 055 246 6105 🕔 Mon–Sat 9:30–5:30, Sun 1–5:30 🚍 23 and C 🎟 Moderate (combined ticket with Santa Croce)

🔟 Museo Horne

The romantic English art historian Herbert Percy Horne was one of

a handful of foreigners living in Florence at the turn of the 20th century who left a profound and lasting impression on the cultural life of the city. Following his death in 1916, he bequeathed his Renaissance palazzo home to the city, together with an eclectic collection of paintings, sculptures, ceramics, furniture, ornaments,

Renaissance cooking utensils and other knick-knacks, all reflecting his passion for the art and history of the city.

There is nothing exceptionally precious here, except a polyptych of *St Stephen* by Giotto. The museum's charm lies more in its hotchpotch of exhibits and the comfortable, informal feel of the palace, previously owned by a wealthy cloth merchant.

🚹 200 C4 ⊠ Via de' Benci 6 ☎ 055 244661; www.museohorne.it
🕔 Mon–Sat 9–1. Last ticket 30 mins before closing 🚍 23, B and C
🎟 Moderate

Left: Museo Horne

Where to...
Eat and Drink

Prices
Expect to pay per person for a meal, excluding drinks and service
€ under €20   €€ €20–€45   €€€ over €45

The area around Santa Croce has some of Florence's best options for eating and drinking. These include the city's three finest and most expensive restaurants – Cibrèo, Pinchiorri and Alle Murate – but also a variety of good mid-price options. You can eat in lively, modern surroundings – notably in Baldovino – or in the simple, old-fashioned trattoria-style restaurant typified by Benvenuto. Bars and cafes are also excellent, thanks to the fact that this part of the city has several emerging districts, such as Sant'Ambrogio, that have witnessed the arrival of new bars, night-spots and interesting shops.

Acqua al Due €–€€

Acqua al Due has been a fixture of the Florentine culinary scene for over 30 years, yet has managed to retain a reputation as one of the new breed of Florentine restaurants. Its ambience combines a pretty stone-walled medieval interior covered with displays of plates with a bright and lively atmosphere. Traditional Tuscan and other Italian dishes are presented but in modern combinations that are modern with an innovative twist. Dishes might include *pasta alle melanzane* (pasta with aubergines/eggplant), *tagliata alla arancia* (slices of beef with orange) and *penne ai quattro formaggi* (penne pasta with a four-cheese sauce). A good way to start your meal is with the *assaggi di primi*, a selection of tasters. Acqua al Due also run a new diner just around the corner at Via Acqua 2r.

🕂 200 B5 ⊠ Via della Vigna Vecchia 40r ☎ 055 284170; www.acquaal2.it 🕔 Daily 7:30pm–1am. Closed for a week mid-Aug

Alle Murate €€€

Alle Murate ranks among Florence's top three or four restaurants – with Oliviero (▶ 131), Cibrèo and the Enoteca Pinchiorri – but its cool and elegant approach can border on the aloof. This said, the food is generally excellent, combining contemporary takes on Florentine classics with creative interpretations of other Italian and international dishes. Menus change frequently, but might include dishes such as stuffed pigeon, seafood ravioli or bass fillet in a crust of celeriac. You'll probably encounter tastes here you won't have experienced before. Puddings are sublime, and the wine list – with about 150 mainly Tuscan wines – is good.

🕂 201 D5 ⊠ Via Proconsolo 16r ☎ 055 240618; www.allemurate.it 🕔 Tue–Sun 7:30pm–11pm

Angels €–€€€

Currently one of the city's hottest venues, Angels is a combination of *enoteca*, or wine bar, with a traditional beamed ceiling; an American-style bar that serves some of Florence's best cocktails; and an expensive restaurant that, despite its Oriental styling, serves a range of Tuscan food, including fish and meat dishes. If you don't want to eat, this is still a good place for an evening drink, and to watch moneyed Florentines at play.

🕂 195 F1 ⊠ Via del Proconsolo 29–31 ☎ 055 239 8762; www.ristoranteangels.it

Florence's best and most expensive restaurant, with three Michelin stars and one of the finest wine cellars in Europe. The prices for the highly refined and elaborate Italian dishes and international food are high – very high – while the service and the surroundings are uncompromising in their formality (men should wear a jacket and tie to feel comfortable). Yet there's nowhere better if you want the Florentine gastronomic treat of a lifetime.

➕ 200 C5 ☒ Via Ghibellina 87 ☎ 055 242757; www.enotecapinchiorri.com ☷ Tue–Sat 12:30–2, 7:30–10. Closed Aug Sun, and lunch Tue and Wed

Finisterrae €€

This exotic, beautiful palazzo on Piazza Santa Croce serves an imaginative menu of modern Mediterranean cuisine in a series of dining rooms, each decorated in the style of a different country or region – Spain, Greece, North Africa… In the centre is a sultry Moroccan-

muted. Don't forget the other parts of the Cibrèo mini-empire – the delicatessen and cafe (➤ 78). Reserve a table several days in advance for weekends.

➕ 197 E1 ☒ Via Andea del Verrocchio 8r ☎ 055 234 1100 ☷ Tue–Sat 12:50–2:30, 7–11:15. Closed Aug

Da Benvenuto €–€€

This basic trattoria with no-nonsense food – and decoration to match – has been serving dependable Tuscan staples, such as ribollita (thick vegetable soup) and bistecca alla Fiorentina (Tuscan beef, ➤ 10), on this street corner not far from Piazza della Signoria for as long as anyone locally can remember.

➕ 200 B4 ☒ Via della Mosca 16r, corner Via de' Neri ☎ 055 214833; www.trattoriadabenvenuto.it ☷ Mon–Sat 12–2:30, 7–10.30

Enoteca Pinchiorri €€€

An enoteca is usually an inexpensive wine bar, but not here. Pinchiorri is

☷ Daily noon–3 for light lunch, 7–10 (bar until 1am, restaurant until 11:30pm). Closed for two weeks in Aug

Baldovino €–€€

If you're in a dilemma over where to eat lunch or dinner close to Santa Croce, look no further than Baldovino, an informal combination of the modern and traditional. Restaurateur David Gardener has combined good food, which ranges from Tuscan classics to Neapolitan pizzas, innovative salads and other non-Italian novelties, with a bright, young staff, pleasant decor, and a convivial and cosmopolitan atmosphere. Dishes on the inspired menu might include fresh, grilled fish, tagliatelli agli asparagi (pasta with asparagus) or risotto al funghi di bosco (risotto with wild mushrooms). Reservations are strongly recommended, especially on Friday and Saturday.

➕ 201 D4 ☒ Via San Giuseppe 22r ☎ 055 241773; www.baldovino.com ☷ Daily 11:30– 2:30, 7–11:30. Closed Mon Nov–Mar

Cibrèo €€€

If you don't want to pay Pinchiorri's prices (➤ 77), and don't want the formality of Alle Murate (➤ 76), then Cibrèo provides a happy medium. Many Tuscan gastronomes rate it Florence's best restaurant, thanks to its imaginative and constantly changing interpretations of traditional "peasant" Florentine food. Dishes might include delicious soups of fish or porcini mushrooms, polenta alle erbe (polenta with herbs), baccalà (salt cod) or a superb ricotta e patate con sugo di carni bianche (ricotta cheese and potatoes with a sauce of white meat juices). The dining area is simple – rustic tables and plain painted walls – and the service and atmosphere are informal. Prices are set for each course (and include service), but be sure to leave room for some of the excellent puddings. You can eat at lower prices in the adjoining trattoria, known as the Vineria Cibreino, but the atmosphere here is somewhat style bar. Be sure to try the house cocktail – a wicked concoction containing absinthe.

➕ 200 5C ◻ Piazza Santa Croce 12
☎ 055 263 8675 ⏱ Tue–Sun noon–11:30 or later

Osteria dei Benci €€

This is one of Florence's new breed of bright and informal restaurants, distinguished by a single attractive dining room painted in warm colours and crowned by a medieval brick vault. The staff are young, the service relaxed, and the Tuscan food well-prepared and imaginative – dishes might include tasty vegetable soups and simple grilled meats (lamb in season is excellent). Menus change regularly.

➕ 200 B4 ◻ Via de' Benci 13r ☎ 055 234 4923 ⏱ Mon–Sat 1–2:45, 7:30–10:45. Closed for a period in Aug

Osteria del Caffè Italiano €€–€€€

This combination of wine bar, restaurant and trattoria just west

of Santa Croce offers a choice of dining experiences and prices. All three linked eating areas have the same distinctive medieval Florentine decor – terracotta floors, whitewashed walls and heavy beamed or vaulted ceilings – set in the restored 14th-century Palazzo Salviati. You can come here for a quick and tasty light lunch, a full meal, or just a glass of wine and snack at any time of the day. Food is typically Tuscan, whether it's salamis and cheeses or a more substantial main course of *bistecca alla fiorentina* (➤ 10).

➕ 200 C5 ◻ Via Isole delle Stinche 11–13r ☎ 055 289368; www.caffeitaliano.it ⏱ Tue–Sun 12:30–3, 7:30–midnight

Ristorante Paoli €€

Open since 1824, this restaurant stands out for having preserved its traditional Tuscan cuisine; allow yourself to be tempted by "La Magnifica" Florentine steak or cuttlefish from the Mediterranean, and for dessert spoil your taste

buds with stewed apples, prunes and pears prepared like the Florentine women of the past used to cook them. You are seated at tables covered with rose-coloured tablecloths under a beautiful vaulted ceiling, together with frescoes and Liberty-style ceramics. It can be a bit of a squeeze and quite loud but that's all part of the atmosphere.

➕ 195 F1 ◻ Via de' Tavolini ☎ 055 216215; www.casatrattoria.com ⏱ Daily 12–5:15, 7–11

BARS AND CAFES

Boccadama €–€€

Despite its busy location on one of the city's key squares, this *osteria*-wine bar maintains a warm welcome and high standards, opening for breakfast, simple lunches and evening meals, but with the chance to drink a glass of wine or similar throughout the day. A typical light lunch might include spinach *crespolini* (small

filled pancakes), fresh tomato *bruschetta* or chicken liver *crostini* (toasts), and dried tomato and anchovy salad.

➕ 201 D4 ◻ Piazza Santa Croce 25–26r ☎ 055 243640 ⏱ Wed–Mon 8am–10:30pm, Tue 8–3:30, but kitchen closes 3:30–7

Caffè Cibrèo €

It's hard to think of a prettier cafe in Florence. The wood-panelled interior dates from 1989 but could just as easily have been lifted from somewhere at least 200 or 300 years older. The cafe is close to the Sant'Ambrogio market (➤ 81) and is a civilized and cosy place, with the added incentive that snacks and cakes (including a famed chocolate torte with bitter orange sauce) come from the celebrated kitchens of the co-owned Cibrèo restaurant nearby (➤ 77). There's outside seating for those long, hot summer days, but the street is, unfortunately, not particularly pretty.

➕ 197 E1 ◻ Via Andrea del Verrocchio 5r ☎ 055 234 5853 ⏱ Tue–Sat 8am–1am

Cantinetta dei Verrazzano €€

This is a superb place for a snack or light meal, and all the better for being central – it lies just a few paces off Via dei Calzaiuoli. When you walk in, all manner of sandwiches and other tasty delights such as pizza and *foccacia* (most baked on the premises) immediately catch your eye under a huge glass-fronted display on your left. You can buy this food to take away or nibble on the bench by the door, or settle down for a more leisurely drink or meal in the cafe-wine bar to the rear. The place is owned by the Castello di Verrazzano estate, one of Chianti's leading vineyards, so the wine here is also good.

➕ 195 F1 ✉ Via dei Tavolini 18–20r
☎ 055 268590 ⏰ Mon–Sat 8am–9pm.
Closed Aug

Del Fagioli €

Amid the plethora of cheap restaurants and wine bars in and around Piazza Santa Croce, many of them pandering (poorly) to visitors, Del Fagioli stands out for its refusal to compromise on the authenticity or quality of its cooking. South of the piazza, it retains the look and feel of a trattoria of the old school, with friendly waiters, informal air, and reasonable prices (note that it does not accept credit cards). The menu is thoroughly Tuscan, with simple standards such as *crostini* (toasts), *ribollita* (a thick vegetable soup), *bollito misto in salsa verde* (mixed meats with a green, herby sauce) and *cantuccini con Vin Santo* (almond biscuits to dip in sweet wine) to round off the meal.

➕ 200 C4 ✉ Corso Tintori 47r
☎ 055 244285 ⏰ Mon–Fri 12:30–2:30, 7:30–10:30

Gustavino €–€€

Just a few moments from Piazza della Signoria, this modern, clean-lined wine bar and restaurant is at odds with the more rustic-looking establishment typical of Florence. You can have full meals in the sleek restaurant section (Gustavino) – glass-top bar, steel chairs and open kitchen – but the wine bar area next door (Canova di Gustavino), with its shared tables and racks of wine bottles, is cosier and less expensive. Here you can sample a variety of simple Tuscan staples.

➕ 199 F5 ✉ Via della Condotta 37r
☎ 055 239 9806; www.gustavino.it
⏰ Gustavino Mon–Fri 7–11.30, Sat–Sun 12:30–3:30, 7:30–11:30. Canova di Gustavino daily 12:30–3:30, 7:30–11:30

Il Francescano €

Formerly an offshoot of nearby Baldovino (▶ 77), but now independently owned, Il Francescano shares many of its mentor's qualities – an informal atmosphere, a pleasingly simple interior (but with outside tables for dining in good weather), and reliable and fairly priced Tuscan food (if anything prices here are a touch lower than Baldovino).

➕ 201 D4 ✉ Largo Bargellini 16 ☎ 055 241605; www.ilfrancescano.com ⏰ Daily noon–2:30, 7–11. Closed Tue Oct–Feb

Perchè No! €

Perchè No! (Why Not!) has been selling superlative ice-cream since 1939, and provides central Florence's only serious rival to Bar Vivoli (▶ 73). The selection of flavours is usually in excess of 50, and varies according to the season.

➕ 195 F1 ✉ Via dei Tavolini 19r
☎ 055 239 8969; www.percheno.firenze.it
⏰ Summer Mon, Wed–Sun 11am–midnight, Tue noon–8; winter Mon, Wed–Sun noon–7:30. Closed for some of Nov

Rivoire €–€€

It's hard to resist Rivoire's outside tables, overlooking Piazza della Signoria. When it opened in 1872, it specialized in hot chocolate, but these days most dishes are available. Prices are high, however, and the food rarely more than average. This said, it's worth paying for the view.

➕ 199 F5 ✉ Piazza della Signoria 5r
☎ 055 214412 ⏰ Nov to mid-Mar Tue–Sun 8am–9pm; mid-Mar to Oct 8am–midnight. Closed two weeks in Aug

Where to... Shop

Shopping in eastern and central Florence requires a sense of adventure, for apart from one or two key streets with many varied shops – notably Via dei Calzaiuoli and Borgo degli Albizzi – this is an area where the more individual and interesting stores are scattered far and wide. Some of the specialist quirky, off-beat shops lie in the Sant'Ambrogio district. Sant'Ambrogio is also home to a good local food market, surrounded with lively cafes and restaurants. The streets around Santa Croce are worth exploring.

CLOTHES

Raspini

Raspini is one of Florence's largest clothes stores, selling a wide range of designer and other clothes, including less expensive "diffusion" lines by the big names of Italian fashion. The main store is in Via Roma, but there are three other outlets, including Raspini Junior for children in Via Por Santa Maria and the latest Raspini Vintage in Via Calimarussa.

➕ 196 A1 ✉ Via Roma 25r ☎ 055 213077 🕐 Apr–Oct Mon 3–7:30, Tue–Sat 10:30–7:30, Sun 2–7; Nov–Mar Mon 3–7:30, Tue–Sat 9:30–1, 3:30–7:30 ✉ Via Por Santa Maria 70r ☎ 055 215796 🕐 Mon 3:30–7:30, Tue–Sat 10:30–7:30, Sun 2:30–7:30 ✉ Via de' Martelli 5r ☎ 055 239 8336 🕐 Mon 3:30–7:30, Tue–Sat 9:30–1, 3:30–7:30, last Sun of month 2–7 ✉ Via Calimaruzza 17r ☎ 055 213901 🕐 Mon 3:30–7:30, Tue–Sat 10:30–7:30, Sun 2:30–7:30

DEPARTMENT STORES

Coin

Coin offers the best one-stop shopping in Florence, partly because it has a central location, and partly because of the quality across its wide range of clothes, linens and other household goods. Clothes include own-label and designer items, conservative Italian classics (for men and women), and younger fashion items. Note the Sunday opening, useful if you're in Florence for a long weekend.

➕ 195 E1 ✉ Via dei Calzaiuoli 56r ☎ 055 280531; www.coin.it 🕐 Daily 10–8

FASHION

Bemporad

One of Florence's oldest family businesses founded in 1885, which dresses some very important clients from the huge selection of classic, elegant men's and women's wear that never goes out of fashion, some created by top fashion houses.

➕ 196 A1 ✉ Via dei Calzaiuoli 11, 13, 15, 17r ☎ 055 216833 🕐 Mon–Sat 9–1, 3:30–7:30

FOOD AND WINE

Vestri

Leonardo Vestri is Florence's leading chocolatier, though many of his exquisite creations are conjured up in his workshops in the town of Arezzo. His creations include chocolate flavoured with anything from chilli and orange to espresso and apricot, and in summer you can indulge in chocolate ice-cream tinged with mint, hazelnut and other flavours. Be sure to try the delicious *cioccolata da bere*, or hot or cold drinking chocolate.

➕ 196 C1 ✉ Borgo degli Albizi 11r ☎ 055 234 0374; www.vestri.it 🕐 Mon–Sat 10:30–8. Closed Sun except in the lead-up to Easter and Christmas

Pegna

Florentines have been visiting this temple to fine food in a little street south of the Duomo since 1860. You can buy excellent cheeses, salamis, coffees, teas, olive oils, wines, cakes, chocolates and other gastronomic treats – 7,000 different items in all – from Italy and many other countries around the world.

➕ 196 B1 ⊠ Via dello Studio 8r ☎ 055 282701 or 055 282702; www.pegna.it ⏰ Mon–Tue, Thu–Sat 9–1, 3.30–7.30, Wed 9–1. Closed Sat afternoon in summer but open Wed afternoon in summer

LEATHER

Scuola del Cuoio

At the rear of the Santa Croce, this leather school, run by Franciscan monks, demonstrates the best in leather craftsmanship in the variety of items made here, which blend tradition with contemporary style.

➕ 201 C5 ⊠ Via San Giuseppe 5r ☎ 055 244533; www.leatherschool.com ⏰ Mon–Fri 9.30–6, Sat 9.30–6, Sun 10–6 (closed Sun Nov–Mar)

JEWELLERY

Torrini

It's hard to argue with the quality or reputation of a jewellers that first registered its trademark – a distinctive half clover-leaf with spur – as long ago as 1369. This is still one of the best places in Florence to buy jewellery, and gold jewellery in particular.

➕ 195 F2 ⊠ Piazza del Duomo 10r ☎ 055 230 2401; www.torrini.com ⏰ Tue–Sat 10–1:30, 2:30–7:30, Mon 3–7:30. Apr–Oct Mon 8–7:30

Sant'Ambrogio

Sant'Ambrogio is the city centre's main food market after the Mercato Centrale (▶ 111), but looks and feels more like a neighbourhood market – it mostly serves the residents. It is also becoming the focus of a rejuvenated quarter housing small specialist stores, cafes and restaurants.

➕ 197 E1 ⊠ Piazza Lorenzo Ghiberti, off Via de' Macci ⏰ Mon–Sat 7–2

PAPER AND STATIONERY

Pineider

Pineider is Italy's – and possibly Europe's – ultimate stationers, founded in 1774. All in their time have been beguiled by the company's exquisite pens, stationery, diaries and other associated items – actress Elizabeth Taylor once ordered blue-violet stationery to match her eyes.

➕ 199 E5 ⊠ Piazza della Signoria 13–14r ☎ 055 284655; www.pineider.com ⏰ Mon–Sat 10–7, Sun 10–2, 3–7

MARKETS

Piazza dei Ciompi

The small collection of bric-a-brac stalls at Florence's flea market, or Mercato delle Pulci (*pulci* are fleas), just north of the Casa Buonarroti (▶ 74), is fairly modest. However, on the last Sunday of each month, a larger bustling antiques market fills the piazza and crowds into the many surrounding streets.

➕ 197 D1 ⊠ Piazza dei Ciompi, off Via Pietrapiana ☎ No phone ⏰ Daily 9–7:30

Zecchi

Artists won't be able to drag themselves away from this superb emporium just south of the Duomo, which sells every art-related raw material and accoutrement imaginable.

➕ 196 B1 ⊠ Via dello Studio 19r ☎ 055 21147O; www.zecchi.com ⏰ Mon–Fri 8:30–12:30, 3:30–7:30, Sat 8:30–12:30. Closed Aug and Sat in Jul

PERFUMES AND TOILETRIES

Antica Officina del Farmacista Dr Vranjes

This shop sells a range of scents, essential oils and aromatherapy products. All are handmade from essential oils and natural products. Try scents such as "Tuscan Garden" or "Fiori di Sicilia". You can also visit Dr Vranjes' workshop at Via San Gallo 69r.

➕ 197 E1 ⊠ Borgo La Croce 44r ☎ 055 241748; www.drvranjes.it ⏰ Antica Officina Mon 3:30–7:30, Tue–Sat 10–1, 3.30–7:30. Workshop Mon–Fri 10–7

Where to...
Be Entertained

Eastern Florence contains the venues or headquarters of several of the city's major orchestras and classical music associations, as well as several of its trendiest night-time bars, its best jazz club, and one or two of its most popular clubs.

CLASSICAL MUSIC

Tuscany's regional orchestra, the **Orchestra della Toscana**, has its headquarters at Via Verdi 5 (tel: 055 234 0710 or 055 234 2722; www. orchestradellatoscana.it) and plays concerts (main season Dec–May) at the nearby **Teatro Verdi** (Via Ghibellina 99–101, tel: 055 212320; www.teatroverdionline.it). Buy tickets from the Teatro Verdi box office or the Box Office ticket agency outlets (▶ 46). Florence's city orchestra, the **Filarmonica di Firenze "Gioacchino Rossini"** (Via Villamagna 41, tel: 055 653 3084; www.filarmonicarossini.it) performs at various venues during its main season (Jan–Feb), but also presents a series of outdoor concerts in Piazza della Signoria in summer months. Consult tourist information centres for details (▶ 39).

The **Orchestra da Camera Fiorentina**, or Florence Chamber Orchestra (Via Monferrato 2, tel: 055 783374; www.orcafi.it) is based in the north of the city, but performs regular concerts in the central **church of Orsanmichele** (▶ 72). Buy tickets from the above number, from Box Office (▶ 46), online at www.boxol.it or from Orsanmichele an hour before each performance. The **Amici della Musica**, one of the city's leading classical music associations, is based at Via Pier Capponi 41 (tel: 055 608420 or 055 607440; www. amicimusica.fi.it), but organizes concerts at the Teatro della Pergola (Via della Pergola 18, tel: 055 226 4353; www.teatrodellapergola.com) – built in 1656 and reputedly Italy's oldest surviving theatre – northeast of the Duomo.

JAZZ

For a different sort of music, head for the long-established and informal **Jazz Club** (Via Nuova de' Caccini 3, tel: 055 247 9700; www.jazzclubfirenze.com, closed Sun and Mon and Jun–Sep). The scene of live jazz most nights in a medieval cellar: it is on a tiny side street a block south of Via degli Alfani at the corner of Borgo Pinti.

You need to buy "membership" as a formality to enter.

NIGHTCLUBS/BARS

One of the area's best disco bars, **Twice** (Via Giuseppe Verdi 57r, tel: 055 247 356, open daily 9pm–4am) attracts a large crowd for a sedate evening drink while listening to jazz or to strut their stuff on the dance floor as the pace picks up. Also popular is **Red Garter** (Via de' Benci 33r, tel: 055 234 4904, open daily 5pm–2am), where a sea of red greets you, plus music most nights and a good selection of cocktails and beers. Relax in the nearby, ever-popular **Rex Café** (Via Fiesolana 23r, tel: 055 248 0331, open daily 6:30pm–2:30am; closed mid-May to mid-Sep), easily the best of the bars in eastern Florence, for an early evening drink or small-hours nightcap: the interior is striking and alarming – lots of mosaics, mirrors and strange lamps – but the atmosphere is easy-going.

Northern Florence

Getting Your Bearings

This noble district was once home to the Medici family, long-time rulers of Florence who commissioned the greatest architects of the time to create such landmarks as the Palazzo Medici-Riccardi (the first Medici residence and seat of political power), the churches of San Marco and San Lorenzo, and lavish Cappelle Medicee, the last resting place for some 50 members of the Medici family.

The Duomo, one of the world's largest cathedrals and the first port of call for most visitors, lies at the heart of the district. As you explore the surrounding streets, you'll frequently catch glimpses of its multi-coloured marble cladding and the massive dome that dominates the entire city.

V d Dogana

V d La Pira

CAVOUR

San Marco 4

Arazzieri

VIA

V d

V di Giorgio La Pira

Giardino dei Semplici 10

Gen M Fanti

Università

Piazza San Marco

Cesare Battisti

Via

Santissima Annunziata 11

CAVOUR

Ricasoli

3 **Galleria dell' Accademia**

Ferdinando I

Museo dell'Opificio delle Pietre Dure

5

Piazza d Ss Annunziata

13

SAN GIOVANNI

Palazzo Gerini

Via degli Servi

Piazza Brunelleschi

Ospedale degli Innocenti

Alfani

Mercato Centrale

Piazza del Mercato Centrale

Via dell'Ariento

Via S Antonino

Borgo la Noce

Via della stufa

Via del Cinori

i

Via del Canto d Nelli

Mostre di Leonardo

Via del Castellaccio

Via del Castellaccio

Cappelle Medicee 2

2

San Lorenzo

8 **Palazzo Medici-Riccardi**

Via del Giglio

Via de' Conti

Via d'Alloro

Biblioteca Laurenziana

Borgo S Lorenzo

Mercato San Lorenzo

V DE MARTELLI

Via de' Pucci

Palazzo Pucci

Via del Castellaccio

Via de' Castellaccio

Ospedale S Maria Nuova

Via Bufalini

Teatro Niccolini

VIA DE' CERRETANI

Battistero 7

Piazza d S Giovanni

1

9 **Duomo** 1

Piazza del Duomo

7

Piazza S M Nuova

Museo di Firenze com'era 6

Via de' Pecori

Loggia del Bigallo 5

Campanile di Giotto

Museo dell'Opera del Duomo

Via Borromei

Via dell'Oriuolo

Via del Campidoglio

V d Oche

Via d Proconsolo

Piazza della Repubblica

Via Pellicceria

Via Calimala

Via d Calzaiuoli

Via d Corso

| 0 | | 200 metres |
| 0 | | 200 yards |

★ Don't Miss

At Your Leisure

Above right: Detail of the statue of *David* by Michelangelo in Galleria dell'Accademia

Today, the area around San Marco (once leafy, open countryside beyond the city walls, well-suited to the needs of the monks of San Marco and Santissima) is a lively student quarter, full of good bars, restaurants and the huge, colourful San Lorenzo market. It is also home to Florence's most celebrated resident – Michelangelo's *David* – the original of which resides in the Galleria dell'Accademia.

Via Gino Capponi

Via Laura

Museo Archeologico ⓬

Via d. Colonna

Previous page: The cupola crowning the Basilica of Santa Maria del Fiore, the Duomo

Right: The exterior of the Duomo is as grand as its superb interior

In Two Days

If you're not quite sure where to begin your travels, this itinerary recommends a practical and enjoyable two-day tour of Northern Florence, taking in some of the best places to see using the Getting Your Bearings map on the previous page. For more information see the main entries.

Day One

Morning
Start your day at the striking **7 Museo dell'Opera del Duomo** (below, ► 103), and spend a couple of hours admiring the many treasures from the Duomo, Campanile di Giotto and Battistero that are sheltered here for safe keeping.

Sit at one of the cafe-terraces edging the traffic-free Piazza del Duomo and marvel at the monstrous proportions of the mighty marble-coated ❶ Duomo (► 88–94), then explore its vast interior.

Lunch
Head northwards to the district of San Lorenzo.

Buy a picnic at the Mercato Centrale (► 111) to eat on the steps of San Lorenzo, or grab a light lunch at Trattoria Mario (► 109) or Trattoria Gozzi Sergio (Piazza San Lorenzo 8r, tel: 055 281941, open Mon–Sat 12–3).

Afternoon
The plain, unfinished facade of **2 San Lorenzo** (► 95–97) belies the many artistic and architectural jewels within. Be sure to see the Sagrestia Vecchia, then join the queues waiting to enter the dazzling **Cappella dei Principi**, made entirely of marble inlay, and the **Sagrestia Nuova**, with its celebrated Michelangelo sculptures.

Evening
Return to the Duomo and climb the dome for a bird's-eye view of the city at sunset. Remember to take your camera.

Day Two

Morning

The simple, spiritually uplifting masterworks of Fra Angelico (below) housed in the monastery of ▲ **San Marco** (➤ 100–101) provide a gentle start to the day. Once within the peaceful cloisters, it is easy to understand why American novelist Henry James said of Fra Angelico, "immured in his quiet convent, he never received an intelligible impression of evil".

The nearby ➒ **Museo dell'Opificio delle Pietre Dure** (➤ 105), a workshop and museum of marble inlay, provides a fascinating insight into this unique Florentine art, and makes the craftsmanship in the Cappella dei Principi (➤ 96) seem all the more remarkable.

Lunch

You'll be spoilt for choice of cheap, cheerful cafes round here as this is the heart of the university quarter.

Afternoon

After lunch, while away a couple of hours at the ➌ **Galleria dell'Accademia** (➤ 98–99). Established in 1563 with Michelangelo among its founders, the world's oldest art school is today home to a priceless collection of fine art, including Michelangelo's *David*.

Then, make your way down Via Cavour to the ➑ **Palazzo Medici-Riccardi** (➤ 104–105; pictured left). The building was to set the standard for Renaissance villas throughout Europe, and the tiny chapel within, adorned with richly coloured frescoes, is a little-known jewel of the Medici crown.

Evening

Enjoy an early evening aperitif at one of the district's traditional wine bars, Zanobini (➤ 109) and Casa del Vino (➤ 108) are both highly recommended. Then round off your day with some traditional Tuscan fare at Antichi Cancelli (Via Faenza 73r, tel: 055 218927, open Tue–Sun 12–2:45, 6:45–10:45), one of the most popular trattorias in town.

❶ Duomo, Campanile di Giotto and Battistero

The Duomo (cathedral) was the grandest building project ever undertaken in Florence, and the vast russet-coloured dome that dominates the cityscape is considered the greatest engineering feat of the Renaissance. At the time of its construction, it aroused amazement, disbelief and delight. Still today, visitors marvel at this magnificent creation "which soars to the sky and has a shadow wide enough to cover all the people of Tuscany" (Leon Battista Alberti, architect).

Work on the Duomo was begun by the city architect Arnolfo di Cambio in 1296, at a time when medieval Florence was at the height of major political, economic and urban expansion. The Republic wanted it to be one of the largest cathedrals in Christendom, "a building of the highest and most sumptuous magnificence so that it is impossible to make it better or more beautiful with the industry and power of man". They weren't to be disappointed: the result was, for many years, the world's fourth largest church (after St Peter's, Rome; St Paul's, London; and the Duomo in Milan). Its sheer size was typical of the Florentine desire for supremacy and to this day it remains the tallest building in the city.

Building Stages

The Duomo was conceived as a vast, covered piazza where the entire church-going population of Florence could assemble. It has a capacity of more than 20,000 people. Various buildings were demolished (including the old church of Santa Reparata) to make room for it, entire forests were requisitioned to provide timber, and huge slabs of marble were transported along the River Arno in flotillas. Its foundation stone was laid in 1296, but it was to take over 100 years to complete.

Arnolfo died soon after the project started and Giotto took over as city architect. He, however, devoted most of his time to the Campanile (➤ 91), and building of the Duomo ceased for almost 20 years. Eventually, by 1418, the massive base was in place, but the problem of how to construct the dome to cover it remained unresolved.

Brunelleschi's dome – one of the architectural wonders of the world

VITAL STATISTICS
Duomo Length: 153m (167 yards). Width: 90m (98 yards) at the transept.
Dome Height: 91m (299 feet); 106m (348 feet) including the lantern.
Diameter: 42m (46 yards).

Finally, a competition was organized to find a solution. The prize, a princely sum of 200 gold florins (more than a skilled craftsman could earn in two years of work), attracted proposals from craftsmen, masons and cabinet-makers from all over Europe. One of the many bizarre ideas put forward was to build a mound of earth and coins over which the dome could be moulded; then the citizens of Florence would be free to gather up the coins and take the earth away with them at

the same time. Eventually, Florence's own architectural genius, Filippo Brunelleschi, came up with the successful design.

Frescoes depicting the *Last Judgement* decorate the interior of the dome

Brunelleschi's Dome

Brunelleschi made it his life's work to find a solution to this architectural puzzle, and the erection of the world's largest masonry dome was to be his most extraordinary and daring achievement. The key to his success lay in his revival and adaptation of classical building techniques – which by the 15th century were largely forgotten and to this day are not fully understood. Combining this knowledge with both medieval and Renaissance principles, he built the dome up by setting stones and bricks of varying sizes and densities in a self-supporting herringbone pattern – a technique copied from the Pantheon in Rome.

Brunelleschi involved himself in every detail of the construction, from the baking of the bricks to the invention of a complex rainwater drainage system. New tools and devices had to be created: for example, to enable bricks to be raised such considerable heights, he called in a group of clockmakers to design a series of hoists and pulleys that were powered by a pair of horses.

One of the main difficulties that Brunelleschi faced in construction was to ensure that the dome was built with the correct curvature in every phase of the work so that it would ultimately converge at the centre. To prevent the dome from buckling

THE "PIGEON LOFT"

Before entering the Duomo, look up at the outisde of the dome and you'll see there is a ring around its base – an arcaded gallery – which suddenly stops. The story goes that on one occasion Michelangelo remarked "What's that? A pigeon loft?" That day work ceased on the gallery and it was never completed.

under its own weight, he designed a series of wooden rings to encircle the dome in the same way that iron hoops contain the staves of a barrel. These rings were to be "invisible", buried in the dome's masonry.

It was this vision – of a massive dome that seemed to rise heavenwards without any visible means of support – that both inspired and frustrated everyone involved with the project until its eventual completion in 1436, 16 years after construction had begun.

The small, octagonal lantern erected on top of the dome (again by Brunelleschi) completed his creation. One of the highlights of any visit to the Duomo is the climb up to it, via the steps between the inner and outer skins of the dome. At over 100m (328 feet), it offers the loftiest panorama of the city.

The Interior

Inside, the cathedral is gloomy and plain, as many of its finest artworks were removed to the Museo dell'Opera del Duomo (► 103) in the 19th century. Brunelleschi wanted the interior of the dome to be decorated with mosaics but in the 16th century it was decided that a painting of the *Last Judgement* by Giorgio Vasari and Federico Zuccari would be more appropriate. The result is undeniably beautiful but somehow rather too gaudy for Brunelleschi's simple, rational design.

After the lavish facade, the Duomo's interior is surprizingly austere

The apse consists of four tribunes and three minor apses, each crowned by a miniature copy of the dome and housing five chapels. The 15th-century stained glass is by Brunelleschi's great rival, Lorenzo Ghiberti.

A stairway in the aisle near the south door leads down to

the crypt, which contains the excavated remains of the 5th-century Church of Santa Reparata, a bookshop and, behind an iron grille, a plain stone slab inlaid in the floor, simply inscribed: "The body of a man of great genius, Filippo Brunelleschi, Florentine".

Campanile di Giotto

Beside the Duomo stands the elegant, square Campanile (bell-tower), designed by Giotto in 1334 but not completed until 22 years after his death by Andrea Pisano and Francesco Talenti. Most of the original sculptures and reliefs are preserved in the Museo dell'Opera del Duomo (► 103).

Although at 84.7m (278 feet) the Campanile is not as high as Brunelleschi's dome, it nevertheless affords spectacular views of the Florentine rooftops from its summit. It is sheathed in ornate white, green and pink Tuscan marble. The neo-Gothic facade of the cathedral (added in the late 19th century) echoes its style but lacks its finesse and charm.

Battistero

The Duomo is partnered by the Battistero (Baptistery), one of Florence's most important religious establishments and the oldest building in the city. It is dedicated to its patron saint, John the Baptist. According to medieval legend, a Roman temple to Mars, the pagan god of war, once stood here, later becoming a Christian church. Today's building – a characteristic example of Tuscan Romanesque style – dates from the 11th century and was used primarily for baptism ceremonies which, in those days, took place just twice a year. The exterior is clad in white and green marble, and its octagonal shape is said to symbolize the "eighth day" or "eternity".

There is a climb of 414 steps to the terrace atop Giotto's Campanile

The Baptistery's most famous features are its three sets of **bronze doors**. The **south doors** are the oldest, designed by Andrea Pisano between 1330 and 1336. The reliefs portray scenes from the life of St John the Baptist. Over a century later, to mark Florence's deliverance from the plague that struck Tuscany, the Guild of Cloth Merchants decided to commission another set of doors. To find an artist, a competition was staged and leading craftsmen, including rivals Brunelleschi and Ghiberti, submitted trial bronze panels depicting Abraham's sacrifice of Isaac (now housed in the Bargello, ➤ 62–65). Much to Brunelleschi's consternation, he and Ghiberti won the commission jointly. Working together was not a proposition that Brunelleschi could countenance and he gave up sculpture – leaving Ghiberti to work on the doors alone – and concentrated on outdoing him in architectural skill.

Ghiberti began work on the **north doors**, which depict scenes from the life of Christ, in 1403. They were so well received when they were completed in 1424 that he was commissioned to design another set of bronzes for the east doors. Ghiberti took nearly 30 years to complete these but the end result was a triumph of design, dubbed the "**Gates of Paradise**" by Michelangelo. The panels demonstrate the artistic ideas that led to the Renaissance: they are set in square frames and the buildings depicted in the ten Old Testament scenes are in a new "classical" architectural style showing a confident line of perspective. Today's east doors are actually modern copies, but you'll find the original panels in the Museo dell'Opera del Duomo (➤ 103).

Above: Detail of the bells of the Campanile

Below: Detail of Ghiberti's door panel *Moses Receives the Ten Commandments*

At the time of its construction, the **Baptistery's dome**, 26m (85 feet) in diameter, was the largest in Europe. Its interior, covered in glittering mosaics created by Venetian craftsmen, with assistance from Giotto and Giovanni Cimabue, represented a dazzling display of Florence's wealth. The centrepiece shows Christ welcoming the arisen dead into heaven with his right hand, and condemning damned souls to hell with his left hand. Beside him are the Apostles, Mary and John the Baptist, with angelic choirs above. Below the ensemble, the history of the world is portrayed in 59 scenes. The stories progress horizontally, starting above the entrance

door: the highest band shows *The Creation*; the next is *The Life of Joseph*; then *The Life of Christ*; while the lowest band represents *The Life of John the Baptist*.

TAKING A BREAK

Le Mossacce (Via del Pronconsolo 55r, tel: 055 294361, open daily 12–2:30, 7–9:30) is a tiny locals' cafe with wooden tables, paper placemats and hearty home cooking.

➕ 195 F2 ✉ Piazza del Duomo ☎ Duomo, Dome and Campanile: 055 230 2885; www.duomofirenze.it 🕐 Duomo: Mon–Wed, Fri 10–5, Thu 10–3:30 , Sat 10–4:45 (1st Sat of month 10–3:30), Sun 1:30–4:45. Dome: Mon–Fri 8:30–7, Sat 8:30–5:40. Closed some public hols. Campanile: Daily 8:30–7:30. Last tickets at 6:50. Closed some public hols. Battistero: Mon–Sat 12:15–7, Sun 8:30–2. 1st Sat of month 8:30–2. Masses on weekdays at 10:30am and 11am. Cathedral Crypt of Santa Reparata: Mon–Wed, Fri 10–5, Sat 10–4:45. Closed some public hols 🚌 Many routes, including 1, 6, 14, 17 and 23 💶 Duomo: free. Dome: expensive. Campanile: moderate. Battistero: inexpensive. Crypt: moderate

---

DUOMO, CAMPANILE AND BATTISTERO: INSIDE INFO

Top tips Take **binoculars** with you to study the mosaics inside the Baptistery.

■ Neither the dome (below) nor the Campanile has a lift. The **dome has 463 steps** and the **Campanile 414**. Unless you're feeling particularly energetic, choose one or other and climb it either early in the morning before it gets too hot, or at sunset for spectacular photos. The dome is the more

interesting (and higher) climb, as you get an insight into its construction and a bird's-eye view of the cathedral, but it usually has the longer queue. Both offer **breathtaking views of the city** and its surrounding girdle of hills.

■ Inside the Baptistery, ask for the free, highly informative **audio-guide**.

One to miss The ruins of the **church of Santa Reparata** in the crypt are confusing, and unless you are particularly interested, it is not worth paying to see them.

Hidden gems Domenico di Michelino's painting in the left aisle of the Duomo depicts Dante, Florence's greatest poet. *The Divine Comedy* was once read out to large, enthusiastic crowds in the cathedral.

■ Look for Paolo Uccello's *Clock for the Canonical Hours* (1443), to your right as you enter the Duomo. It goes anticlockwise (counterclockwise).

■ In the Battistero, the **tomb of Baldassare Cossa** (deposed Pope John XXIII), sculpted by Donatello and Michelozzo di Bartolommeo Michelozzi, is one of the earliest Renaissance wall tombs (1421–27).

■ The large **octagonal font** in the Baptistery is where many famous Florentines, including Dante, were baptized.

❷ San Lorenzo and the Cappelle Medicee

After the Duomo, San Lorenzo is the city's second most important church. Founded in the 4th century, the original church served as Florence's cathedral for 400 years. In the early 15th century it became the official church of the Medici family and was entirely rebuilt, to designs by Filippo Brunelleschi. The facade remains unfinished to this day, despite various proposals, including one by Michelangelo.

Brunelleschi's elegant interior is one of the supreme masterpieces of the early Florentine Renaissance. It is based on Gothic architectural principles, with a cross-shaped plan and three aisles, but has elements that later became typical features of Renaissance buildings: rounded arches, a coffered central ceiling, and *pietra serena* (grey sandstone from the quarries of Fiesole).

The Cappelle Medicee

The treasure trove of precious artworks contained here was financed mainly by the Medici family. The Sagrestia Vecchia (Old Sacristy), also by Brunelleschi, is an architectural gem, consisting of a geometrically perfect cube topped by a dome. The apsidal ceiling represents the celestial hemisphere, showing the passage of the sun between the constellations above Florence on the night of 4 July, 1442.

The cloisters lead to the Medici's great Biblioteca Laurenziana (Laurentian Library), housing one of the world's most important collections of Italian manuscripts and featuring Michelangelo's highly original *pietra serena* staircase, formed of three separate flights.

Cappelle Medicee

The Cappelle Medicee (Medici Chapels), the family mausoleum of the Medici, consists of three distinct parts, the crypt, the Cappella dei Principi and Sagrestia Nuova.

The remarkable **Cappella dei Principi** (Chapel of the Princes) was begun in 1604 and took 300 years to complete. It consists entirely of marble and precious stones, painstakingly pieced together by craftsmen of the Opificio delle Pietre Dure (► 105). The end result was so spectacular that the Medici family used the chapel (intended as a mausoleum) to receive foreign ambassadors and hold marriage ceremonies.

A narrow corridor leads to the **Sagrestia Nuova** (New Sacristy), designed by Michelangelo along similar lines to Brunelleschi's Old Sacristy, to house the Medici tombs. With clever use of white marble and dark grey stonework, he created an appropriately solemn atmosphere. Michelangelo also produced some of his finest, most famous sculptures for the tombs, including the monumental funerary figures of **Night** (a young woman asleep) **and Day** (a strong, muscular man whose face is roughly hewn), and, on the opposite side of the sacristy, **Dawn and Dusk**, who symbolize, among other things, the passage of time, to which even the bravest of men must submit.

The ceiling of San Lorenzo

Madonna and Child flanked by saints by Michelangelo in the Cappelle Medicee

TAKING A BREAK

At lunch-time, try **Palle d'Oro** (Via Sant'Antonino 45r, tel: 055 288383, open Mon–Sat 12–2:30, 6:30–10) and choose between a quick snack at the bar, a sandwich to take away or a meal in the simple restaurant at the back.

San Lorenzo
✚ 195 E2 ✉ Piazza di San Lorenzo ☎ 055 214042 🕙 Church: Mon–Sat 10–5:30; Mar–Oct only Sun 1:30–5:30. Sagrestia Vecchia: hours vary on availablity of staff. Biblioteca Laurenziana: Mon–Thu 8–5:30, Fri 8–2 🚍 Many routes including 1, 6, 17 and A 💶 Inexpensive

Cappelle Medicee
✚ 195 E2 ✉ Piazza Madonna degli Aldobrandini 6 ☎ 055 238 8602; advance booking 055 294883; www.firenzemusei.it/medicee 🚍 Many routes including 1, 6, 11, 17 and A 🕙 Daily 8:15–5. Closed 1st, 3rd and 5th Mon and 2nd and 4th Sun of the month. Last entry 30 mins before closing 💶 Moderate

---

SAN LORENZO AND THE CAPPELLE MEDICEE: INSIDE INFO

Hidden gems In the nave of the church, look for the **bronze pulpits**, depicting scenes from Christ's Passion and Resurrection. These were the last works of Donatello.

■ *The Martyrdom of St Lawrence* (1659), in the north aisle, is a vast Mannerist fresco by Bronzino (Agnolo Allori detto il Bronzino).

■ *St Joseph and Christ in the Workshop* by Pietro Annigoni (1910–88), at the end of the north aisle, is notable as one of few modern works to be seen in Florence.

■ Today, the *Marriage of the Virgin* altarpiece (1523) by Rosso Fiorentino is used for the blessing of engagement rings. Fiorentino later left Florence to live and work in France.

■ Michelangelo's *Madonna and Child* (1521) in the Sagrestia Nuova is considered to be one of his most beautiful statues.

3 Galleria dell'Accademia

Florence's Academy of Fine Arts was founded in 1563 as the first school in Europe devoted to teaching the techniques of drawing, painting and sculpture. Its art collection was formed in the 18th century to provide students of the academy with inspirational models.

David

Nowadays, everyone comes here to see *David* (1501–04, ► 20–21), the city's most celebrated sculpture. Sculpted by Michelangelo from a single block of marble when he was just 29 years old, the masterpiece, 4.1m (13.5 feet) high, established him as the foremost sculptor of his time. As Giorgio Vasari remarked: "There has never been seen a pose so fluent, or a gracefulness equal to this, or feet, hands and head so well-related to each other with quality, skill and design." The statue shows David in meditative pose preparing for his fight with Goliath, rather than in the traditional pose of triumph (with one foot on the severed head of the defeated giant). Placed in Piazza della Signoria (► 60–61) on completion, *David* soon became a symbol of civic pride and liberty for the Florentine Republic. Amid growing concerns that he was losing his balance and leaning forwards, *David* was moved to the Accademia in 1873. It was a massive undertaking: streets were widened, arches demolished, and the move took 40 men five days to accomplish.

Above: Michelangelo's *Quattro Prigioni*, four dramatic *non-finito* works

GALLERIA DELL'ACCADEMIA: INSIDE INFO

In more depth Look for Giovanni di Scheggia's *Cassone Adimari*, an elaborately painted chest dating from the 15th century. Originally part of a bride's trousseau, it is covered with scenes depicting daily life in Florence.

■ In Lorenzo Monaco's painting *Christ in Pietà* note the symbols of the Passion story: Pilate washing his hands (under the cross on the left); 30 pieces of silver, the ear of Malchus and the torch symbolizing Christ's arrest (under the cross on the right); St Peter's denial (top left) and Judas's kiss (top right).

David – a legend in marble

Other Highlights

Other classic works here by Michelangelo include the dramatic *Quattro Prigioni*, four muscular *non-finito* (➤ 63) "prisoners" struggling to free themselves from the stone, which were intended for the tomb of Pope Julius II. The Accademia is not, however, just the "Museum of Michelangelo", so be sure to see the rest of the collection, including such treasures as Pacino di Buonaguida's *Tree of Life* (1310); Taddeo Gaddi's reliquary cupboard panels showing Stories of *Christ and St Francis of Assisi* (1330–35) from Santa Croce; and (on the first floor) Jacopo di Cione's 14th-century embroidered altar frontal showing *The Coronation of the Virgin* from Santa Maria Novella. Finally, the 19th-century gallery contains plaster busts of key figures, both Florentine and foreign: Machiavelli, Dante, Byron, Liszt and so on. See how many you can identify.

TAKING A BREAK

A good choice for lunch is **Trattoria Mario** (➤ 109), where you can enjoy authentic Tuscan food.

🚹 196 B3 ✉ Via Ricasoli 60
☎ 055 294883;
www.tickitaly.com (reservations);
055 238 8609 (information)
🕐 Tue–Sun 8:15–6:50. Last tickets 30 mins before closing
🚌 1, 17 and C
💶 Expensive

4 San Marco

The monastery of San Marco is one of the most spiritually uplifting places in Florence. Fra Angelico, who lived and worked here, provided much of the decoration, and the beautiful, faded frescoes and paintings are some of his most important works. His use of pale colours and local landscapes as backdrops gives the paintings a mystical serenity. Fra Bartolomeo, St Antonino (Bishop of Florence) and the religious fanatic Girolamo Savonarola also spent time here.

The Exterior

A church and convent had stood on the site since the 13th century, and in 1437 Cosimo Il Vecchio de Medici commissioned Michelozzo to enlarge them to house the Dominican monks from nearby Fiesole. In the 1580s the dark, lofty church was rebuilt, and a new facade (thought to be by Agostino Nobili) was added some 200 years later.

The Interior

It is Fra Angelico's frescoes, though, that are San Marco's real draw. As soon as you enter the first cloister in the museum, you see one of his most important frescoes, the *Crucifixion with St Dominic*. The door to the right of the entrance leads to a small gallery devoted to Fra Angelico's work. After World War I, all of his Florentine paintings

Sant'Antonino cloisters, a place of serenity and contemplation

were amassed here including *The Deposition* (1432), containing a portrait of Michelozzo (the figure in the black hood behind Christ) and the *Linaiuoli Tabernacle* (1433), the most frequently reproduced of all his paintings. His magnificent *Crucifixion* fresco, which graces an entire wall of the chapter house, is unusual in that it contains figures not alive at the time of Christ, among them St Dominic and St Francis.

Continue up to the first floor to the dormitory. Fra Angelico's inspired *Annunciation* (1442), a masterpiece of Renaissance perspective, greets you at the top of the stairs. Beyond lie 44 tiny cells, which form the backdrop for a celebrated series of devotional frescoes.

TAKING A BREAK

Directly opposite San Marco, **Ristorante Accademia** (Piazza San Marco 7r, tel: 055 217343, open 12–3, 7–11) is a lively and welcoming trattoria serving simple Florentine dishes. The *menù del giorno* is particularly good value.

The Church of San Marco, beside the monastery complex	➕ 196 B4 ✉ Piazza di San Marco 1 ☎ 055 238 8608 🕐 Church: daily 7–noon, 4–8. Museo di San Marco: Mon–Fri 8:15–1:50, Sat–Sun 8:15–6:50; closed 1st, 3rd and 5th Sun and 2nd and 4th Mon of the month. Last ticket 30 mins before closing. Closed some public hols 🚇 Major intersection – many routes including 1, 7, 25, 33 and C 💷 Moderate

---

SAN MARCO: INSIDE INFO

Top tips Arrive early to beat the crowds, and begin your visit on the first floor to appreciate the solitariness of the monks' cells.

■ Allow at least **two hours** in the museum.

Hidden gems In the ground-floor gallery, look for the **35 scenes from the** *Life of Christ* by Fra Angelico. These masterpieces, originally cupboard panel decorations, are remarkably intricate in their design.

■ Don't miss Domenico Ghirlandaio's *Last Supper* in the refectory (to the left of the stairs to the first floor).

In more depth Among the most beautiful of the **cell frescoes** are *The Deposition* (cell 2); *The Annunciation* (cell 3); *The Crucifixion* (cell 4); *The Transfiguration* (cell 6); *The Mocking of Christ* (cell 7); and *The Coronation of Mary* (cell 9).

■ Cells 12–15, **Savonarola's quarters** when he was Prior, contain various mementos and a portrait by Fra Bartolomeo.

■ In cells 38–39, which were kept for **Cosimo il Vecchio** when on retreat, look for the *Adoration of the Magi* fresco.

At Your Leisure

5 Loggia del Bigallo

It's easy to miss the Loggia del Bigallo, an exquisitely carved Gothic porch on the corner of Piazza di San Giovanni and Via dei Calzaiuoli. It was constructed in the 14th century for the Misericordia, one of Florence's great charitable confraternities, which still runs an ambulance service and has its headquarters in the square.

For years, the loggia served as a kind of lost-property office for unwanted babies. Abandoned children were displayed here for three days and if their parents didn't come forward to claim them within that time, they were sent to foster homes. In the 15th century, the Misericordia merged with a similar charitable concern called the Bigallo.

Today, a small gallery (open all year) houses various works of art accumulated by both organizations, including a fresco of the *Madonna della Misericordia* (1342) by the school of Bernardo Daddi, containing the earliest-known view of Florence.

An overview of 15th-century Florence in Museo di Firenze com'era

🚩 195 E2 ✉ Piazza di San Giovanni ☎ 055 271 80306 🚍 36, 37 🎟 Loggia: free. Gallery: inexpensive

6 Museo di Firenze com'era

If possible, make this small museum one of your first ports of call. You will see the development and urban transformation of Florence from the Renaissance to the end of the 19th century, through a comprehensive series of maps, drawings, models, paintings and prints.

The museum is housed in a former convent surrounding a grassy courtyard near the Duomo. Its finest exhibits include the famous *Pianta*

[Map labels: Palazzo Pucci · Via de' Pucci · Via Servi · Teatro Niccolini · Via Bufalini · Ospedale S Maria Nuova · Battistero · Museo dell'Opera del Duomo · Museo di Firenze com'era · Duomo · Piazza d S Giovanni · Piazza del Duomo · Via F Portinari · Campanile di Giotto · Loggia del Bigallo · Via d'Oche · Via dell'Oriuolo · Via d Proconsolo · Via d Calzaiuoli · Via d Corso · Via Dante Alighieri · FIORENZA]

Catena (Chain Map, 1470) showing a detailed panorama of the city (the original is in Germany); the exquisite lunettes (1599) by Giusto Utens, cataloguing all the Medici villas and gardens; and *Views of the City* by Giuseppe Zocchi, which provides a vivid impression of Florentine street-life during the 18th century.

One room is devoted to the drawings of Giuseppe Poggi, the city architect who planned to remodel much of central Florence during its brief spell as the capital of Italy (1865–71). Fortunately, his schemes were halted, but not before the 14th-century walls had been destroyed (together with numerous medieval buildings) to make way for Piazza della Repubblica (➤ 127).

➕ 196 B2 ✉ Via dell'Oriuolo 24 ☎ 055 261 6545 ⏰ Jun–Sep Mon–Tue 9–2, Sat 9–7; Oct–May Mon–Wed 9–2, Sat 9–7 🚌 14, 23 and A 💷 Inexpensive

❼ Museo dell'Opera del Duomo

The Cathedral Works Museum, in a striking modern interior just behind the Duomo, contains many precious items removed from the Duomo, Campanile and Baptistery for purposes of preservation. Most notable are the Lorenzo Ghiberti panels from the Baptistery doors (➤ 92–93), which are displayed in the main courtyard (where Michelangelo carved *David*).

Detail of the *Pietà* by Michelangelo in Museo dell'Opera del Duomo

The ground floor contains 14th-century sculptures from the facade of the Duomo, including an unusual *Madonna and Child* by Arnolfo di Cambio, (sometimes known as the *Madonna with the Glass Eyes*). Halfway up the first flight of stairs is a beautiful *Pietà*, sculpted by Michelangelo when he was almost 80. It is an especially significant work as it was meant for his own tomb. He portrayed himself in the figure of Nicodemus, a sculptor and one of the two men who removed Christ from the cross.

Further upstairs, you'll find sketches and models of different facades proposed for the Duomo, showing the change in architectural taste from the 15th to the 19th century. There is also a model of the dome and a picture of King Victor Emmanuel II laying the first stone of the present facade in 1860, together with his trowel and various other Duomo memorabilia. Brunelleschi's funeral mask (1446) and a reconstruction of his workyard, showing the wooden scaffolding and types of tools he used, are also on display.

➕ 196 B2 ✉ Piazza del Duomo 9 ☎ 055 230 2885; www.operaduomo.firenze.it ⏰ Mon–Sat 9–7:30, Sun 9–1:45 🚌 14 and 23 💷 Moderate

8 Palazzo Medici-Riccardi

The innovative style of this massive palazzo, home to the Medici family for nearly 100 years, marked a turning point in Renaissance architecture. Within its bulky walls lies the Cappella dei Magi, one of Florence's most beautiful chapels, still adorned with brilliantly coloured frescoes.

Cosimo il Vecchio, founder of the great Medici dynasty, had a passion for building and is considered among the great innovators of the Renaissance movement in Florence. Having dismissed Brunelleschi's original designs for the palace as too showy, he commissioned his favourite architect, Michelozzo di Bartolommeo Michelozzi, to build a more discreet symbol of his power. Michelozzi's heavily rusticated design, featuring large, rough-hewn blocks of stone, became the model for other Renaissance palaces.

During the time that the palace served as the Medici family home (from 1444 to 1540), the family gradually deprived the old Republican aristocracy of its power. The Duomo (► 88–94) and the Palazzo Vecchio (key symbols of Republican Florence; ► 70–71)

Inside the vast Sala di Luca Giordano

diminished in importance, while the Medici Palace became prominent as the real seat of political power. Nowadays, the Palazzo Medici-Riccardi (incorporating the later owners' name) houses the offices of the Town Prefecture.

The **Cappella dei Magi** is the palace's greatest treasure. Its richly coloured frescoes showing the *Journey of the Magi* were probably commissioned by Cosimo's eldest son, Piero the Gouty, and painted by Benozzo Gozzoli between 1459 and 1463. Set in an idealized Tuscan landscape, they have an almost fairytale quality, with magical scenes of exotic birds, animals, kings and castles. You can identify members of the Medici family by their ostrich-feather emblem – on the right-hand wall, Piero's son, Lorenzo the Magnificent (on the central white horse), is followed by Cosimo (on another white horse), with Piero (hatless) between them, then his brother Lorenzo (in a conical hat, also riding). The artist can be seen in the crowd following the King, with his name inscribed on his small red cap. The Cappella dei Magi is hard to

Map labels

San Marco
Giardino dei Semplici
Università
Gen M Fanti
Piazza San Marco
Galleria dell' Accademia
Museo dell'Opificio delle Pietre Dure
SAN GIOVANNI
Palazzo Gerini
Mostre di Leonardo
Palazzo Medici-Riccardi
Palazzo Pucci
V d Dogana
V d La Pira
V d Arazzieri
Via Giorgio La Pira
CAVOUR
Via Cesare Battisti
Ricasoli
Via degli Alfani
Via della Stufa
Via dei Ginori
VIA
Via dei Servi
Via de' Pucci

– the Cappella dei Principi (➤ 96) – and the city's most spectacular example of the craft.

Now located in the former Convent of San Nicolò, the Opificio delle Pietre Dure is a national institute for teaching this ancient and unique Florentine art.

A small museum on the premises contains an exquisite collection of different marbles, tools of the trade, and a dazzling display of items – cabinets, tables, vases, picture frames, even portraits of the Medici Grand Dukes – all made with semi-precious stone inlay or *scagliola*, a cheaper version of *pietre dure* made with painted plaster rather than costly marble.

🔢 196 B3 ✉ Via degli Alfani 78 ☎ 055 265111 🕐 Mon–Wed, Fri–Sat 8:15–2, Thu 8:15–7 🚌 C ♿ Inexpensive

find. Proceed to the first courtyard, enter the door immediately to your left, then climb the stairs to the second floor, where a small door on the left will lead you into the chapel.

On the first floor the Sala di Luca Giordano, with its lavish gilt stucco work, painted mirrors and chandeliers, is named after the Neapolitan artist who frescoed the ceiling with a splashy baroque *Apotheosis of the Medici*. In an adjoining room, you'll find a demure *Madonna and Child* painting by Filippo Lippi, which was once the altarpiece of the palace chapel. The palace is also used for temporary exhibitions.

🔢 195 F2 ✉ Via Cavour 3 ☎ 055 276 0340 🕐 Thu–Tue 9–7 🚌 1, 6 and 17 ♿ Expensive

🔟 Museo dell'Opificio delle Pietre Dure

The Medicis were the first to promote Florence's special craft of producing inlaid pictures by using *pietre dure* – "hard stones" (marble and semi-precious stones). Ferdinando I de Medici founded the Opificio in 1588 as a workshop for the craftsmen working on the family mausoleum

Right: Ornamental *pietre dure* work dating from the 17th century

🔟 Giardino dei Semplici

Although somewhat unkempt, the Semplici Gardens, Florence's botanical garden, hidden off the well-trodden tourist track beyond San Marco, provides a tranquil and rare green space. It was founded in 1545

by Cosimo I de Medici to grow herbs and other *semplici* (raw ingredients) used by medieval apothecaries in the preparation of medicines. Today it forms part of the University of Florence, containing around 9,000 species of plants. It is especially stunning in springtime.

➕ 196 C4 ✉ Via Micheli 3 ☎ 055 275 7402 ⏱ Mon, Tue, Thu, Fri, Sun 9–1, Sat 9–5 🚌 1, 7 25, 33 and C 💶 Moderate

🔟 Santissima Annunziata

The most striking thing about this church is the feeling that you've entered it at the wrong end, as half the pews face the doorway!

Immediately to your left, above the silver altar, is one of the city's most venerated shrines – a painting of the Virgin Mary. The story goes that in 1252 a monk, struggling to paint the Virgin's face, fell asleep and on waking found the fresco had been finished by an angel.

The church's interior, with its mass of coloured marble, gilt and frescoed side chapels, is magnificent. The Feroni Chapel (Cappella Feroni), in particular (first on the left), is considered a jewel of Florentine baroque, with decoration by Giovanni Battista Foggini. The entrance porch was added to the

Fresco by Andrea del Sarto in Santissima Annunziata

church at a later date and decorated by up-and-coming young artists Pontormo, Fiorentino, Baldovinetti and Andrea del Sarto.

Outside, the piazza is considered among the city's most elegant squares, frequently described as "an extended Renaissance courtyard". An equestrian statue of Duke Ferdinando I by Giambologna graces the centre of the square, together with two Mannerist bronze fountains. Each year a fair here celebrates the Feast of the Annunciation (25 March), and on the Feast of the Rificolona (7 September) Florentines process through the city with colourful paper lanterns to give thanks to the Madonna of Santissima Annunziata.

➕ 196 C3 ✉ Piazza della Santissima Annunziata ☎ 055 266181 ⏱ Daily 7:30–12:30, 4–6:30 🚌 6, 31, 32 and C 💶 Free

🔢 Museo Archeologico

The remarkable collections of ancient art in the Archaeological Museum provide a refreshing change from Florentine Renaissance art. They include Italy's most important Etruscan artefacts and its second most important Egyptian collection.

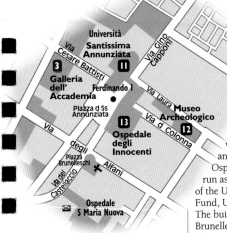

The museum was damaged during the 1966 flood (► 32–33), and many items are not yet on display.

Star exhibits include an Egyptian chariot made of wood and bone (14th century BC, found near Thebes); the François vase, depicting scenes from Greek mythology (570BC, found in an Etruscan tomb near Chiusi); and the Etruscan bronze chimera (5th century BC), a peculiar mythical creature with a lion's body, a goat's head and a serpent for a tail.

✚ 197 D3 ✉ Via della Colonna 36 ☎ 055 23575 🕔 Mon 2–7, Tue, Thu 8:30–7, Wed, Fri, Sat, Sun 8:30–2 🚌 6, 31, 32 and C 🖐 Moderate

13 Ospedale degli Innocenti

Europe's first orphanage – the Hospital of Innocents – was founded here in 1445, following the delivery of Agatha Emerald on 25 January. From that day, mothers could place unwanted children anonymously on the *rota* (a rotating stone wheel) here and ring the bell. The stone was then turned around and the child was taken in. Ospedale degli Innocenti is still run as an orphanage, and offices of the United Nations Children's Fund, UNICEF, are on the premises. The building, designed by Filippo Brunelleschi, is a prime example of restrained Classical design. The arcaded loggia is based on the repetition of the exact same measurement (the slender columns are equal in height to the width of the arches), and enhanced by the alternation of light plaster and dark ribbing. The charming ornamental rondels by Andrea della Robbia on the facade show babies wrapped in swaddling clothes.

Two elegant cloisters and a gallery of paintings are also open to visitors, including Ghirlandaio's *Adoration of the Magi*, once in the adjoining church.

✚ 196 C3 ✉ Piazza della Santissima Annunziata 12 ☎ 055 203 7308 🕔 Cloisters and Gallery: Mon–Sat 8:30–7, Sun 8:30–2. Last tickets 30 mins before closing 🚌 6, 31, 32 and C 🖐 Moderate

Baby identity tags from the museum in the Ospedale degli Innocenti

Where to...
Eat and Drink

Prices

Expect to pay per person for a meal, excluding drinks and service
€ under €20   €€ €20–€45   €€€ over €45

Casa del Vino €

The Casa del Vino, or House of Wine, is just that – a place to come to drink or buy wine. It is often busy, thanks to its location close to the Mercato Centrale (► 111), but usually only with locals rather than visitors.

You can choose wine to buy by the bottle to take home with you, or wash down *crostini* (toasts) or *panini* (rolls) at the bar with one of many wines which are available by the glass.

➕ 195 E3 ⊠ Via dell'Ariento 16r
☎ 055 215609 ⏰ Mon–Fri 9:30–7.30,
Sat 10–3

Coquinarius €€

This is a must if you're in Florence but be sure to book or you'll have a long wait. Giant framed posters against whitewashed walls create a cool and relaxed atmosphere for the awesome food to come. The vegetable pie is superb and the goat cheese and pear ravioli is to die for.

➕ 196 A1 ⊠ Via dell' Oche 15r ☎ 055 230
2153 ⏰ Mon–Sat 9am–11pm

Gozzi Sergio €–€€

This simple trattoria prides itself on its generous portions of hearty Florentine cuisine made with the finest produce from the nearby

Mercato Centrale (► 111). The menu is small but boasts such staples as *minestone di verdura* (vegetable soup), *bistecca alla fiorentina* (► 10), with *cantucci e vin Santo* for dessert, all washed down with a robust house wine. There is also tripe on Mondays and Thursdays and fresh fish on Tuesdays and Fridays. Excellent value for money.

➕ 195 E2 ⊠ Piazza San Lorenzo 8r
☎ 055 281941 ⏰ Mon–Sat noon–3.
Closed Aug

Gran Caffè San Marco €–€€

Just around the corner from the Galleria dell'Accademia, Gran Caffè San Marco is one of the oldest coffee houses in Florence and traditionally a meeting place for artists, painters, professors and students from the nearby university. A wide choice of delicacies is offered, either off the menu or self-service from the counter, and can be eaten outside in the pretty garden, which is covered and heated in winter.

➕ 196 B4 ⊠ Piazza San Marco 11r ☎ 055
215833; www. grancaffesanmarco ⏰ May–
Sep daily 6pm–1am; Oct–Apr 6am–12am

La Mescita Fiaschetteria €

A *fiaschetteria* is a traditional wine bar, which means a place that sells wine by the glass along with an inexpensive selection of snacks, pastas and simple hot meals.

This place is especially popular at lunchtime, when it fills up with students enthusiastically tucking into the reasonably priced dish of the day.

➕ 196 B3 ⊠ Via degli Alfani 70r,
corner of Via dei Servi ☎ No phone
⏰ Mon–Sat 11–3

Nerbone €

There's no cheap-and-cheerful Florentine eating establishment more authentic than this tiny place in a busy corner of the Mercato Centrale. Market traders and local shoppers throng its tables and counters, filling up on a selection of tasty snacks and simple hot lunch

...dishes (pastas, stews, soups) whose range and recipes have been tried and tested since the place opened in 1872.

＋ 195 E3 ☒ Mercato Centrale ☎ 055 219949 ⓦ Mon–Sat 7am–2pm

q.b. €€

A sleek, contemporary wine bar and restaurant not far from the Palazzo Medici-Riccardi. The q.b. stands for *quanto basta*, translating as "how much is enough". The lunchtime buffet is good value, with an array of cured meats and delectable cheeses, accompanied by a glass or two from the extensive wine list.

＋ 195 A3 ☒ Via de Ginori 10r ☎ 055 211427; www.quantobasta.eu ⓦ Wine bar Wed–Sun 12:30–3.30, 6:30–10:30; restaurant Wed–Sun 7–11

Taverna del Bronzino €€€

This is northern Florence's smart and expensive option, an elegant place with vaulted ceilings and terracotta floors. It has been around for years, but still seduces the great and the good (local and foreign alike) with its charming setting and refined regional cuisine – the meats and fresh fish are invariably excellent. The regular menu is full of Florentine and Tuscan staples such as *bistecca alla fiorentina*, but the daily menu is often more creative and adventurous. You might be able to sample imaginative and mouth-watering dishes such as *rombo al forno con olive* (oven-cooked turbot with olives) or *rigatoni al ragù bianco d'anatra* (pasta with duck sauce). Although the restaurant lies some way north of the city centre, near the Museo di San Marco (▶ 100), it is well worth seeking out.

＋ 195 F5 ☒ Via delle Ruote 25r ☎ 055 495220 ⓦ Mon–Sat 12:30–2:30, 7.30–10:30. Closed Aug

Trattoria Mario €

Mario is a Florentine institution that makes few concessions to interior decor or to stylish dining. Rather it's a rough-and-ready eating place just north of the Mercato Centrale that provides cheap, authentic and good-quality Tuscan food (lunch only) to students, shoppers and market traders. You'll find tripe on Mondays and Thursdays, fish on Fridays and just one pudding week-round – *cantucci* with *vin Santo* (biscuits with dessert wine).

＋ 195 E3 ☒ Via Rosina 2r- Piazza del Mercato Centrale ☎ 055 218550 ⓦ Mon–Sat 12:30–3. Closed Aug

Zanobini €

Zanobini is much like its near-neighbour, the Casa del Vino (▶ 111). It's a simple wood-panelled wine bar patronized almost entirely by locals (always a good recommendation). Its local popularity is despite the fact that Zanobini lies just off streets filled with visitors crowding the San Lorenzo market (▶ 111). It makes a good place to have a hunk of bread with cheese or salami and drink a glass of wine. There's also a fine selection of wines by the bottle to buy in the back room.

＋ 195 E3 ☒ Via Sant'Antonino 47r ☎ 055 239 6850 ⓦ Mon–Sat 8:30–2, 3.30–8. Closed public holidays

Zà-Zà €

This long-established, once low-key place is in a convenient location, close to the Mercato Centrale, and as a result is extremely popular, and the chances are you'll have to wait in line patiently for a table at busy times. You can see the appeal, however: low prices (you choose from one of several tempting set-price menus); a rustic stone dining-room lined with pictures and fascinating old photographs (there is a larger eating area downstairs); and good, expertly cooked, basic food. Try the justifiably celebrated hot *antipasti* (starters) or the tasty *crostini* (toasts) with taleggio cheese, oil, pepper and vinegar.

＋ 195 E3 ☒ Piazza del Mercato Centrale 26r ☎ 055 215411; www. trattoriazaza.it ⓦ Mon–Sat 9am–11pm. Closed Sun, except last of the month

Where to... Shop

Shopping in northern Florence is dominated by two markets: the Mercato Centrale, a food market, and San Lorenzo, a general street market. The district is home to excellent bookshops and fine food and wine outlets.

BOOKS AND CDS

Alberti

Alberti is Florence's best shop for CDs and DVDs. Opera, classical and jazz are found in the Borgo San Lorenzo shop, while the Via de' Pucci outlet is devoted to contemporary dance, pop and rock.

➕ 195 E2 ⊠ Borgo San Lorenzo 45–49r and Via de' Pucci 16r ☎ 055 284346 ⏰ Both stores Mon 3:30–7:30, Tue–Sat 9–7:30

Feltrinelli Librerie

Feltrinelli belongs to a nationwide chain of bookshops. Invariably busy, its various floors are filled not only with Italian titles, but also a few English and other foreign-language books – though the sister store (▶ below) is better for such titles. This branch just west of the Duomo has a good selection of guides and maps.

➕ 195 E2 ⊠ Via Cerretani 30r ☎ 055 238 2652; www.feltrinelli.it ⏰ Mon–Fri 9:30–8, Sat 10–8, Sun 10:30–1:30, 3–7:30

Feltrinelli

A short walk from the Duomo, this specialist branch of the excellent Feltrinelli chain of bookshops deals in English and other foreign-language titles, as well as maps, guides, magazines and good art and photography sections. It also sells the useful *Firenze Spettacolo* listings magazine (▶ 46).

➕ 196 B3 ⊠ Via Cavour 12–20r ☎ 055 219524 ⏰ Mon–Sat 9–7:30

Paperback Exchange

This long-established second-hand bookshop just south of Piazza del Duomo has a good selection of English titles with an art, art history or Italian connection. It also has an exchange scheme for second-hand paperbacks.

➕ 197 D2 ⊠ Via dell'Oche 4r ☎ 055 293460; www.papex.it ⏰ Mon–Fri 9–7:30, Sat 10:30–7:30; closed Sat afternoon Jul–Aug

FOOD AND WINE

Fonte dei Dolci

Since 1954, the "Fountain of Sweets" just west of the Mercato Centrale has been selling a vast range not only of sweets, but also cakes, chocolate, nougat and other goodies. Many are made in the shop's own kitchens. The store also carries a range of oils, wine, pasta sauces and other savoury items.

➕ 195 D3 ⊠ Via Nazionale 120–122r ☎ 055 294180; www.fontedeidolce.com ⏰ Daily 9–7:30

Robiglio

Robiglio is an old-fashioned *pasticceria*, or cake and pastry shop, with three outlets in Florence: this is the main one, and makes an elegant place to enjoy tea, coffee and other drinks. It also sells exquisite cakes. Another outlet can be found just south of the Duomo on Via de' Tosinghi.

➕ 196 B2 ⊠ Via dei Servi 112r ☎ 055 214501; www.robiglio.it ⏰ Mon–Sat 7:30–8

HOUSEHOLD

Bartolini

Bartolini was founded in 1921, and has become such a fixture that locals refer to the junction where it stands as the *angolo* Bartolini or "Bartoloni corner". It sells just about every item of kitchenware you could wish for, as well as fine china, porcelain and glassware from some of the best names worldwide (Alessi, Wedgwood, Spode, Riedel and so on).

🚹 196 B2 🖂 Via dei Servi 30r, corner of Via Bufalini ☎ 055 289223 or 055 211895; www.dinobartolini.it 🕓 Tue–Sat 9–12:30, 3:30–7, Mon 3:30–7

Frette

Famous throughout the world, this Italian company is renowned for producing the finest luxury bedding, tableware and other soft furnishings for the home. The unforgettable styles, textures and patterns are always at the forefront of design.

🚹 196 A2 🖂 Via Cavour 2 ☎ 055 211369 🕓 Mon–Sat 9–1, 3:30–7:30

Mercato Centrale

Florence's magnificent central food market deserves almost as much attention from visitors as the city's museums and galleries.

Opened in 1874, it is Europe's largest covered food hall, a wonderful stone, iron and glass building designed by Giuseppe Mengoni, the architect responsible for Milan's celebrated covered shopping galleries.

The market divides into two: the upper level is devoted mostly to fruit and vegetables. On the ground floor, by contrast, stalls (stands) display cheese, ham, meats, dried goods, olive oils, pasta and a cornucopia of other basic and gourmet foodstuffs. This is a great place to come for treats and gifts to take home, for picnic provisions, or for snacks and light meals in places such as Nerbone (▶ 108), but if you want to buy wine, you should visit wine bar-shops such as Zanobini (▶ 109) and the Casa del Vino (▶ 108).

🚹 195 E3 🖂 Via dell'Ariento ☎ No phone 🕓 Jul–Aug Mon–Sat 7–2; Sep–Jun Mon–Fri 7–2, Sat, 7–5

San Lorenzo

The San Lorenzo market fills the area around the Church of San Lorenzo. Mid-price leather jackets, shoes, ties, handbags, luggage, T-shirts and inexpensive clothing are for sale. The quality of the leatherware can be surprisingly good, and prices correspondingly high given that this is a market. The competition for buyers means you may be able to haggle over prices. Note that goods are cheaper at the weekly market in Cascine Park (▶ 134). The streets can be uncomfortably crowded, with pickpockets operating.

🚹 195 E2 🖂 Piazza di San Lorenzo–Via Canto de' Nelli ☎ No phone 🕓 Daily 9–7:30

Scriptorium

A few paces north of the Duomo, this delightful shop is devoted to paper, books and calligraphy, selling fine inks, handmade plain-leaf books, pens, personalized stationery, sealing wax, seals, old-fashioned twine and *carta paglia* (wrapping paper).

🚹 195 F2 🖂 Via dei Servi 5r ☎ 055 211804; www.scriptoriumfirenze.com 🕓 Mon–Sat 10–2, 3:30–7:30

Farmacia SS Annunziata

The origins of the products in the ancient wooden cabinets of this lovely vaulted shop can be traced to 1561, when the herbalist Domenico di Vincenzo Brunetti moved his business to this site just south of the junction of Via dei Servi and Via degli Alfani. All the many products for men, women and children, from rosemary soap and sage toothpaste to camomile baby shampoos and bilberry aftershave, are handmade to the original recipes, and come in the company's simple yet chic black-and-white packaging (▶ 24).

🚹 196 B2 🖂 Via dei Servi 80r ☎ 055 210738; www.kerit 🕓 Mon–Fri 9–1, 4–8. Open occasional Sat

Where to...
Be Entertained

Northern Florence may attract a sizeable daytime population of students and visitors, but its nightlife is relatively quiet as most people prefer to head east or across the river to the Oltrarno. This said, the area does have a handful of places to listen to live music or enjoy a late drink, as well as one or two churches and auditoria where you may catch a classical recital.

JAZZ AND FOLK

Classical, jazz and other musical recitals are occasionally held in the **Lyceum** (Via degli Alfani 48r, tel: 055 247 8264; www. lyceumclubfirenze.net). Churches such as San Lorenzo and the

Duomo also sometimes host concerts, choirs or organ recitals – for details check with tourist information centres (▶ 39) or look out for posters outside the venues.

LIVE MUSIC AND BARS

Florence's best Latin bar is the hugely popular **Girasol** (Via del Romito 1, tel: 055 474948; www.girasol.it, open Tue–Thu 7pm–2am, Fri–Sat 7pm–3am), though you'll need to take a taxi from the centre, as it's located north of the Fortezza da Basso. It offers live Brazilian, Cuban and other Latin music, as well as powerful cocktails, salsa classes and DJs.

Further north still, **Auditorium Flog** (Via Michele Mercati 24b, tel: 055 487145, box office 055 210804; www.flog.it) has been around for over 20 years and continues to be a favourite with live music fans who come here to see the most popular Italian and international bands.

If you prefer to stay more central, **Astor Café** (Piazza Duomo 20r, tel: 055 239 9000), offers hip surroundings with the Duomo in the background, for an aperitif and buffet snack before the DJ or occasional life band set-up in the back room.

Somewhere that doesn't have to worry about a high-rent central location is **Tenax** (Via Pratese 46r, tel: 055 308160; www.tenax.org), which lies out in the northern suburbs near Peretola airport. This large, long-established disco and live-music club is one of the city's most celebrated nightspots. It's worth the trip on the nights when there is live music if you want to catch good local bands or the occasional big-name international

act. See listings in newspapers or fly posters for forthcoming events. At other times DJs, music – from house to Latin – and theme-nights change nightly. There is plenty of room, with lots of bars and seating.

THEATRE AND CONCERTS

Teatro della Pergola (Via della Pergola 12/32, tel: 055 22641; www.pergolafirenze.it) stages well-known theatre productions on a regular basis in one of its two sumptuous halls. Some **Maggio Musicale** (▶ 46) concerts are performed here and the theatre is a principal venue for classical music.

On the edge of the city centre, cars and buses rush around all sides of the **Fortezza da Basso** (Viale Filippo Strozzi, tel: 055 36931), an enormous fortress originally built in 1534. Today the citadel and its additional modern complexes act as a multipurpose centre for cultural events, exhibitions and music concerts.

Western Florence

Getting Your Bearings

This is the oldest, most eclectic district of Florence. Traces of Roman Florentia can still be seen, together with the ancient grid of medieval lanes – today graced by the impressive buildings of the city's Renaissance heyday, when the wealthiest families vied to create the most beautiful palazzi, churches and monuments.

This area stretches from the main railway station, a rare example of the city's modern architecture, to the Ponte Vecchio, the oldest bridge in Florence and a veritable jewel in its crown. Between these two extremes, you'll find a mixed bag of attractions. Santa Maria Novella, for example, is one of the city's largest and most prestigious churches, crammed with sacred art; the Palazzo Davanzati provides a fascinating insight into the luxurious lifestyles of medieval merchants; while grandiose cafe-lined Piazza della Repubblica harks back to Florence's brief spell as the capital of Italy.

It is also among the best shopping districts, with the likes of Gucci, Prada and Bulgari in Via de' Tornabuoni – the city's prime shopping street.

Left: Detail of the decoration on the 15th-century facade of Santa Maria Novella

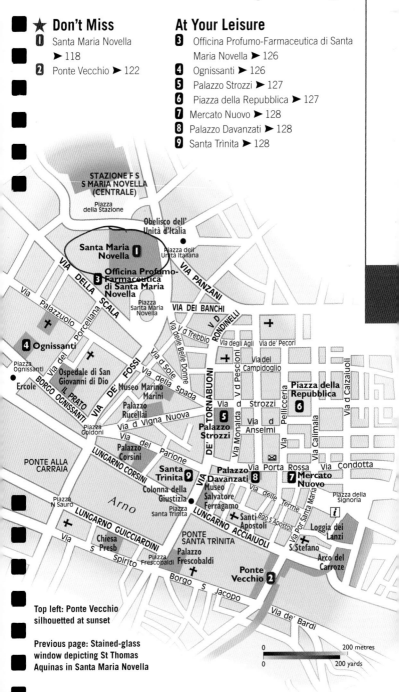

★ Don't Miss

At Your Leisure

Top left: Ponte Vecchio
silhouetted at sunset

Previous page: Stained-glass
window depicting St Thomas
Aquinas in Santa Maria Novella

In a Day

If you're not quite sure where to begin your travels, this itinerary recommends a practical and enjoyable day out in Western Florence, taking in some of the best places to see using the Getting Your Bearings map on the previous page. For more information see the main entries.

10:00am

Allow plenty of time to visit the Gothic church of **1 Santa Maria Novella** (➤ 118–121). Its complex contains an astonishing wealth of sacred treasures, including some of the most important works of art in Florence (frescoes in the Spanish Chapel, left). The adjoining **Museo di Santa Maria Novella** (➤ 120) in the cloisters is also worth a glimpse.

11:30am

Relax with a coffee in one of the popular cafes fringing **6 Piazza della Repubblica** (➤ 127), an imposing square centred on a bombastic arch. It was laid out as part of the grandiose plans to remodel Florence during the city's brief stint as the nation's capital. Pause awhile and consider how different Florence might have looked today had architect Giuseppe Poggi been allowed to continue with his plans, which would have destroyed a large number of Florence's finest buildings.

Noon

No visit to Florence is complete without indulging in some shopping. After all, this is the home of such legendary names as Gucci and Ferragamo (➤ 14–17, 132–133 and 135; picture right). You'll find everything in this part of town from top couturiers to markets, including a flower market on Thursday mornings under the portico in Piazza della Repubblica. In the narrow lanes, look out for local artisans who continue Florence's tradition of fine craftsmanship. Their skills range from textile-making and pottery production to stone-cutting and restoration work.

1:30pm

Head to the small but frenetic **7 Mercato Nuovo** (➤ 128) and join local market-workers in a traditional lunch of *trippa* (tripe). Alternatively, try Caffè Gilli (➤ 130) in nearby Piazza della Repubblica.

3:00pm

Continue your shopping spree as you head down the crowded Via Por Santa Maria to marvel at the **2 Ponte Vecchio** (above, ► 122–125), one of the most picturesque sights in Florence. Aglitter with jewellers' shops, the bridge you see today presents a scene that has hardly changed since 1593.

4:00pm

Take time to visit the church of **9 Santa Trìnita** (► 128–129). Compared with Santa Maria Novella, it receives surprizingly few visitors, yet it contains one of Florence's most fascinating fresco cycles – *Scenes from the Life of St Francis* by Domenico Ghirlandaio. As with many Renaissance frescoes, important personages of the era can be identified in the painting, but here Ghirlandaio goes one step further than his contemporaries and includes several Florentine landmarks, including the church itself.

5:30pm

You should have time for a bit more shopping in Via de' Tornabuoni (► 132–135), the most elegant street in Florence. The glamorous window displays lining this majestic avenue are a delight to behold, but take a look too at the prestigious palaces – the former homes of wealthy Renaissance bankers and merchants. There are also several tempting tea rooms along the way.

8:00pm

Round off the day with dinner at Oliviero (► 131), where you can enjoy innovative Tuscan and other Italian cuisine.

❶ Santa Maria Novella

The strikingly beautiful Gothic church of Santa Maria Novella contains some of Florence's most important artworks by such masters as Giotto, Brunelleschi, Domenico Ghirlandaio and Filippino Lippi, while the adjoining cloisters form a fascinating museum of precious frescoes.

The mighty church we see today had very humble beginnings. In 1221 Dominican friars established a small chapel called Santa Maria delle Vigne (of the vines) set among vineyards beyond the city walls, but with a large open space in front of it, ideal for preaching to large congregations. In 1278 two friars, Fra Sisto and Fra Ristoro, started to convert the original chapel into the largest monastery complex in Florence. The buildings were completed in the mid-14th century and the church was consecrated in 1420, but the delicate marble facade remained incomplete until 1458, when architect Leon Battista Alberti was commissioned to finish it. Rather than start afresh, he cleverly blended the existing Gothic elements with new Renaissance features – such as the two large volutes (spiral scrolls) in the upper section of the facade designed to conceal the side chapel roofs – creating an elegant and well-balanced whole.

The Interior

The interior of Santa Maria Novella is one of the finest examples of Florentine Gothic architecture. Light and lofty, it was designed not only for silent meditation but also as a meeting place for large congregations. At first glance, the nave appears to be exceptionally long, but in fact this is an optical illusion, created by spacing the pillars closer together as they approach the chancel. The walls were once smothered by frescoes but many were lost in the 16th century when the interior was whitewashed and the windows were shortened to make way for side chapels.

Halfway down the left-hand aisle you'll find one of the church's most influential works of art – Masaccio's pioneering fresco of *La Trinità* (1427). In the centre is Christ on the Cross, at the bottom are the Madonna and St John, and at the top God the Father with the Holy Spirit in the form of a dove beneath his beard. The two extra figures in the bottom corners are members of the Lenzi family, who commissioned this work of masterful perspective.

Continue to the raised **Cappella Strozzi** in the left transept. The 14th-century frescoes here were based on

Above: The elegant facade of Santa Maria Novella

Dante's epic poem, *The Divine Comedy*. At the centre is the *Last Judgement*, on the left *Paradise* and on the right *Hell*. Dante himself is portrayed in the *Paradise* fresco, amid angels, saintly figures and members of the Strozzi family.

The sanctuary's main chapel, the **Cappella Tornabuoni** (behind the high altar), was financed by the Tornabuoni family, following the Black Death of 1348. Giovanni Tornabuoni was the uncle of the great Medici Lorenzo the Magnificent. The frescoes (1485–90) here by Domenico Ghirlandaio include *Scenes from the Life of the Virgin* (on the left wall) and *Scenes from the Life of St John the Baptist* (on the right), they also provide an invaluable record of life in Florence at that time, with portraits of dignitaries and the blatant glorification of the Tornabuoni family (shown worshipping on the far wall). Their representation in the frescoes, combined with the fact they were related to the Medici, so outraged Girolamo Savonarola (➤ 8–9) that he condemned the cycle as an example of frivolous and profane art.

The next chapel to the right – **Cappella di Filippo Strozzi** – contains further dramatic frescoes (1489–1502) by Filippino Lippi, one of Florence's earliest Mannerist painters. The chapel's stained-glass window is also attributed to him. The sacristy contains a masterpiece by Giotto: a painted wooden crucifix.

Museo di Santa Maria Novella

The cloisters form a small museum, with a separate entrance, alongside the church. It has two main attractions: the **Cappellone degli Spagnoli** (Spanish Chapel) and the **Chiostro Verde** (Green Cloister), named after the greenish hue of Paolo Uccello's sadly fading frescoes of the early 15th century. The Spanish Chapel was built as the chapter house of the monastery, but in the 16th century, Eleonora of Toledo, wife of Cosimo I, designated it a place of worship for her Spanish entourage. The walls are completely covered in frescoes by Andrea di Bonaiuto (known as Andrea di Firenze), exalting the role of the Dominicans in the struggle against heresy. In one section, on the right-hand wall, they are portrayed as "hounds of God" (in Latin *Domini canes*, a pun on the Order's name), leading their followers, the stray sheep, back to the fold.

The decoration of the chapel represents one of the largest painted areas of the late 14th century. As art critic John Ruskin (1819–1900) wrote: "It will literally seem to you one of the grandest places roofed without a central pillar that you ever entered. And you will marvel that human daring ever achieved anything so magnificent."

Ghirlandaio's magnificent frescoes in the Tornabuoni Chapel provide an insight into life in 15th-century Florence

TAKING A BREAK

Caffè Gilli (Via Roma 1r, on the corner of Piazza della Repubblica 36–39r, tel: 055 213896, open Wed–Mon 8:30–midnight) is one of four cafes on the piazza where you'll be able to enjoy a hot drink (especially their hot chocolate) and a snack (➤ 130).

Nuns in the cloister of Santa Maria Novella, outside the Spanish Chapel

➕ 194 C2 ✉ Piazza di Santa Maria Novella ☎ Church: 055 219257. Museo di Santa Maria Novella: 055 282187 🕐 Church: Mon–Thu, Sat 9–5, Fri, Sun 1–5. Museo e Chiostri Monumentali di Santa Maria Novella: Mon–Thu, Sat 9–5. Last ticket 30 mins before closing 🚌 Many routes including 6, 11, 12, 36, 37 and A 💶 Inexpensive (church and museum on separate inexpensive tickets)

SANTA MARIA NOVELLA: INSIDE INFO

Top tips Arrive early to avoid the worst of the crowds.
- Bring **loose change** to illuminate the frescoes and **binoculars** to see the details of the frescoes.

Hidden gems Filippo Brunelleschi dismissed Donatello's wooden crucifix in Santa Croce (➤ 66–69) as resembling "a peasant on a cross", so Donatello challenged him to do better: the **wooden *Crucifix*** (1420) in the Cappella Gondi was the result.

In more depth Paolo Uccello's **frescoes in the Chiostro Verde** depict stories from Genesis, including *The Creation of the Animals, Adam and Eve, The Original Sin, The Labours of the Ancestors, Cain and Abel, Lamech and Noah's Ark, The Flood* and *The Drunkenness of Noah*. Uccello was obsessed with perspective and the frescoes are remarkable for their figures and perspective devices. Unfortunately, some were irreparably damaged by the 1966 floods.

❷ Ponte Vecchio

The Ponte Vecchio (Old Bridge), located at the heart of the city, is one of Florence's most famous landmarks. Lined on both sides with higgledy-piggledy shops supported over the river with timber brackets (*sporti*) and painted in vivid shades of orange and yellow ochre, it is particularly photogenic and lively at sunset when Florentines gather for their evening *passeggiata*. The bridge's three stone arches cross the River Arno at its narrowest point, linking the historic city centre with the Oltrarno (➤ 137–156).

The Ponte Vecchio was the only bridge in the city to escape destruction in World War II, spared by retreating Nazi forces in 1944, possibly on Hitler's orders. There has been a bridge here since Roman times, but the current Ponte Vecchio dates from 1345 when it was built to replace the former wooden structure that was swept away while the river was in full spate. It was probably designed by Taddeo Gaddi. In 1565 an elevated walkway, the Corridoio Vasariano (➤ 54), was built along the eastern side of the bridge.

Today the bridge is lined with glitzy jewellery shops, but in the Middle Ages it was very different. Butchers and fishmongers had their shops here, as did leather-workers who hung hides in the water for up to eight months before tanning them with horse's urine. A gap was created in the row of shops on one side to make the bridge easier to clean. These trades were eventually banished by Grand Duke

Saved from destruction in World War II, the bridge today looks much as it did in the 16th century

A DEVASTATING FLOOD

Over the years the Ponte Vecchio has withstood floods, battles and bombing. However, it didn't fare so well on 4 November, 1966, when a freak cyclone swept across the region, destroying part of the bridge (► 32). This was Florence's worst flood, and the damage to the city's artistic heritage was immense: treasures in the Museo Archeologico, the Biblioteca Nazionale and 8,000 Renaissance paintings stored in the basement of the Uffizi were damaged, and Santa Croce was submerged under mud and water.

Ferdinando I, who would cross the bridge daily en route to the Palazzo Pitti. The Duke found the stench so offensive that in 1593 he replaced the tradesmen with the jewellers and goldsmiths who have been there ever since.

TAKING A BREAK

Buca dell'Orafo (Volta de' Girolami 28r, tel: 055 213619, closed Sun–Mon), a tiny basement restaurant, has long been a Florentine favourite.

✚ 199 E4 ⊠ Ponte Vecchio 🚌 B and D 🎫 Free

An artist captures the character of the Ponte Veccio

Right: Shutters protect shop fronts on Ponte Vecchio out of hours

A FATEFUL MURDER

In 1215, nobleman Buondelmonte de' Buondelmonti was murdered at the entrance to the bridge following a quarrel between two Florentine *consorterie* (groups of noble families). The event sparked off a bitter conflict between the Guelph middle classes, who had played an important role in promoting the economic development of Florence, and the old Ghibelline nobles, who wished to maintain their feudal privileges. Despite periods of Ghibelline power, the city was predominantly controlled in the 13th century by the Guelph faction. Divisions within the Guelph faction, between the Blacks (who supported the Pope) and the Whites (who were opposed to papal influence) eventually led to civil war. In 1302, numerous Whites were forced into exile, including Dante (► 26–27), convicted for alleged corruption.

PONTE VECCHIO: INSIDE INFO

Top tip For the **best photos** of the bridge, stand either on the Ponte Santa Trìnita, or on one of the river embankments near by, at sunset.

Hidden gem In 1900 **Benvenuto Cellini**, one of the most famous of Florence's Renaissance goldsmiths, was commemorated with a bust (right), which stands in the middle of the bridge.

At Your Leisure

❸ Officina Profumo-Farmaceutica di Santa Maria Novella

Not far from Santa Maria Novella is one of the oldest pharmacies in the world established by Dominican friars in 1221. In their gardens, the monks grew the herbs they needed for medicines and ointments used in the monastery's infirmary, including a rosewater disinfectant – considered useful in times of plague.

In 1612, the pharmacy opened to the public – its reputation rapidly grew and its products became known throughout the whole of Europe. Today, the beautiful hand-wrapped cosmetics, pot-pourri and fragrances (➤ 24–25) are still made to the ancient recipes.

✚ 194 C2 ✉ Via della Scala 16 ☎ 055 216276; www.smnovella.it ◷ Mon–Fri 10–5, Sat by appointment only. Closed Aug ▣ 6, 11, 12, 36, 37 and A 🎫 Free

❹ Ognissanti

The church of Ognissanti (All Saints) was established by a Benedictine order of monks in the 13th century. In later years it came under the patronage of the Vespuccis, a wealthy merchant family whose most famous member, Amerigo, gave his name to the New World. Amerigo can be seen in Domenico Ghirlandaio's beautiful fresco, the *Madonna della Misericordia*

Medicines and ointments are still for sale at Officina Profumo-Farmaceutica di Santa Maria Novella

(1472), in the second chapel on the right. He is the young boy immediately to the left of the Virgin.

Halfway down the nave on the right, an intense fresco of *St Augustine* (1480) by Sandro Botticelli is complemented by Ghirlandaio's *St Jerome* (1480) on the opposite wall. Other treasures include Botticelli's tomb, a monk's habit reputedly worn by St Francis when he received the stigmata, and, in the adjoining refectory, a moving *Last Supper* (1480) by Ghirlandaio.

✚ 194 B2 ✉ Borgo Ognissanti 42 ☎ 055 239 8700 ◷ Daily 7–12:30, 4–8. *Last Supper* Mon, Tue and Sat only 9–12 ▣ B, D 🎫 Free

---

DESIGNER SHOPPING

■ **Via de' Tornabuoni** is the place for designer-label shopping: choose from Prada, Trussardi, Beltrami, Bulgari, Ferragamo, Gucci, Pucci, Tiffany, Louis Vuitton and Hermés.

■ **Via della Vigna Nuova** is equally sophisticated and expensive but has more choice of home-grown designer talent.

5 Palazzo Strozzi

The Palazzo Strozzi is the largest palace in Florence. It was built by the egocentric banker Filippo Strozzi in the 15th century in an attempt to outdo the Medici family, his arch enemies. Determined to prove that he was the richest and most influential man in the city, Strozzi purchased and demolished 15 buildings to make way for this monumental palace. Leaving nothing to chance, he even called in astrologers to determine the most favourable day on which to lay the foundation stone.

Unfortunately, he never lived to see the end result – an astonishing masterpiece of Renaissance art. Although only three storeys high, each floor is as tall as a normal palazzo. As with many contemporary palazzi, the exterior is heavily rusticated, according to Michelozzo, "to unite an appearance of solidarity and strength with the light and shade so essential to beauty under the glare of the Italian sun". Today, the palace contains various cultural institutes, and the first floor is used for major art exhibitions.

✚ 195 D1 ✉ Piazza degli Strozzi ☎ 055 277 6461; www.palazzostrozzi.org ◷ Opening hours vary with each exhibition 🚌 A

6 Piazza della Repubblica

Piazza della Repubblica has long been at the heart of Florentine history. It was once the site of the Forum, the main square of the Roman city of Florentia, and in medieval times the city's principal food market was held here. A single column topped by a statue of *Abundance* – all that remains of the ancient market – still stands in the square. Later the square became the centre of the Jewish ghetto. Today's piazza, with its triumphal arch, was laid out as part of Giuseppe Poggi's grandiose plans to remodel Florence. Many locals consider the square an eyesore, but its cafes have always been hugely popular.

✚ 195 E1 ✉ Piazza della Repubblica 🚌 A 👋 Free

A decorative street lamp outside Palazzo Strozzi

Leather bags for sale in Mercato Nuovo

🟦 Mercato Nuovo

There has been a market here since the 11th century, but this New Market was constructed in the mid-16th century as a place for gold and silk merchants and bankers to conduct their business.

Today leatherware, knick-knacks and souvenirs are sold, and the lovely loggia is a popular venue for street musicians on summer evenings. You'll also usually find a couple of *tripperie* – mobile stalls selling *trippa* (tripe) in a *panini* (bread roll), which can be washed down with a glass of local wine.

Under the loggia, a marble wheel in the middle of the floor marks the spot where dishonest merchants were put into the stocks to be bombarded with rotten fruit and vegetables. On the southern edge of the market stands a bronze of a wild boar, *Il Porcellino* (a 17th-century copy of the Roman marble original, now in the Uffizi). The base of the small fountain beneath him is smothered in minute bronze flowers, frogs, snails, a bee and other enchanting details. Rubbing the nose of the boar will bring you luck and ensure a return visit to Florence.
➕ 199 E5 ✉ Loggiato del Porcellino, Via Porta Rossa 🕐 Daily 9–7:30 🚌 A
🎟 Free

🟦 Palazzo Davanzati

This stately 14th-century palace and former home of the wealthy Davizzi family has been converted into the Museo della Casa Fiorentina Antica (Museum of the Old Florentine House), providing a rare and vivid insight into the life of city merchants, artists and noblemen during the Middle Ages. A visit to the palace comprises the ground-floor loggia and first floor with lovely rooms (Salone Madornale, Sala dei Pappagalli, Sale dei Merletti Studiolo), the Camera del Pavoni and two rooms devoted to lace. The second floor rooms are at present only open by appointment.
➕ 199 E5 ✉ Via Porta Rossa 13 🕐 055 238 8610 🕐 Daily 8:15–1:50. Closed 1st, 3rd and 5th Mon, and 2nd and 4th Sun of the month 🚌 6, 11, 36, 37 and A
🎟 Free

🟦 Santa Trìnita

With so many noble palazzi in the streets surrounding Santa Trìnita, it's hardly surprising the local parish church contains private chapels dedicated to wealthy Florentines, among them the Strozzi, Davanzati,

---

FOR KIDS

- Rubbing the nose of *Il Porcellino* in the Mercato Nuovo and spotting the different types of insects around him.
- **Palazzo Davanzati** (▶ above), which gives a vivid insight into the lifestyle of medieval merchants and nobles.
- Hide-and-seek on the **Ponte Vecchio** (▶ 122–125).

Spini and Doni families. Each is embellished with elaborate frescoes, reliquaries and tombs in an attempt to outdo its neighbours. Built in the 11th century, the original church was unadorned and austere but, over the years, it gradually became more ornate. The baroque facade was added in 1593.

The second chapel of the left transept boasts one of Florence's most beautiful tombs, a marble monument of Benozzo Federighi, Bishop of Fiesole (1454–57), by Luca della Robbia. It is framed by a border of painted floral terracotta tiles.

The undisputed pièce de résistance of Santa Trìnita, however, is the **Cappella Sassetti** (second chapel of the right transept) with its delightful frescoes by Domenico Ghirlandaio depicting scenes from the life of St Francis of Assisi (1483–86). They tell the story of a child who fell out of a window (in the background on the left-hand side), and how St Francis came to resurrect him.

The backdrop for this miracle is 15th-century Florence and it is possible to identify the buildings (including the earlier Gothic facade of Santa Trìnita), as well as some

One of Ghirlandaio's St Francis frescoes in Santa Trìnita

contemporary figures (among them Sassetti's friend, Lorenzo the Magnificent). The donors of the chapel, Francesco Sassetti and his wife, are portrayed praying on either side of the altar.

✚ 199 D5 ✉ Piazza Santa Trìnita ☎ 055 216912 🕐 Mon–Sat 8–noon, 4–6, Sun 4–6. Services: Mon–Sat 7:30am, 6:30pm, Sun 7:30am, 11am, 6:30pm 🚌 6, 11, 36, 37 and A 🎫 Free

CAFES AND CAKE SHOPS

- **Giubbe Rosse** (Piazza della Repubblica 13–14r): a stylish early 20th-century cafe, once a popular haunt of artists and intellectuals.
- **Giacosa** (➤ 131): this elegant cafe-cum-cake shop on Via di Spada invented the Negroni aperitif cocktail (Martini, gin and Campari).
- **Procacci** (➤ 133): a smart cafe full of shoppers carrying their designer purchases. Try the *tartufati* (truffle rolls).

Where to...
Eat and Drink

Prices
Expect to pay per person for a meal, excluding drinks and service
€ under €20   €€ €20–€45   €€€ over €45

Western Florence does not have the number or variety of restaurants you'll find elsewhere in the city, though there are some that are worth a special journey, Oliviero for dinner and Rose's, Caffè Amerini or Belle Donne for lunch, as well as several other excellent cafes for snacks or drinks.

If you are on a tight budget, head for the area around the Santa Maria Novella railway station where there is a plethora of fast-food and other cheap eating places.

Belle Donne €–€€

On entering Belle Donne you will immediately be struck by the decor, consisting of huge piles of fruit, vegetables and flowers laid out in almost sculptural arrangements. The place is small, turnover of covers is quick and the setting relaxed – you share wooden tables with fellow diners, eat off paper tablecloths, and choose from a list of daily tempting Florentine specials chalked up on a board. It makes an excellent place for lunch, but is perhaps rather too informal for all but an early or impromptu dinner.

✚ 195 D2 **⊠** Via delle Belle Donne 16r **☎** 055 238 2609 **⊙** Daily 12–3, 7–11; closed 10 days in Aug

Caffè Amerini €

Like the not-so-distant Rose's (▲ 131), Caffè Amerini is different from most Florentine eating places. While it has the familiar medieval brick-arched ceiling, its paint-effect walls, furniture and fittings provide a more modern and slightly eccentric edge. It's an easy-going place, good for breakfast or lunch. You simply point out which of the sandwiches, salads or other good snacks you want from the glass-fronted bar just inside the door and then take a seat to be served – you pay only a small premium for sitting down.

✚ 194 C1 **⊠** Via della Vigna Nuova 61–63r **☎** 055 284941 **⊙** Mon–Sat 8–8

Caffè Gilli €

Piazza della Repubblica is not the most attractive square, and is redeemed only by its four large and historic cafes – Gilli, Giubbe Rosse, Donnini and Paszkowski – of which the Caffè Gilli is the most notable. The original Gilli opened in 1733 on Via degli Speziali, but moved to its present site in 1910. Today, it still preserves its stunning belle époque interior – worth seeing in its own right – but on warm days you should choose the large outside terrace. In cold weather, Gilli's famous hot chocolate is the drink to go for – it comes in five flavours: almond, coffee, orange, gianduia and cocoa. If you enjoy this type of large and old-style cafe, try the Giubbe Rosse (founded in 1897), the next-best of the square's quartet.

✚ 195 E1 **⊠** Via Roma 1r, corner of Piazza della Repubblica 36–39r **☎** 055 213896; www.gilli.it **⊙** Wed–Mon 7:30am–1am

Cantinetta Antinori €€

This so-called Cantinetta, or "Small Wine Cellar", belongs to Antinori, one of the most celebrated and venerable of central Italy's wine dynasties. Much of the food, olive oil and wine served comes from the family's various vineyards and estates. The large single dining room forms part of the historic Palazzo Antinori, providing a suitably elegant setting for the high-quality snacks and light meals available, including hearty classic Tuscan dishes such as *pappa al pomodoro* (bread and tomato soup) and *ribollita* (vegetable soup). The service and ambience are lively, but it's worth dressing up a little to live up to the fine surroundings.

♦ 195 D1 ⊠ **Piazza Antinori 3** ☎ **055 292 234; www.cantinetta-antinori.com** ⊕ **Mon–Fri 12:30–2:30, 7–10:30. Closed Aug**

Garga €€–€€€

Garga is patronized almost entirely by Florentines, but don't let that intimidate you. The atmosphere and appearance of the place are pleasant and welcoming – pastel-coloured walls, soft lighting, wooden ceilings and some curious frescoes. The food is Tuscan,

with a mixture of fish and meat: dishes might include *pesce spada* (swordfish), grilled meats such as lamb served with rosemary or redcurrants, risotto with asparagus or *baccalà* (salt cod) with a tomato and basil sauce. The wine list features good Tuscan wines.

♦ 195 F1 ⊠ **Via del Moro 48r** ☎ **055 239 8898** ⊕ **Tue–Sun 7:30pm–11pm**

Giacosa €€–€€€

If you have been to Rivoire in Piazza della Signoria (▶ 79) you'll know what to expect in the co-owned Giacosa. Both are equally smart and refined, and both have an illustrious pedigree – the cafe was much favoured by 19th-century nobility, and the celebrated Negroni aperitif cocktail, a combination of gin, Campari and Martini, was invented here. It offers light snacks, a tremendous selection of cakes and high-quality chocolates.

♦ 195 D1 ⊠ **Via di Spada 10r** ☎ **055 277 6328** ⊕ **Mon–Fri 7:30am–8:30pm, Sat 8am–9pm**

Oliviero €€€

Oliviero is the best restaurant in this part of the city made famous during the "Dolce Vita" years of the 1960s. The cooking embraces Tuscan and other Italian influences, but often adds an innovative touch. Meats include wild boar and fresh fish – unusually for a Florentine restaurant – is also often available, all complemented by good Tuscan wine.

♦ 199 E5 ⊠ **Via delle Terme 51r** ☎ **055 287643; www.ristorante-oliviero.it** ⊕ **Mon–Sat 7:30pm–midnight**

Rose's €

There may come a time when you want a change from the classic Florentine restaurant or cafe and its rustic decor and reliable regional cooking. In this respect, Rose's is a breath of fresh air, a bright, modern and stylish bar-restaurant that wouldn't be out of place in New York or Sydney: there is even an art gallery attached. The menu is similarly diverse, and

while there are plenty of Italian dishes to choose from, you can also opt for sushi or inventive salads and snacks.

♦ 195 D1 ⊠ **Via del Parione 26r** ☎ **055 287090; www.roses.it** ⊕ **Mon–Sat 12pm–1:30am**

Trattoria 13 Gobbi €€

Dim lighting, soft music and a cosy atmosphere make 13 Gobbi a great place to come for a romantic meal. Overflowing with Florentine charm, this trattoria has never strayed from genuine Tuscan dishes full of delicate flavours and cooked with great care and attention. Try the grilled meats, which are exceptionally tender, especially the beef fillet in sauce, and the desserts will leave you with something to savour. Don't be put off by the large choice of wine labels, as the waiters are always willing to help you decide.

♦ 194 C2 ⊠ **Via del Porcellana 9r** ☎ **055 284015; www.casatrattoria.com** ⊕ **Daily 12–2:30, 7:30–11**

Where to... Shop

Western Florence has broader streets than other parts of the city, streets that are suited to larger shops and more shoppers. Via de' Tornabuoni and surrounding streets such as Via della Vigna Nuova still have the lion's share of Florence's designer and other fashion, shoe and accessory shops. Many are closed on Monday mornings.

Further afield, streets such as Borgo Ognissanti and Via del Porcellana have smarter stores and discreet individual designers' ateliers, not to mention the artisans' furniture and other workshops tucked away in quiet corners. Finally, around the Santa Maria Novella railway station, you'll find a rash of souvenir and clothes shops.

BOOKS

Edison

Edison is one of Florence's best bookshops – a high-tech superstore with video screens showing the latest news, internet points, a cafe and an excellent travel section.

⊞ 195 E1 ⊠ Piazza della Repubblica 27r
☎ 055 213110; www.libreriaedison.it
🕑 Mon–Sat 9am–midnight, Sun 10am–midnight

Alinari

The world's first photographic company, established in 1852, has a collection of photography books and exhibition catalogues and an excellent selection of books on history, art and landscapes, and multimedia products.

⊞ 195 D3 ⊠ Largo Fratelli Alinari 15
☎ 055 23951; www.alinari.it 🕑 Mon–Fri 9–1, 2–6

CLOTHES AND ACCESSORIES

A Ugolini & Figli

This historic men's clothing shop has traded in the heart of Florence since 1896. Soft colours and wood furnishings create a refined ambience for the timeless, classical styles that attract gentlemen with good taste.

⊞ 195 F1 ⊠ Via Calzaiuoli 65r
☎ 055 214439 🕑 Mon–Fri 10–7, Sat 10.30–7.30

Armani

Giorgio Armani's understated and elegant clothes need little introduction. The designer's Via de' Tornabuoni shop is his flagship Florentine store: the less expensive Emporio Armani outlet is near by.

⊞ 193 D1 ⊠ Via de' Tornabuoni 48r
☎ 055 219041; www.giorgioarmani.com
🕑 Mon–Fri 10–7, Sat 10.30–7:30

⊞ 195 D1 ⊠ Piazza degli Strozzi 16r
☎ 055 284315; www.giorgioarmani.com
🕑 Mon–Fri 10–7, Sat 10.30–7:30. Last Sun of month in winter open 3–7

Cellerini

Few leather and other bags are as elegant or covetable as those from Cellerini, most of whose stock is handmade on the premises.

⊞ 195 D1 ⊠ Via del Sole 37r
☎ 055 282533; www.cellerini.it
🕑 Tue–Sat 9–1, 3–7, Mon 3–7. Closed Sun and Mon am

Gucci

The famous Gucci label (▶ 14–15) was founded at this address, which still acts as a prestigious showroom for the company's clothes, shoes and accessories. Quality and cutting-edge cool are assured.

⊞ 195 D1 ⊠ Via de' Tornabuoni 73r
☎ 055 264011 🕑 Mon–Sat 10–7, Sun 2–7

Infinity

The Italo-American couple who run this shop have been offering belts, bags, purses and other leather items for over 20 years. There are hundreds of styles and colours, and you can choose on the spot and have a belt made while you wait. Bags can be made up in a week. Alternatively, bring in your own design, or choose more exotic leathers such as deer, elk, snakeskin, alligator or crocodile.

🚹 199 E5 🖂 Borgo SS Apostoli 18r
☎ 055 239 8405; www.infinityfirenze.com
🕓 Mon–Fri 10–7:30, Sat 10:30–7:30. Closed Sun and a period in Aug

Luisa Via Roma

A cult boutique that always has the last word on *alta moda* fashion, not only through its collections, but also through the space they are displayed in. The window dressing is surreal, and inside wall-screens dazzle customers with video art while they navigate through the store using touch-screen monitors.

🚹 195 E1 🖂 Via Roma 19–21r
☎ 055 9064116; www.luisaviaroma.com
🕓 Mon–Sat 10–7:30, Sun 11–7

Pucci

The aristocratic Marchese Emilio Pucci made his name in the 1950s and 1960s in Italian designer fashion with his bright and hugely distinctive printed silks (▲ 16–17). His star waned somewhat, however, until the 1990s, when the same colourful, patterned silks again became fashionable. Today, Pucci is the doyen of Florentine designers, and is much fêted in the city's fashion circles.

🚹 195 D1 🖂 Via de' Tornabuoni 20–22r
☎ 055 265 8082 🕓 Mon–Sat 2–7. Last Sun of month 2–7

DEPARTMENT STORES

Rinascente

Rinascente is one of a nationwide chain of department stores. It has a more upmarket reputation and more spacious appearance than its nearby rival Coin (▶ 80), yet in reality the selection of goods seems inferior and their presentation dowdier than Coin. That said, this

is still a good place to come one-stop shopping for stylish Italian clothes, kitchenware, linens and other department store staples if your stay in Florence is limited to a short time.

🚹 195 E1 🖂 Piazza della Repubblica 1
☎ 055 219113; www.rinascente.it
🕓 Mon–Sat 9–9, Sun 10:30–8

FABRICS

Casa dei Tessuti

Florence has a long tradition of trading in sumptuous fabrics (as you would expect of a city which still owes much of its prosperity to textiles). For more than 50 years this conveniently located shop, just west of Piazza del Duomo, has been a place of pilgrimage for Florentines and visitors alike in search of the finest silks, cottons, velvets, damasks and wools.

🚹 195 E2 🖂 Via de' Pecori 20–24r
☎ 055 215961; www.casadeitessuti.com
🕓 Mon 3:30–7:30, Tue–Sat 9–1, 3:30–7:30

FOOD AND WINE

Arte del Cioccolato

At this tiny space chocolatier Roberto Catinari's amazing array of products are laid out before you, guaranteed to amaze your eyes and as well as your palate.

🚹 195 D1 🖂 Via Porta Rossa (corner of Via de' Tournabuoni) ☎ 055 217 136;
www.artedelcioccolato.it 🕓 Tue–Fri, Sun 1–8, Sat 10am–midnight

Bottega della Frutta

You need look no further than this fine fruit and vegetable shop if you want to buy the freshest provisions for a delicious packed lunch or picnic, or just a snack.

🚹 195 D1 🖂 Via de' Federighi 31r ☎ 055 239 8590 🕓 Mon–Tue, Thu–Sat 8–7:30, Wed 8–1:30. Closed Jun–Aug Sat pm

Procacci

This is the place to buy truffles in season (October to March), one of the world's rarest foodstuffs. At other times of the year, buy the bottled or tinned versions or stop by for a famous truffle-flavoured roll – *un panino tartufato*.

🕀 195 D1 ⊠ Via de' Tornabuoni 64r 🕿 055 211656; www.antinori.it ⏱ Mon–Sat 10–8

Tassini

Decades of experience lie behind this shop's selection of fine Tuscan foods and wines. Pastas, dried porcini mushrooms, the best olive oils and a host of other gastronomic treats are available, along with vintages from some of the region's premier wine-growing areas – notably Montalcino, Chianti and Montepulciano.

🕀 199 E5 ⊠ Borgo SS Apostoli 24r 🕿 055 282696 ⏱ Mon, Tue, Thu–Sat 8:30–2, 4:30–7:30, Wed 8:30–2

Vini & Delizie

This is a tempting shop for serious wine-buyers but also for those who simply want a bottle of grappa to take home. Murgia also sells Tuscan and other Italian olive oils.

🕀 195 D2 ⊠ Via dei Banchi 45r 🕿 055 215686 ⏱ Mon–Sat 9–7 (may close for lunch on some days 1–2:30)

JEWELLERY

Tharros Bijoux

This tiny but beautiful shop specializes in period jewellery inspired by the rings, brooches, pendants and so forth that you see in many of the city's Renaissance paintings. Prices are surprisingly reasonable, though you will pay more for the designs that incorporate precious and semi-precious stones such as rubies, sapphires and emeralds.

🕀 200 A5 ⊠ Via della Condotta, corner of Vicolo de' Cerchi 2r 🕿 055 284126; www.tharros.com ⏱ Mon–Sat 10–1, 3:30–7:30

MARKETS

Cascine

The Cascine is the biggest of Florence's markets, and takes place every Tuesday morning in the Parco delle Cascine, a large park close to the River Arno to the west of the city centre. It's a long walk to get here, so take a taxi or jump aboard the "B" electric bus to Piazza Vittorio Veneto and change there to the "P" electric bus – the latter runs through the park on Viale degli Olmi. The outdoor market consists of hundreds of stalls (stands) of all descriptions, from inexpensive clothes and shoes to food and general household goods. Prices here are among the best in the city.

🕀 194 off A2 ⊠ Viale Abraham Lincoln, Parco delle Cascine 🕿 No phone ⏱ Tue 8–2

Mercato dei Fiori

The practical side of getting your blooms home may stop you buying anything from Florence's small weekly flower market, but it's still worth making a detour to admire the displays if you're in the vicinity of Piazza della Repubblica on a Thursday morning.

🕀 195 E1 ⊠ Via della Pellicceria-Piazza della Repubblica 🕿 No phone ⏱ Thu 8–2

Mercato Nuovo

▶ 128 for a description.

🕀 199 E5 ⊠ Loggiato del Porcellino, Via Porta Rossa 🕿 No phone ⏱ Daily 9–7:30

PAPER AND STATIONERY

Cozzi

Cozzi is primarily a book-binding business, but sells a selection of beautiful diaries, notebooks and other leather- or plain-bound books covered in marbled paper.

🕀 203 D5 ⊠ Via del Parione 35r 🕿 055 294968 ⏱ Mon–Fri 9–1, 3–7

PERFUMES AND TOILETRIES

Olfattorio

More of a showroom than a shop, most of the fragrances and scented candles sold here are handmade. Take a seat at the counter and let an expert customize a perfume to suit you. Out the back of the shop is a small collection of early 20th-century powder boxes.

🚇 195 D1 ☒ Via de' Tornabuoni 6
☎ 055 286925 🕐 Tue–Sat 11–7:30

Spezierie Erboristeria Palazzo Vecchio

This old-fashioned apothecary, with a magnificent frescoed interior, sells fine soaps, perfumes and other gloriously scented toiletries made to ancient recipes by Tuscan monks and nuns.

🚇 199 E5 ☒ Via Vacchereccia 9r
☎ 055 239 6055; www.spezieriefirenze.com
🕐 Mon–Sat 9–7.30, and 1st and last Sun of every month 11–9

PRINTS AND ENGRAVINGS

Ducci

This shop between the Carraia and Trinita bridges does not have the old-fashioned charm of Baccani (▶ right), but its selection of historical and other prints and engravings is good.

In addition, it sells a selection of other goods that make excellent gifts, notably a variety of objets d'art in marble, some superb woodcraft items and elegant Florentine boxes covered in gold leaf and handmade marbled paper.

🚇 195 D1 ☒ Lungarno Corsini 24r
☎ 055 214550; www.duccishop.com
🕐 Tue–Sat 9:30–1, 4–7:30; times may vary. Closed Nov–Apr Mon am; May–Oct Sat pm

Giovanni Baccani

Florence is dotted with enticing shops selling prints and engravings, but none is quite as alluring as this company founded in 1903. There's a huge selection of framed and unframed prints on a range of subjects and they are all sold at prices to suit every budget. Florentine and other Italian scenes and maps are particularly good buys.

🚇 194 C1 ☒ Borgo Ognissanti 22r
☎ 055 214467 🕐 Tue–Sat 9–1, 3:30–7:30, Mon 3:30–7:30

SHOES AND LEATHER GOODS

Bisonte

Italians like a designer label, and in Bisonte's shoes and leather goods they have one that is growing ever more popular both at home and abroad. All the company's products are stamped with a distinctive bison motif, and though you will pay a lot for goods with this trademark, the products are extremely durable and well made.

🚇 199 D5 ☒ Via del Parione 31r
☎ 055 215722; www.ilbisonte.net
🕐 Mon–Sat 9.30–7

Bonora

This shop has made exquisite handmade and ready-to-wear shoes in classic styles – especially for men – since 1878. The prices are high, but these are some of the best shoes in Florence, which is to say some of the best shoes in Italy.

🚇 195 D1 ☒ Via del Parione 11–15r
☎ 055 283280 🕐 Mon 3–7, Tue–Sat 10–1, 2–7

Ferragamo

Salvatore Ferragamo made his name in the United States making shoes for Hollywood stars (▶ 17). His descendants still run the company, and their Via de' Tornabuoni shop has a tremendous showroom not only for shoes – on which Ferragamo's reputation still largely rests – but also for clothes and leather accessories.

🚇 195 D1 ☒ Via de' Tornabuoni 4–14r
☎ 055 292123; www.ferragamo.com
🕐 Mon–Sat 10–7:30, Sun 2–7

J P Tod's

No one in Italy took much notice of J P Tod's until their distinctive driving shoes became must-have accessories in the United States. Now the label is going from strength to strength and broadening its range – prices here are also generally lower for the same item than elsewhere in Europe or the US.

🚇 195 D1 ☒ Via de' Tornabuoni 103r
☎ 055 219423; www.tods.com 🕐 Mon–Sat 10–7, Sun 2–7. Closed Sun Feb, Jun–Aug

Where to...
Be Entertained

Western Florence is home to a wide range of bars and clubs, and to the Teatro Comunale, the city's principal performance space for classical music, dance and theatre productions. The district's farthest fringe is also the site of several major dance clubs, including Tuscany's largest disco.

THEATRE

For drama, good food and music all rolled into one, go to **Opera et Gusto** (Via della Scala 17r, tel: 055 288190; www.operaetgusto.com). Dramatic red velvet curtains encircle the dining area, which is laid out in front of the stage: later the dining area transforms into a bar with live music.

The **Teatro Comunale** (Corso Italia 16r, tel: box office 055 287222, information 055 277 9350) is a drab-looking building well to the west of the city centre. It is Florence's main theatre and auditorium, and provides its own orchestra, chorus and dance companies, together with visiting orchestras and performers. It also hosts many of the performances of the annual Maggio Musicale, one of Italy's leading music festivals. For tickets contact the box office (Tue–Fri 10–4:30, Sat 10–1), or book online at www.maggiofiorentino.com). Outside the Maggio Musicale, the main season for concerts, opera and ballet runs from January to April and September to December.

NIGHTCLUBS

One of the area's best-known nightspots is **Space Electronic** (Via Palazzuolo 37r, tel: 055 293082; www.spaceelectronic.net, open daily 10pm–2am or later), a huge and fairly trashy disco – it claims to be Europe's largest – but fine if all you want to do is dance and aren't too bothered by a lack of cutting edge music or style.

Much the same can be said about the almost equally large **Meccanò** (Viale degli Olmi 1r, tel: 055 331371, open days vary month to month 11:30pm–6am) in Casine Park. This is the city's most famous disco, and the one to visit if you're going to sample only one Florentine club. People come from across Tuscany for a night out here, so it's likely to be crowded, though in summer the action spills outdoors: dress is fairly smart and the music played safe and commercial.

The third of the area's trio of key dance clubs is **Yab** (Via Sassetti 5r, tel: 055 215160; www.yab.it, evenings may vary, call info line; closed Jun–Sep), which generally pursues a more adventurous music policy than many of its rivals. It also operates a "card" system whereby admission is usually free but during the evening you have to spend a minimum amount (recorded on your card) on drinks – fail to spend enough and you have to pay up before leaving.

BARS

For early evening cocktails, try sleek and showy **Slowly** (Via Porta Rossa 63, tel: 055 264 5354; www.slowlycafe.com. Club and bistro daily 7pm–2:30am, buffet lunch Mon–Sat 12:30–3. Closed Jul–Aug), which attracts a young and trendy crowd. At the other extreme is the **Fiddler's Elbow** (Piazza di Santa Maria Novella 7r, tel: 055 215056; www.thefiddlerselbow.com, daily noon–2am), a small "Irish pub" that is busy and animated.

Oltrarno

Getting Your Bearings

The name Oltrarno means "beyond the Arno", and this small district along the south bank of the river presents a different Florence. Quieter, greener, more relaxed, and with less traffic, it is one of the most rewarding areas to explore.

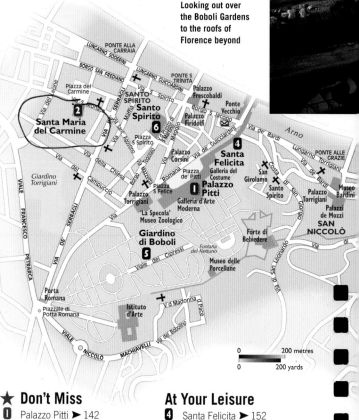

Looking out over the Boboli Gardens to the roofs of Florence beyond

★ Don't Miss

1. Palazzo Pitti ➤ 142
2. Santa Maria del Carmine – Cappella Brancacci ➤ 148
3. San Miniato al Monte ➤ 150

At Your Leisure

4. Santa Felicita ➤ 152
5. Giardino di Boboli ➤ 152
6. Santo Spirito ➤ 153

For a long time the Oltrarno was considered an inferior neighbourhood, inhabited only by those with insufficient wealth to live in the city centre. This soon changed, however, when the household of the Medici Grand Dukes moved from the north bank to the Palazzo Pitti in 1550, from where they ruled much of Tuscany for years to come. Several Florentine aristocrats followed suit, building luxurious palazzi near the Medici Palace.

But to discover the true character of Florence, step into the side streets, brimful of tiny authentic restaurants, boutiques, antiques shops and artisans' studios. Among the sights, the Cappella Brancacci stands out for its fabulous fresco cycle, while, on a grassy hilltop overlooking the city, San Miniato counts among Tuscany's finest Romanesque treasures. Here, on the southern fringes of the Oltrarno, you'll find city and countryside merging together with some quite exceptional views.

Previous page: Rooftops of the Oltrarno, and spire and dome of Santo Spirito

In a Day

If you're not quite sure where to begin your travels, this itinerary recommends a practical and enjoyable day out in Oltrarno, taking in some of the best places to see using the Getting Your Bearings map on the previous page. For more information see the main entries.

9:00am

Make sure you arrive early at the **❶ Palazzo Pitti** (➤ 142–147) to get a head start on the hundreds of visitors who trail through the palace daily. You would be advised to devote most of your morning to the various museums here: take your time and be selective, but be sure to include the paintings of the Galleria Palatina in your itinerary.

Noon

Stroll through the magnificent **❺ Giardino di Boboli** (below, ➤ 152–153). They were once the Pitti's private gardens, but now they are the city centre's largest public park and a foremost example of Italianate gardening.

1:00pm

Grab a quick lunch at Caffè Pitti (➤ 154) near the entrance to the Palazzo Pitti or head for the picturesque **Piazza di Santo Spirito** (➤ 153) to purchase a picnic lunch of *antipasti,* cheeses, cold cuts, salad and fruit from the daily market to eat on the steps of the **❻ church of Santo Spirito**.

3:00pm

Visit **2 Santa Maria del Carmine** (► 148–149) to see the beautiful, emotionally charged frescoes by Masaccio and others in the Cappella Brancacci (below), which had a profound influence on the direction of art in the Early Renaissance. The church is located in a particularly individual part of the Oltrarno – the parish of San Frediano, once the wool-dyers' and leatherworkers' district which, together with the adjacent area around Santo Spirito, still has its own dialect. The side streets are packed with fascinating workshops, local stores and small cafes.

4:30pm

Save your visit to **3 San Miniato al Monte** (► 150–151) until the heat of the day subsides because it involves a lengthy uphill climb. Your efforts will be richly rewarded, however, by one of Florence's most beautiful churches, the picturesque countryside of the hinterland and outstanding city views.

7:30pm

After a long and tiring day, treat yourself to a meal on the panoramic terrace at **La Loggia** (► 151).

Palazzo Pitti

The Palazzo Pitti, the most monumental of all Florence's palaces, was the chief residence of the Medici from the mid-16th century. Later it was home to their successors, the Lorraines, then briefly became the royal palace of the Savoy dynasty (1865–71), when Florence was the nation's capital. Today, its lavish rooms house several important museums of Medici treasures, including the Galleria Palatina with its prestigious collection of High Renaissance and baroque paintings.

The palace was originally built for Luca Pitti, a rich banker and rival of the Medici. It was begun in 1457, to a design by Filippo Brunelleschi, at a time when all eminent Florentine families were vying to build the biggest and best residences – symbols to reflect their standing in society. Determined to outdo even the great Medici, Pitti insisted that his massive palace windows were to be larger than the doors of the Medici Palace (now the Palazzo Medici-Riccardi, ➤ 104–105). These grandiose ideas proved to be his downfall, however, as building costs bankrupted him and in 1465 construction was halted. Ironically, the palace was bought by the Medici in 1549.

It was Cosimo I's wife, Eleonora di Toledo, who, in ill health, persuaded her husband that she might benefit from the more rural setting of the Oltrarno, until then considered the "wrong" side of the river to live. She employed Bartolommeo Ammannati to add two wings to the palace and a stately courtyard opening on to the magnificent Giardino di Boboli (➤ 152–153). The palace that you see today is three times its original size, due to subsequent enlargements and embellishment: the facade alone is over 200m (219 yards) in length.

The Fontana del Carciofo (Fountain of the Artichoke) was designed by Francesco Susini

The Collections

Inside the palace, you'll find no fewer than six museums: the Galleria Palatina (Palatine Gallery), the Galleria d'Arte Moderna (Modern Art Gallery, ➤ 146), the

A modern sculpture outside the main entrance to the Palazzo Pitti

Museo degli Argenti (Silver Museum), the Appartamenti Monumentali (State Apartments), the Galleria del Costume (Costume Gallery, ➤ panel below), and the Museo delle Carozze (Coach Museum), which houses a small collection of state carriages and sedan chairs, and is open by appointment only. The Museo delle Porcellane (Porcelain Museum) can be accessed only through the Giardino di Boboli (➤ 152).

Don't be put off by the palace's immense size, or daunted by its many museums and wealth of fine works of art. The secret is to be selective. Pick just one or maybe two collections that interest you and concentrate on those. If the going gets tough, seek retreat in the landscaped gardens.

Galleria Palatina

The Palatine Gallery was created by the Lorraine Grand Dukes at the start of the 19th century simply by converting the former Medici private quarters, crammed with paintings, into public reception rooms. The display spans Florentine art from the Early Renaissance to Mannerism (➤ 152), and includes key works from other contemporary Italian and European

GALLERIA DEL COSTUME

The collection is housed in the Palazzina della Meridiana, a wing of the palace accessed through the Giardino di Boboli (➤ 152). Tel: 055 238 8713. Open: Jun–Aug daily 8:15–7:30; Sep–Oct daily 8:15–6:30; Jan, Feb, Nov, Dec daily 8:15–4:30. Closed 1st and last Mon each month. Last tickets one hour before closing. Admission: (combined ticket with Museo degli Argenti, Museo delle Porcellane and Giardino di Boboli), expensive.

masters, including Raphael, Titian, Tintoretto, Rubens and Van Dyck. Unlike the Uffizi (► 52–59), the paintings are not displayed in a chronological order, but hung as the Medici Grand Dukes wished – in a purely decorative manner more or less regardless of subject, style or date.

The ceilings in rooms 24–28 are painted with ebullient frescoes (1641–47) by Pietro da Cortona allegorizing the education of young Cosimo III de Medici by the gods. Start from Room 28 and work backwards: in the Sala di Venere, Minerva (Knowledge) tears the prince from the love of Venus; in the following rooms he is taught science from Apollo (Sala di Apollo), war from Mars (Sala di Marte) and leadership from Jupiter (Sala di Giove); finally, the aged Cosimo is taken

Cortona's celebrated ceiling fresco in the Sala di Marte of Cosimo III de Medici learning about war from Mars

Right: One of the palace's exuberant State Apartments

HIGHLIGHTS

- Sala di Prometeo: *Virgin and Child* (Filippo Lippi); *Portrait of a Young Woman* and *Portrait of a Young Man* (Sandro Botticelli); *Adoration of the Magi* (Jacopo Pontormo)
- Sala dell'Educazione di Giove: *Sleeping Cupid* (Michelangelo Merisi da Caravaggio)
- Sala dell'Iliade: *La Gràvida – The Pregnant Lady* (Raphael)
- Sala di Saturno: *Madonna of the Chair* (Raphael)
- Sala di Giove: *La Velata – Veiled Woman* (Raphael); *Deposition* (Fra Bartolomeo)
- Sala di Marte: *The Consequences of War*; *The Four Philosophers* (Rubens)
- Sala di Apollo: *Mary Magdalene* (Titian); *The Holy Family* (Andrea del Sarto)
- Sala di Venere: *La Bella* (Titian)

to Saturn, father of the gods, by Mars and Prudence, and crowned by Fame and Eternity (Sala di Saturno).

Appartamenti Monumentali

The opulent State Apartments, on the first floor of the south wing, are a must see – home to the Medici, then the Lorraine Grand Dukes and, from 1865 to 1871, the official residence of King Victor Emmanule II. You can see his throne under a large canopy in the Sala del Trono.

These princely rooms are extravagantly decorated with bold colour schemes, ornate gold and white stucco-work ceilings and period furnishings, with the Sala Bianca (White Room), the palace ballroom, as the pièce de résistance.

Museo degli Argenti

The Silver Museum is housed in the Grand Dukes' summer apartments (on the ground and mezzanine floors beneath the Palatine Gallery) and contains a fantastic and eclectic collection of Medici treasures. You'll find not only silverware, but also a dazzling array of gold, amber, glass and other fine arts. Lorenzo the Magnificent's collection of 16

GALLERIA D'ARTE MODERNA

The Gallery of Modern Art (on the second floor of the palace) features Italian art from 1784 to 1924. Among the 2,000-odd paintings and sculptures are works of neo-classicism and Romanticism (rooms 1–12); the Florence-based Macchiaioli ("spotmakers", similar to French Impressionists, rooms 16–18); and Tuscan post-Impressionism (rooms 28–30).

Tel: 055 238 8616. Open: Tue–Sun 8:15–6:50. Last tickets 45 mins before closing. Admission: (combined ticket with Galleria Palatina and Appartamenti Reali) expensive.

pietre dure vases in the Sala Buia includes Roman and Byzantine pieces and should certainly not be missed. The Medici jewellery collection, on the mezzanine floor, is also superb.

TAKING A BREAK

Caffè Pitti (Piazza de' Pitti 9r, tel: 055 239 9863), virtually opposite the Palazzo Pitti, serves pasta, salads, snacks, cocktails and other refreshments. On one or two evenings a week, you can sit and enjoy live jazz.

➕ 199 D3 ✉ Piazza Pitti 🚌 D

Galleria Palatina and Appartamenti Monumentali

☎ 055 238 8614 🕐 Tue–Sun 8:15–6:50; closed Jan. Last tickets 45 mins before closing 💷 Combined entrance fee: expensive

Grand Ducal Treasures Museum (Museo degli Argenti)

☎ 055 238 8709 🕐 Jan–Feb and Nov–Dec daily 8:15–4:30; Mar 8:15–5:30; Apr–May, Sep–Oct 8:15–6:30; Jun–Aug 8:15–7:30 💷 Expensive (combined ticket with Museo della Porcellane and Giardino di Boboli)

Above: Canova's *Venus Italica* coyly watches visitors in the Sala di Venere, in the Galleria Palatina

Left: Elaborate decoration in the Galleria Palatina

PALAZZO PITTI: INSIDE INFO

Top tips Try to **arrive early** and be prepared to queue.

- If you intend to visit three or more museums within the palace, consider buying the *Cumulativo* ticket for the entire palace complex (plus Giardino di Boboli). It's valid for three days and saves queuing at the ticket office each time you visit. Tickets may cost more during special exhibitions.

Hidden gems Galleria Palatina: Napoleon's neo-classical bathroom.

- Museo degli Argenti: Exquisite **pearl ornaments**, modelled into various animal forms; frescoed state rooms, including an exuberant Medici allegory by Giovanni da San Giovanni and two staggering *trompe-l'oeil* "palace within a palace" frescoes in the Public Audience Chamber.
- Galleria d'Arte Moderna: Paintings from the **Staggia School**, the first school of landscape art in Tuscany (Room 14).

2 Santa Maria del Carmine – Cappella Brancacci

The magnificent frescoes by Masaccio in the Cappella Brancacci, in the south transept of Santa Maria del Carmine, constitute the single most influential sequence of paintings of the Early Renaissance.

In 1423, Felice Brancacci, an important political figure in Florence and a wealthy silk merchant, commissioned two artists – Masaccio and Masolino da Panicale – to paint his family chapel with 12 scenes from the life of St Peter (who is portrayed in orange robes throughout). However, work was interrupted in 1428 when Masaccio moved to Rome (he died a few months later, aged just 27) and the Brancacci family was exiled from Florence by the Medici. The beautiful pastel-coloured cycle was eventually completed by Filippino Lippi some 50 years later.

Differences in Style

An immediate contrast between the works of Masaccio and Masolino is obvious in their two depictions of **Adam and Eve** on the upper entrance piers. Masolino's portrayal is simple and decorative, while the intensity of Masaccio's makes it one of the most emotional images in Western art. It was this realism, in particular, that set Masaccio's painting worlds apart from the courtly, elegant style of his contemporaries. A strategically placed fig leaf was added to his Adam at a much later date, but this was removed during restoration work in the 1980s. Also by Masaccio is the **Tribute Money** (left wall, top row), unusual in that it contains three pictures in one: Christ (centre) instructing St Peter to catch a fish (left) in whose mouth he will find

THE FRESCOES: WHO PAINTED WHAT

Left-hand side
Top row: *Expulsion of Adam and Eve* and the *Tribute Money* (Masaccio); *St Peter Preaching* (Masolino)

Bottom row: *St Peter Visited by St Paul* (Lippi); *Resurrection of the Emperor's Son* (Masaccio/Lippi); *St Peter Enthroned* and *St Peter Healing the Sick* (Masaccio/Lippi)

Right-hand side
Top row: *St Peter Baptising the Converts* (Masaccio); *St Peter Healing the Cripple, Raising Tabitha* and *The Temptation of Adam and Eve* (Masolino)

Bottom row: *St Peter and St John Giving Alms* (Masaccio); *Crucifixion, Before the Proconsul* and *The Release of St Peter* (Lippi)

CAPPELLA BRANCACCI: INSIDE INFO

Top tips To reach the **Cappella Brancacci**, go through a side door of Santa Maria del Carmine, along the peaceful late 16th-century cloisters, then into the sacristy.
- Be prepared to **queue** and to book your place on a guided tour. Visitor numbers and the time you can spend in the chapel are limited.

Hidden gems The only known **contemporary portrait of architect Filippo Brunelleschi** is in the scene of *St Peter Enthroned* (left wall, bottom row). He can be seen in the doorway on the right in a black hood.
- In the background of Masolino's *St Peter Healing the Cripple* (right wall, top row), you can see a lovely view of 15th-century Florence.
- The **two roundels** of ladies' faces behind the altar are remarkable for their depth of colour and delicate complexions.

the tribute money to pay the tax collector (right). In ***The Resurrection of the Emperor's Son*** (left wall, bottom row, centre), Masaccio added various Brancacci family members to the scene, but when they were exiled from Florence their portraits were eliminated. Filippino Lippi repainted them though, in 1481–82.

TAKING A BREAK

Try **Angiolino** (➤ 154), an atmospheric trattoria serving such Florentine staples as *ribollita* (Tuscan vegetable soup), tripe and grilled meats in jolly, rustic surroundings.

The nave of Santa Maria del Carmine ✚ 198 B4 ✉ Piazza del Carmine ☎ Church 055 212331; chapel 055 276 8224 🕔 Chapel Mon and Wed–Sat 10–5, Sun 1–5. Last tickets 30 mins before closing 🚌 6 and D 💶 Church free; chapel moderate

❸ San Miniato al Monte

One of Florence's oldest and most beautiful churches, and the most sublime example of Romanesque architecture in Tuscany, San Miniato was founded in 1018 near the tomb of Minias, a rich Armenian merchant who had travelled to Florence to spread Christianity. Minias was beheaded for his beliefs in AD250 and, according to legend, picked up his severed head and marched up the hill with it, keen to be buried where he'd lived as a hermit.

The Exterior

After climbing the steep steps to the church's lofty hilltop terrace, you hardly know what to admire first: the dazzling bi-coloured facade with its geometric marble patterning typical of the Romanesque style, or the sweeping vistas of Florence. The mosaic in the pediment of *Christ with the Virgin and St Minias* dates from the early 13th century, and atop the entire ensemble sits a gilded copper eagle clutching a bale of wool – the symbol of the Arte di Calimala, the powerful guild of wool importers who financed the church during the Middle Ages.

The vault of Michelozzo's 15th-century tabernacle is decorated with blue glazed-terracotta tondi

The Interior

The interior is every bit as impressive as the exterior. It is strikingly arranged on three levels – the nave, a raised choir containing the main altar and, beneath it, the crypt, designed so the central altar could lie directly above St Minias's relics. In the raised section, the intricately carved pulpit was set sideways so it could be seen by both the congregation and the monks segregated by the magnificent screen. The nave contains exquisite 13th-century **marble mosaic panels** depicting signs of the zodiac, and the apse is dominated by a further Byzantine-style mosaic of *Christ with the Virgin and St Minias*. The surrounding windows are covered with thin layers of alabaster to soften the light, enabling the monks to pray here

Above: The view across Florence from the ramparts surrounding San Miniato al Monte

with greater concentration. The oldest and most fascinating part of the church is the **12th-century crypt**. It rests on 36 marble columns, each one different and all salvaged from ancient Roman buildings. Services usually take place here – including an atmospheric Vespers, often conducted in Gregorian chant.

TAKING A BREAK

Enjoy gastronomic alfresco dining on the terrace of **La Loggia** (Piazzale Michelangelo 1, tel: 055 234 2832; www.ristorantelaloggia.it, open daily 12–3, 7–10:30), a 19th-century neo-classical villa.

Top left: Detail of the 13th-century facade mosaic

🚇 201 D1   ✉ Via del Monte alle Croci   ☎ 055 234 2731   🕐 Apr–Oct daily 8–7; Nov–Mar daily 8–12, 3–6. Closed during services. Services (usually in the crypt): Mon–Sat 8:30am, 10am, 11:30am, 5:30pm, Sun 8:30am, 5:30pm   🚌 12 and 13   💲 Free

---

SAN MINIATO AL MONTE: INSIDE INFO

Top tips Try to come when the church is at its quietest – **either early** morning or towards **the end of the day**.

■ Visit the **monks' small shop** for lavender, honey, herbs and a variety of homeopathic remedies.

Hidden gems Cappella del Cardinale del Portogallo (Chapel of the Cardinal of Portugal), inspired by Filippo Brunelleschi's Sagrestia Vecchia in San Lorenzo (▶ 95–97), is striking in its simpicity of design.

■ The Cappella del Crocifisso (Chapel of the Crucifix) is intricately carved and decorated with terracottas by Luca della Robbia.

■ The sacristy has colourful frescoed scenes from the life of St Benedict.

At Your Leisure

4 Santa Felicita

Santa Felicita's most precious treasure is the Cappella Capponi just inside the church on the right, decorated by Jacopo Pontormo with two of the greatest works of Mannerist art ever produced: the *Annunciation* and the *Deposition*. Painted between 1525 and 1528, these sophisticated works have a luminescent quality, which reflects the work's emotional intensity. The *Deposition*, with its iridescent palette of colours and its entwined yet graceful bodies, is widely acknowledged as Pontormo's greatest work, yet in many ways his *Annunciation* is even more moving in its simplicity.

As you leave the church notice the unusual exterior. The edifice has been remodelled numerous times since its Romanesque origins and the dome was destroyed in the mid-16th century to make way for Giorgio Vasari's great Medici corridor (➤ 54), now embedded in the rebuilt facade.

➕ 199 E4 ✉ Piazza di Santa Felicita
☎ 055 213018; www.santafelicita.it ⏰ Mon–Sat 9–12, 3:30–5:30; closed Sun and during services. Services: Mon–Sat 6pm, Sun 9am, 11am 🚌 D 🎫 Free

5 Giardino di Boboli

The extensive Boboli Gardens climbing the hill behind the Palazzo

MANNERISM

Mannerism was derived from the Italian word *maniere* (meaning style or elegance) and, as with the term Renaissance, it applies to a diverse movement of art characterized by exaggerated elegance, heightened colour combinations, free-flowing lines and technical flair. It developed out of the High Renaissance and lasted approximately 60 years (1520–80), with Pontormo's frescoes in Santa Felicita paving the way.

Pitti are a magical retreat on a hot summer's day. Highlights include the Neptune Fountain and the unforgettable Bacchus Fountain (Cosimo I's court jester as the Roman god of wine, astride a turtle); the Orangery, filled with sweet-smelling citrus plants; and the elegant avenue of cypress trees leading down to L'Isolotto (Little Island), a moated garden bedecked with statuary and fountains. There's even a rococo-style pavilion, from where there are exceptional views over the city and surrounding countryside.

At the top of the gardens, an 18th-century ballroom houses the Museo delle Porcellane (Porcelain Museum) with its important ceramic collection, including pieces from Sèvres, Vienna and Meissen. The views of Florence from the upper terraces are superb.

➕ 198 C2 ✉ Accessed from the Palazzo Pitti ☎ 055 238 8786 ⏰ Jun–Aug daily 8:15–7:30; Apr–May, Sep–Oct 8:15–6:30; Mar 8:15–5:30; Nov–Feb 8:15–4:30. Closed 1st and last Mon of every month. Last tickets one hour before closing 🚌 D 🎫 Expensive (combined ticket with Argenti, Costume and Porcellane museums)

The collections in the Museo delle Porcellane are superb

Museo delle Porcellane
✚ 199 D2 ✉ Accessed from the Palazzo Pitti ☎ 055 238 8605 ⏱ Same as Boboli Gardens (▶ 152). 💶 Expensive (combined ticket)

6 Santo Spirito
Don't be put off by the austere, unfinished facade of Santo Spirito. This was Filippo Brunelleschi's last great church, described by Bernini as "the most beautiful church in the world" – light, airy and harmoniously proportioned with a colonnaded nave, graceful archways and 38 intimate side chapels, all in soothing grey and white stone.

But Santo Spirito is more than just a church: it is a splendid picture gallery filled with artistic masterworks. Each side chapel is a treasure trove of art, including several beautifully painted wooden altar frontals; Filippino Lippi's cherished *Madonna and Child with Saints* (1494) in Chapel 11; and Raffaellino del Garbo's 16th-century interpretation of the same subject in Chapel 30. Be sure to see the vestibule with its stylish barrel-vaulted ceiling, which leads to the sacristy – a veritable Renaissance gem designed by Giuliano da Sangallo – and a charming fountain-splashed cloister.

Next door, the Cenacolo (Refectory) di Santo Spirito is all that remains of the monastery that once stood here. It contains Andrea de Cione Orcagna's famous *Crucifixion* fresco, a rare example of High Gothic art in a predominantly Renaissance

city, and a good collection of Romanesque sculpture.

The atmospheric Piazza di Santo Spirito, dominated by the yellow facade of the church, resembles a cool garden with its plane trees and fountain. In the mornings, the tastes,

The Sagrestia in Santo Spirito

fragrances and colours of the vibrant market here (Mon–Sat 8–2) provide a feast for all the senses. On Sundays there are interesting antiques and second-hand stalls. By night it is a popular meeting place, its bars and cafes spilling out on to the cobbles and remaining lively until the early hours.

Church
✚ 198 C4 ✉ Piazza di Santo Spirito 🚇 D ☎ 055 210030 ⏱ Mon–Tue, Thu–Sun 10–12:30, 4–5.30. Closed during services. Services: Mon–Fri 9am, Sat 5:30pm, Sun 9am, 10.30am, noon, 5:30pm 💶 Free

Cenacolo
✚ 198 C4 ✉ Piazza di Santo Spirito 29 🚇 D ☎ 055 287043 ⏱ Sat 10:30–1:30 💶 Inexpensive

Where to...
Eat and Drink

Prices

Expect to pay per person for a meal, excluding drinks and service

€ under €20 €€ €20–€45 €€€ over €45

The Oltrarno has always been a traditional and no-nonsense part of Florence, a fact that is reflected in its straightforward and inexpensive restaurants, which are often family-run.

It is also an area with an up-and-coming reputation, something that is reflected in several new, informal places to eat and drink, particularly on and around its two principal squares, Piazza del Carmine and Piazza di Santo Spirito.

The San Frediano area is also becoming increasingly trendy, but it lies well to the east of the heart of the Oltrarno.

and plump pumpkins adorn the bar, and dried flowers and chillis hang from the old brick-vaulted main dining room. Checked tablecloths and wicker-covered wine bottles complete the picture. The menu offers simple Tuscan mainstream dishes – crostini (toasts), hams, salami, bistecca (beef), pappa al pomodoro (bread and tomato soup) and other pastas, grilled meats and soups.

➕ 198 C5 ☒ Via di Santo Spirito 36r ☎ 055 239 8976 ☻ Daily 12:30–2:30, 7:30–10:30

Le Barrique €

If Angiolino (▶ above) is not quite what you want after admiring the Cappella Brancacci, then turn the corner into Via del Leone and wander into this small and attractive wine bar, where you can choose from several hot or cold dishes of the day or wash down bread, cheese and other snacks with a glass of wine from the bottles on the bar.

4 Leoni €–€€

Relatively few casual visitors stumble across this trattoria, which lies in a piazza just a few steps from the Palazzo Pitti. The interior is rustic, with rough stone walls and colossal beams hung with dried flowers. The food is Tuscan, and in summer can be enjoyed under umbrellas on the square outside.

➕ 199 D4 ☒ Via dei Vellutini 1r-Piazza della Passera ☎ 055 218562; www.4leoni.com ☻ Daily 12–3, 7–12. Closed Aug

Angiolino €–€€

A traditional trattoria, this has a pretty interior: strings of tomatoes

➕ 198 A5 ☒ Via del Leone 40r ☎ 055 224192; www.enotecalebarrique.com ☻ Tue–Sun 7pm–midnight or later

Borgo Antico €–€€

This is one of the Oltrarno's newer-style eating places. It's hugely popular, so it gets quite crowded and noisy, though this is less of a problem if you can find an outside table. Service can be slow and the food – which runs the gamut of pasta, pizza, meat, fish, vegetables and salads – is rarely exceptional, although the portions are huge. However, you come here for the convivial and lively atmosphere more than anything else.

➕ 198 C4 ☒ Piazza di Santo Spirito 6r ☎ 055 210437; www.borgoanticofirenze.com ☻ Daily 12:30–3, 7–midnight

Caffè Pitti €

The piazza in front of the Palazzo Pitti offers several cafe options, of which this – the southernmost in the square – is by far the best

Sant' Agostino 23 €€

This hidden gem is a great find in the atmospheric streets around Santo Spirito. The five young owners are hands on and their modern take on a trattoria has injected new life into the area, but the emphasis is still on expertly prepared, simple Tuscan cooking.

✚ 198 C4 ☒ Via Sant'Agostino 23r
☎ 055 210208; www.sa23.it ☺ Tue–Sun
12:30–2:45, 7:30–10:45

Le Volpi e L'Uva €

This is a modern and first-rate *enoteca*, or wine bar, hidden in a small square just over the Ponte Vecchio. Its selection of wines by the glass is especially good – with many unusual vintages – and changes every few days. The snack food offered – including *crostini* (toasts), *panini* (filled rolls), bread and cheese – is also excellent.

✚ 199 E4 ☒ Piazza dei Rossi 1r,
off Piazza di Santa Felicita
☎ 055 239 8132; www.levolpieluva.com
☺ Mon–Sat 11–9

Hemingway €

Hemingway is a modern cafe just off Piazza del Carmine. It is unlike anything else in Florence, thanks to its specialities: tea, coffee and chocolate. You can indulge in a high tea, choosing from many different special teas; sample more than 20 types of coffee; try a tea-based cocktail; or gorge on the sensational cakes and chocolates. More conventional fare is also available.

✚ 198 A5 ☒ Piazza Piattellina 9r
☎ 055 284781; www.hemingway.fi.it
☺ Daily 3.30pm–1am

Maracana' Grill €€

For something slightly more novel, this Brazilian *churrascaria* (steakhouse) fits the bill; the lively, modern look and authentic dishes will have you convinced you are in Rio. Try the *churrasco*, six meats barbecued at the table and served with rice, black beans and salad.

✚ 198 C4 ☒ Borgo Tegolaio 17r (off
Santo Spirito) ☎ 055 238 2290; www.
maracanagrill.com ☺ Tue–Sun 7–10:30

thanks to its pretty and old-fashioned interior.

✚ 199 D3 ☒ Piazza de' Pitti 9r
☎ 055 239 9863; www.caffepitti.it
☺ Daily 11am–2am

Caffè Ricchi €

Most neighbourhoods or big squares have their pivotal bar, and in Piazza di Santo Spirito it's the Caffè Ricchi, a good place for breakfast, mid-morning coffee, a sandwich, a light lunch, an evening drink or a late nightcap. In good weather you can sit at outside tables on the traffic-free piazza and watch the world go by.

✚ 198 C4 ☒ Piazza di Santo Spirito 9r
☎ 055 215864 ☺ Bar: Mon–Sat
7am–1.30am in summer; Mon–Sat
7am–10pm in winter. Restaurant: Mon–Sat
12:30–2:45, 7:30–10

Casalinga €

This old-fashioned neighbourhood trattoria still offers the good basic Tuscan food, brisk and friendly service and animated atmosphere

you'd expect of a restaurant that's been run by the same family for a couple of generations. Try eating here as an alternative to the nearby Borgo Antico (▶ 154) and Osteria Santo Spirito.

✚ 198 C4 ☒ Via del Michelozzi 9r,
off Piazza di Santo Spirito ☎ 055 218624
☺ Mon–Sat 12–2:30, 7–10

Fuori Porta €

Fuori Porta means "outside the door or gate", in this case the Porta San Miniato. As such, this celebrated wine bar makes a good place to take a break if you're walking to or from the outlying church of San Miniato. The bar has some 600 different wines, including around 40 available by the glass, plus whiskies, grappas and other more unusual drinks. The snack food is superb, and the menu also runs to a limited selection of delicious hot dishes.

✚ 200 C3 ☒ Via del Monte alle Croci 10r
☎ 055 234 2483; www.fuoriporta.it ☺ Daily
12:30–3:30, 7–12:30

Where to...
Shop

The Oltrarno is not an area blessed with many shops likely to interest visitors. It is full of food and other stores designed to serve the neighbourhood.

JEWELLERY

One historic shop is a cut above most of Florence's many jewellers: **Lapini** (Borgo San Frediano 50r, tel 055 277 6452, Mon–Fri 9–1, 3:30–7:30), which uses the finest materials and has unusual designs.

ART AND ANTIQUES

Art and antiques can be found in the area around Via Maggio. Via Maggio, in particular, has any number of well-stocked galleries

and antiques shops, notably **Mara Zecchi** (No 34r, tel: 055 293368, closed Sat pm in summer, Mon am in winter), filled with pieces dating from the Renaissance and earlier, and **Guido Bartolozzi** (No 18r, tel: 055 215602) and **Paulo Paoletti** (No 30r, tel: 055 214728), both excellent sources for period furniture and objects. Make time to visit **Castorina** (Via di Santo Spirito 13–15r, tel: 055 212885, open Mon–Fri 9–1, 3–7, Sat 9–1), remarkable for its huge number of decorative gilt picture frames, cherubs and ornate mouldings, and baroque or baroque-style items. Another fine old-fashioned shop is **Guilio Giannini & Figlio** (Piazza de' Pitti 37r, tel: 055 212 621), a traditional book-binder (▶ 24).

Where to...
Be Entertained

Much of the entertainment in the Oltrarno is casual, offered by high-spirited restaurants, bars and cafes that stay open until the small hours.

BARS AND CLUBS

Dolce Vita (Piazza del Carmine, tel: 055 284595, open daily 10am–2am in summer; Tue–Sun 6pm–2am in winter) is one of the city's most frequented bars. Forgo the over-slick interior in favour of a table outside on the piazza. **Cabiria** (Piazza di Santo Spirito 4r, tel: 055 215732, open daily 8am–1.30am. Closed Tue in winter) is moodier and funkier, and appeals to a more "alternative" clientele. It only really comes into its own in the evening.

There are tables outside in summer. **Zoe** (Via dei Renai 13r, tel: 055 243111, open Mon–Sat 8:30am–1 or 2am, Sun 6pm–2am) is a popular, elegant and relaxed cocktail bar (with dancing later in the evening) in the eastern margins just beyond the Ponte alle Grazie. In summer you can sit outside. Neighbouring bars such as Negroni are also good. Mauve is the colour at the **Cavalli Club** (Piazza de Carmine 8r, tel: 055 211650, www.cavalliclub.com, open nightly 7–late) and Roberto Cavalli's style and signature animal prints are here in abundance. Inside a former 15th-century church, the upper level is a restaurant and downstairs is a futuristic bar where the dance floor is lowered after midnight.

Excursions

Excursions

The Tuscan countryside provides a perfect escape from the intensity, the hustle and bustle and, in summer, the sheer heat of Florence. Should you tire of the capital's countless charms, why not set out to sample the rural pleasures of the region? Alternatively, visit the magical towns and cities of Lucca, Pisa, San Gimignano and Siena, all within easy reach.

Towns and Cities

As the critic Ervenat remarked, "The stones of cities mark the great hours of history", and nowhere is this more true than in Tuscany. Every Tuscan town, however humble, has at some point experienced a golden age, hence the abundance of beautiful palazzi, churches and grand piazzas – an artistic heritage that extends to even the remotest village.

You'll find that many of the towns and villages have similar features. Most have a main square flanked by their principal religious and civic buildings – the church, town hall, a loggia

(built to provide shelter from the sun or rain, now commonly the site of the local market) and a towering campanile. These bell-towers were built high so that the bells could be heard far and wide. They were rung to summon townsfolk to Mass or to public meetings in the square, to sound the curfew and, when rung furiously (a *stormo*), to signal danger. Their significance gave rise to the expression *campanilismo*, used to define the strong Tuscan character trait of parochialism.

The main square of most Tuscan towns and villages is also the scene of local festivities and the daily *passeggiata* when the entire population promenades in their finery, gazing in shop windows and admiring each other. The people of the cities of Tuscany, in common with many Italians, are keen to practise

Previous page: Detail of a colonnaded section of Pisa's Campanile

Above: Rolling Tuscan countryside near Monte Oliveto Maggiore

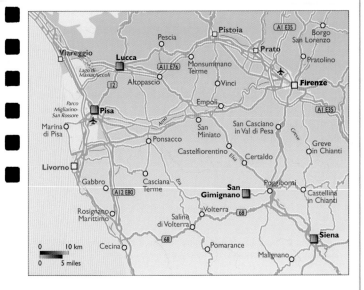

the art of *fare bella figura* (looking and being seen to look good).

Tuscans are fiercely proud of their heritage, their countryside, and also their ancestry, which dates back to the Etruscans. But they are determined not to allow their great cities to become museum pieces given over entirely to tourism. Instead, they have cultivated thriving service sectors, especially in the fields of finance, architecture and conservation. Glass, marble and motorcycles count among the main industrial products, while Tuscany's crafts, olive oil and wines are respected worldwide. Living in a hard-working and economically independent region, the locals scorn, like many Italians, the government in Rome, with its ceaseless bureaucracy. Many of them would prefer the autonomy they enjoyed before the unification of Italy in 1870.

The Countryside

But don't just visit Lucca, Pisa, San Gimignano, Siena and Tuscany's many hilltop towns and villages. The region's true identity is to be found in its beautiful countryside – its seductive, softly hued landscapes of undulating green hillsides splashed with wild flowers, hiding sun-bleached farms within their folds; picturesque lemon- and apricot-coloured villas; olive groves; vineyards; fields of lavender, corn and bare terracotta earth; and single lines of cypresses. For this is quintessential Tuscany – an intoxicating backdrop to the cities that harbour the greatest art treasures of the Italian Renaissance; the archetypal Italian countryside, which for centuries has had a bewitching effect on visitors.

Siena

Siena is arguably the most beautiful city in Tuscany. Its appearance is distinguished from Florence by its hilltop site, its predominance of rich red brick as the main building material rather than honey-coloured stone, and its medieval monuments, which are a perfect foil to Renaissance Florence. As an alderman here once remarked: "For those involved in governing the city, the main problem is one of beauty."

According to folklore, Siena was founded by Senius, son of Remus, one of the two legendary founders of Rome – hence the abundant statues of the she-wolf who suckled Romulus and Remus. Since then the city has played a distinguished role in history, which is reflected in its rich cultural heritage. Its heyday came in the Middle Ages, when it was one of Europe's wealthiest cities. Not only did it boast a thriving textile trade but, much to the envy of Florence, it also established the first international banks, raking in money from the whole of Christendom on behalf of the papacy. Local painters (including Andrea Pisano, Simone Martini, the Lorenzetti

The view from Torre del Mangia over Siena's main square, the Campo

brothers and Duccio di Buoninsegna) were at the forefront of Italian art. Their minute attention to detail and their early experimentation with techniques of perspective were widely respected and they were in demand throughout Tuscany.

However, the Black Death of 1348 dealt Siena a cruel blow: three-quarters of the population died, and the city never really fully recovered. For centuries it languished in the shadows of the then-thriving Florence and even in the late 19th century Henry James found it a "cracking, peeling, fading, crumbling, rotting" city. But today, Siena is an elegant, old-fashioned provincial city, grown rich on banking and tourism, with plentiful art treasures, stylish shops and fantastic cellar restaurants – all encased within ancient city walls. There's a charming, almost medieval atmosphere in its uneven cobbled lanes, its dark stepped alleyways and the way in which the city is still divided into ancient districts called *contrade*, a system common throughout Italy.

At the height of its power the city was split into over 40 such districts, but since the 17th century there have been just 17. Each is still a village at heart, with its own symbols, traditions, social club, museum, church and fountain, where newborn babies are baptized into the *contrada*. The inhabitants are fiercely proud of their wards, leading to inevitable competition that reaches its climax each year at the Palio (► 164), Tuscany's best-known festival.

Piazza del Campo

No matter which way you turn in the labyrinth of medieval streets, even the darkest, most tortuous alleyway seems to lead back to Siena's main square, undoubtedly one of the most striking designs of Italian town planning. This vast, fan-shaped open space of red brick is divided into nine segments by long spokes of white marble. The natural rose-coloured palazzi flanking the square was built according to strict 13th-century regulations, laid down to preserve the dignity of the city's great showpiece. The majestic Palazzo Pubblico and its bell-

Above: Siena's Duomo rising over the surrounding streets

tower, the second highest medieval tower in Italy, dominate the square. By day, the Campo is a popular meeting place, but by night it has an almost magical atmosphere, abuzz with crowds dining alfresco in the restaurants and cafes that fringe the uniquely seashell-shaped square.

Palazzo Pubblico

The Palazzo Pubblico, at the lower end of the Campo, has been the seat of government since the 13th century. Part of it (the **Museo Civico**) is open to the public, and contains some of Tuscany's finest Sienese paintings. Ambrogio Lorenzetti's dazzling pair of frescoes, *The Allegories of Good and Bad Government* (1337–39), in the Sala della Pace are considered among the world's most important medieval secular paintings.

The Torre del Mangia bell-tower, at 102m (335 feet), lords it over the Campo below. It was built as a symbol of the freedom of the city-state to mark the end of the feudal era, and was named after its first bell-ringer, nicknamed *Mangiaguadagni* (literally "eat the profits") because of his idleness. Do climb the 505 steps to the top. You'll be rewarded by unforgettable views.

Duomo

The spectacular black-and-white striped marble cathedral (built between 1215 and 1376) and matching campanile stand proud atop Siena's highest hill. The Sienese had hoped to make it the largest church in Christendom, intending the vast nave we see today to be merely the transept of a far greater building. In 1339, with this in mind, they began to build a new nave to the south, but plague struck the city, wiping out not only the funds but the congregation too, so the church remained unfinished. The incomplete nave now houses the **Museo dell'Opera del Duomo**, containing the sculptures by Giovanni Pisano that once adorned the facade

Left: View across Siena to the hills beyond

THE PALIO

The Palio (above), a fiercely contested bareback horse race between the *contrade* (districts) of the city, takes place in the Campo each year on 2 July and 16 August. It was first recorded in 1283. Each horse is blessed by the priest of the local *contrada*, then by the Bishop at the Duomo, amid great pageantry, with parades of drummers, trumpeters, flag-throwers and mace-bearers all dressed in medieval costume. The massive crowds cram into the Campo, where straws are drawn to decide the heats. The actual races are over in a flash – each lost and won in just three laps of the square. The victor is awarded a *palio* (banner) and, in the evening, the winning horse takes place of honour at an enormous open-air candlelit banquet in the winning *contrada*. It's a wonderful spectacle.

You can see the Palio for free if you're prepared to stand, but you'll need to arrive early and be prepared for a long, hot wait. Tickets for numbered seats and balcony places are expensive and sell out many months in advance. Advance bookings can be made through Palio Viaggi, Piazza Gramsci 7 (tel: 0577 280828).

of the cathedral, and Duccio's masterwork, a multi-panelled *Maestà* (enthroned Madonna). The abandoned wall of the Duomo, accessed through the museum, affords great views of Siena and the surrounding countryside.

The cathedral facade is a lavish confection of pink and white marble with an intriguing (and, some say, tasteless) blend of medieval statuary and 19th-century mosaic. The interior is equally ornate, described by John Ruskin as "overstriped, over-crocketed, over-gabled…a piece of faithless vanity". Highlights include Giovanni Pisano's carved pulpit panels depicting scenes from the life of Christ; the inlaid marble pavement illustrating stories from the Bible; and Duccio's magnificent stained-glass windows in the apse.

Tourist Information Office
✚ 202 B3   ✉ Piazza del Campo 56
☎ 0577 280551; www.terresiena.it   🕐 Daily 9–7

Museo Civico and Torre del Mangia
✚ 202 B3   ✉ Piazza del Campo 1
☎ 0577 226230 or 0577 41169   🕐 Tower: Nov–Mar daily 10–4; Apr–Oct 10–7. Museum: Jan to mid-Mar, Nov–Dec daily 10–6; mid-Mar to Oct 10–7
🎟 Museum: expensive; tower: moderate

Duomo

✚ 202 A3 ✉ Piazza del Duomo ☎ 0577 283048; www.operaduomo.siena.it
🕐 Mar–May, Sep–Oct Mon–Sat 10:30–7:30, Sun 1:30–5:30; Jun–Aug Mon–Sat
10:30–8, Sun 1:30–7; Nov–Feb Mon–Sat 10:30–6:30, Sun 1:30–5:30
🎟 Inexpensive

Museo dell'Opera del Duomo

✚ 202 A2 ✉ Piazza del Duomo 8 ☎ 0577 283048 ; www.operaduomo.siena.
it 🕐 Mar–May, Sep–Oct daily 9:30–7; Jun–Aug daily 9:30–8; Nov–Feb daily
10–5 🎟 Moderate

SIENA: INSIDE INFO

Top tips The city centre is **closed to traffic**, so be prepared to do a lot
of walking! Thankfully, though, all the main sights are within easy reach
of each other.
■ Climb the Torre del Mangia or the old cathedral wall to get a feel for **Siena's
size and layout**. The city, encircled within medieval city walls, is built on
three ridges, which all meet at Piazza del Campo.
■ Try the delicious **local specialities**, *panforte di Siena* (a dark, dense cake
made with candied fruit, nuts, cinnamon and cloves) and *ricciarelli*
(sweets made from ground almonds, orange peel and honey).

One not to miss The **Enoteca Italiana Permanente** (National Wine Library) in the
former munition cellars of the Fortezza promotes Italian wines. It claims to
hold every variety of wine the country produces. What's more, its bar (open
daily noon–midnight) offers all the wines by the glass or bottle. Salute!

Hidden gems The **Pinacoteca Nazionale** (Via San Pietro 29, tel: 0577
286143, open: Mon 8:30–1:30, Tue–Sat 8:15–7:15, Sun 8:15–1:15;
admission: moderate) contains paintings from the Sienese School.
■ **Santa Maria della Scala** (Piazza del Duomo 2, tel: 0577 224811, open:
mid-Mar to Oct daily 10:30–6:30; rest of year 10:30–4:30), housed in
the ancient medieval hospital building, boasts a fascinating collection of
15th-century frescoes (admission: moderate).
■ The only known **authentic portrait of St Catherine of Siena** hangs in San
Domenico church (Piazza San Domenico, tel: 0577 286848, open:
Apr–Oct daily 7:30–1, 3–6:30, Nov–Mar 9–1, 3–6:30).

Getting there In the early 19th century it took two days to travel the 70km
(43 miles) from Florence to Siena. Thankfully, today, it's much easier.
■ The **fastest route from Florence is by car** (about one hour) on the toll-free
Superstrada de Palio. The scenic Chiantigiana SS222 takes longer but
passes through "Chianti Country" and some of Tuscany's most beautiful
countryside. Cars are prohibited in the city centre, but there are plenty
of clearly signposted carparks.
■ SITA operates a regular **coach service** (about one an hour) from Florence's
train station to Piazza San Domenico in Siena (tel: 800 373760 in Italy
only; www.sitabus.it).
■ **Trains** run from Florence most hours and take about 90 minutes. Some
involve changing at Empoli. The station is 1.5km (1 mile) from the city
centre so, on arrival, you'll need to catch a bus from the station to Piazza
Matteotti, near the city centre.

San Gimignano

Perched on a hilltop beyond olive groves, cypresses and vineyards, San Gimignano is one of the most picturesque towns in Tuscany, famous for its elegant, soaring towers. These *belle torri* were the skyscrapers of the medieval Tuscan world, hence the town's popular epithet, "Manhattan of the Middle Ages".

In San Gimignano's prime, there were a staggering 72 towers in the town, of which just 14 survive. They were built, mainly in the 12th and 13th centuries, as much as status symbols as for defence, with every noble family eager to demonstrate its prestige. The town thrived as an important trading post on the Via Francigena pilgrim route from northern Europe to Rome, and its population was double the size of today. But the plague of 1348, followed by the diversion of the pilgrim route, led to its decline. In later years many of the towers were demolished and the stone used to build citadels.

André Suarès, on his Grand Tour of Europe at the turn of the 19th century, considered San Gimignano the most fascinating town in Italy. During his visit he also noted, "there is hardly a foreigner to be seen on this beautiful, languid August afternoon of torrid heat". Regrettably, this is no longer the case. The town's picturesque setting and proximity to Florence and Siena have made it into something of a tourist trap, with daily invasions of coach parties thronging the immaculately maintained streets and souvenir shops. However, at sunset, after the last of the day trippers have left, the town takes on a magical, timeless atmosphere.

The Piazzas

Walking through the two interlocking main squares – **Piazza del Duomo** and **Piazza della Cisterna** – is rather like walking on to a stage set, such is the magnificence of the surrounding buildings. Pause for an espresso or an ice-cream, absorb the atmosphere and marvel at the medieval palazzi surrounding you. It is easy to see why,

The view from Torre Grossa in San Gimignano

Startling skyline – the city of beautiful towers

this urban jewel has been a UNESCO World Heritage Site since the 1960s.

The Piazza della Cisterna is named after the well at its centre, the focal point of activity for over eight centuries. On the stone parapet you can see the ancient grooves made by the taut ropes once used to draw water.

In Piazza del Duomo you'll find the **Palazzo del Podestà**, whose tower (1239) is probably the town's oldest, and the grand town hall, **Palazzo del Popolo**, which houses the Museo Civico on the upper floors.

Museo Civico

Here in the frescoed Sala del Consiglio, Dante, acting as ambassador for the Guelph cause (➤ 125), tried to persuade the town to join an alliance with Florence in 1300 against Pisa, Siena, Arezzo and Volterra. San Gimignano's "reward" for co-operation was the loss of its independence and a gradual tightening of Florentine control. Today, the hall is dominated by a glorious *Maestà* by Lippo Memmi. The remaining galleries contain treasured paintings by Filippino Lippi, Benozzo Gozzoli, Pinturicchio (Bernardino di Betto Vagio), Taddeo di Bartolo and Memmo di Filippuccio.

The museum also affords access to the **Torre Grossa**, with memorable views over the pantiled roofs.

Collegiata

The plain Romanesque facade of San Gimignano's former cathedral belies the extravagant interior, modelled on Siena's cathedral and decorated with four major fresco cycles. Those to look out for include Bartolo di Fredi's amazingly detailed 26 *Old Testament Scenes* (1367), which describe the stories of Genesis; Lippo and Federico Memmi's *Scenes from the Life of Christ* (1333–41); and Taddeo di Bartolo's *Last Judgement, Paradise and Hell* (1393), notable for its luridly graphic and entertaining detail.

The adjoining **Cappella di Santa Fina** is a veritable Renaissance masterpiece, with frescoes by Domenico Ghirlandaio describing some of the miracles worked by Fina (a young girl) from her sick bed.

Looking across the rooftops of the medieval hill town

Tourist Information Office
✉ Piazza del Duomo 1 ☎ 0577 940008

Museo Civico and Torre Grosso
✉ Piazza del Duomo ☎ 0577 990348 ⏰ Nov–Feb daily 10–5; Dec 10–5; Jan 12:30–5; Mar–Oct 9:30–7:30 ✋ Moderate or expensive (combined ticket with four other museums)

Collegiata
✉ Piazza del Duomo ☎ 0577 940316 ⏰ Jan, Mar, Nov–Dec Mon–Sat 9:30–4:40, Sun 12:30–4:40; Apr–Oct Mon–Fri 9:30–7:10, Sat 9:30–5:10, Sun 12:30–5:10 ✋ Moderate

---

SAN GIMIGNANO: INSIDE INFO

Top tip If you are short of time, concentrate on the frescoes in the Collegiata and bypass the paintings in the Museo Civico, making your way instead straight to the top of the Torre Grossa to enjoy the impressive views.

Hidden gems The **garden at the "Rocca" fortress** at the top of the town, with fig and olive trees and wonderful views, is an ideal spot to write those postcards or have an afternoon siesta.
■ Look for **Benozzo Gozzoli's detailed fresco cycle**, depicting the life of St Augustine (1464), in the church of Sant'Agostino in Piazza Sant'Agostino.

Getting there The easiest way to reach San Gimignano, 57km (35 miles) southwest of Florence, is **by car**. On arrival, you'll find there are plenty of parking spaces outside the main walls.
■ By **public transport**, catch a train or a coach (SITA, Via Santa Caterina di Siena 15, tel: 800 373760 in Italy only; www.sitabus.it) to Poggibonsi, then a Train bus (tel: 0577 204246; www.trainspa.it) to San Gimignano.

Lucca

There's an undeniably special charm to Lucca. Secure within splendid Renaissance ramparts lies an enthralling tangle of perfectly preserved medieval streets and squares graced by exquisite churches, gardens and palazzi. For Henry James (*Italian Hours*, 1909), Lucca was "overflowing with everything that makes for ease, for plenty, for beauty, for interest and good example".

In 180BC, the town of Lucca became a colony of ancient Rome, and the legacy of this era is still evident in the organized grid pattern of its streets. For years the two cities fought against Pisa and Florence, hence the handful of fortified palaces (which were once the homes of feudal lords) with watchtowers such as Torre Guinigi – one of the last towers in Italy to retain the old custom of having a tuft of holm oak crown its summit.

The lords grew wealthy from olive oil and silk, and they used diplomacy rather than force to keep Lucca an

The view across Lucca from the Torre Guinigi

independent republic, while other Tuscan powers succumbed to the Spanish and the French. But, unlike their tourist-courting neighbours the Pisans and Florentines, the Lucchesi seem oblivious to their town's cultural heritage. As a result, Lucca remains remarkably unspoilt and relatively devoid of visitors.

Duomo di San Martino

To accommodate the adjoining belfry, Lucca's Duomo has an unusual, asymmetrical marble facade. Nevertheless, with its lace-like arcading and rich decoration, it remains a sublime example of the popular Pisan-Romanesque style. St Martin, the Duomo's patron saint, is depicted on the facade in various scenes, including one where he cuts his cloak with a sword to share with a beggar.

Statue of Giacomo Puccini outside Museo Casa di Puccini

The interior contains the *Volto Santo*, a revered 13th-century wooden effigy believed to have been carved by Christ's follower Nicodemus at the time of the Crucifixion, and one of Italy's finest pieces of funerary sculpture – Jacopo della Quercia's *Tomb of Ilaria del Carretto* (1406–13), depicting the youthful bride of Paolo Guinigi, a member of the powerful Guinigi family, which ruled the city in the 15th century.

Piazza Anfiteatro

During Roman times this was the site of the amphitheatre, and its perfect oval plan has been preserved – even the entrances to the piazza are exactly where the gladiators would once have entered. Today, this is Lucca's best-loved square, an evocative circle of old medieval houses in faded shades of terracotta and yellow, with washing hanging out from the upper floors above the restaurants and cafes that spill out onto the square. There is a Christmas market here every December.

San Michele

This is the finest of Lucca's many churches built in the exuberant Pisan-Romanesque style. The facade is so lavishly decorated you could be forgiven for mistaking it for the Duomo, with its riot of superimposed arcades, intricate pillars and barley-sugar columns. Unusually, the second arch is open to the sky, as is the light and airy two-stage pediment, surmounted by a statue of St Michael (framed by a pair of trumpet-blowing angels) crushing the dragon.

Piazza di San Michele in Foro is Lucca's main square, more central than Piazza del Duomo. Its name "in Foro" indicates that it stands on the original site of the Roman forum – the city's main square, even in ancient times.

Cycling round the city walls

Tourist Information Office
✉ San Donato Porto ☎ 0583 419689; www.luccaturismo.it 🕐 Nov–Jan daily 9:30–7:30; Mar–Oct 9–7

Duomo di San Martino
✉ Piazza del Duomo ☎ 0583 957068 🕐 Mid-Mar to Oct Mon–Fri 9:30–5:45, Sat 9:30–6:45, Sun 9:30–10:45, 12–6; Nov to mid-Mar Mon–Fri 9:30–4:45, Sat 9:30–6:45, Sun 9:30–10:45, 12–5 📖 Cathedral: free; sacristy: inexpensive

San Michele
✉ Piazza di San Michele in Foro 🕐 Apr–Oct 9–12, 3–6; Nov–Mar 9–12, 3–5. Closed for services

---

LUCCA: INSIDE INFO

Top tip For an **overview of Lucca**, walk or cycle the 4km (2.5-mile) circuit of the city walls. The wide ramparts, now a raised park, shaded by trees, offer a superb view of the surrounding countryside and the jagged Apuan Alps, their summits white with snow in winter. Bikes can be rented from several outlets.

Hidden gems Casa di Puccini (Corte San Lorenzo 8, Via di Poggio 30, tel: 0583 584028; May–Sep daily 10–6; Oct–Apr Tue–Sun 10–1, 3–6; inexpensive) is the birthplace of the composer Giacomo Puccini.
■ Look out for the **art nouveau shop-fronts and interiors** along Via Fillungo, and have an espresso in Caffè di Simo at No 58.

Getting there There are a couple of **trains** an hour from Florence to Lucca. The journey takes around 1.5 hours and the railway station is outside the walls (south of the city) in Piazza Ricasoli.
■ Regular **coaches** (journey time 1 hour) run from Florence. They are organized by Lazzi (Piazza Stazione 4r, tel: 055 215155; www.lazzi.it).
■ If you go by **car**, they are prohibited in the city centre. The best car park is Le Tagliate, in the west near Porta San Donato and the tourist office.

Pisa

Together with Venetian gondolas and the Colosseum in Rome, the Leaning Tower has become a symbol of Italy and is the main port of call for first-time visitors to Pisa.

Yet, there's more to Pisa than the tower. It is the gateway to Tuscany, with an international airport (➤ 36), and Italy's second busiest port. From the 11th to the 13th centuries, at the height of its power, Pisa's formidable navy dominated the western Mediterranean and, until its harbour silted up 600 years ago, the languid River Arno was the city's lifeblood. Today, this bustling, industrious city still contains vestiges of its former glory – medieval towers, Romanesque architectural gems and mercantile palazzi.

If you stroll the narrow streets and wide cobbled piazzas, join in the *passeggiata* under the arcades of the main shopping street, Borgo Stretto, visit the elegant Piazza dei Cavalieri, the historic heart of Pisa, and shop with locals at the provincial market in Piazza Vettovaglie, you will find a side of the city that many visitors, obsessed by the tower, overlook.

Campo dei Miracoli
Pisa's remarkable Field of Miracles, a great green swathe of lawn in its northwestern corner, boasts one of the most ambitious building programmes of the entire Middle Ages. The four main elements – the Duomo, the Battistero, the Camposanto cemetery and the famed Torre Pendente (Leaning Tower) – complement each other, dressed in dazzling white marble, with the city walls as a backdrop.

Also in the Field of Miracles, you'll find two small museums: the **Museo delle Sinopie**, displaying sketches and fragmented remains of the fresco cycle from the Camposanto, and the **Museo dell'Opera del Duomo**, in the cathedral's chapter house, containing treasures from the Duomo and Battistero.

The **Leaning Tower** provides an irresistible pull for millions of visitors who come to marvel that gravity hasn't yet caused it to tumble. Indeed, the fascination of the tower is not its gleaming white marble, nor its six elegant registers of classical columns, but rather its defect. Pisa's tower has never stood upright. Eight centuries ago it was already tilting, probably as a result of an unstable water table, and the authorities believe the tilt is increasing by 7mm (0.25 inches)

The legendary Torre Pendente and Duomo on the Campo dei Miracoli

A bell in the Leaning Tower

a decade. Remedial work, during which the tower was encased in huge scaffolding of steel wires, struts, supports and counterweights, was completed in 2003.

Pisa's **Battistero** is the largest in Italy and a veritable jewel, blending elegant Romanesque arcades with a Gothic crown. The interior is austere with simple, striped walls. Climb up to the gallery (and if you're feeling really energetic, up to the superior gallery) for a bird's-eye view of the piazza.

Behind the Baptistery, the **Camposanto** cemetery is an ideal place for meditation. Unfortunately, Allied bombing destroyed some of the frescoes in the cloister, leaving its white marble bare.

The **Duomo**, 100m (109 yards) long, begun in 1063, took two centuries to complete. Its lace-like facade, made of white Carrara marble with superimposed registers

AN HISTORIC TUG OF WAR

Every year special regattas and jousting competitions are organized in memory of Pisa's ancient maritime prowess. The grandest spectacle takes place on 27 June on the Ponte di Mezzo, when the ancient rivalry between north and south is re-enacted in the highly contested *gioco dei ponte* (tug of war) across the bridge.

of columns, set the pattern for the Romano-Pisan style of architecture that spread to the rest of Tuscany and beyond.

Battistero/Camposanto

✉ Piazza dei Miracoli ☎ 050 560547
🕐 Battistero: Jan–Feb daily 10–4:30; Mar, Oct 9–6:30; Apr–Sep 8–8; Nov–Dec 10–4:30. Camposanto: as above 💶 Battistero: moderate. Camposanto: moderate

Duomo

✉ Piazza dei Miracoli ☎ 050 560921
🕐 Apr–Sep daily 8–8; Oct–Mar Mon–Sat 10–12:45, 3–4:45, Sun 3–4:45 💶 Inexpensive

Leaning Tower

Guided tours only, pre-book at www.opapisa.it or tourist office

Museo dell'Opera del Duomo

✉ Piazza Arcivescovado 8 ☎ 050 560547
🕐 Jan–Feb daily 10–5; Apr–Oct 9–7

Museo delle Sinopie

✉ Piazza del Duomo ☎ Number as for Museo dell'Opera
🕐 Hours as for Museo dell'Opera

Houses surrounding Piazza dei Cavalieri

PISA: INSIDE INFO

Top tips The **tourist information office** (Piazza Arcivescovado 8, near the Duomo, tel: 050 42291; www.pisaturismo.it; daily 10–7) provides useful maps. There are other offices at Pisa airport and at Piazza Vitorrio Emanuele II 6.

■ Consider **hiring a bicycle** to tour the town. They are available for hire from Eco Voyager, Via della Faggiola 41, tel 050 561839; www.ecovoyager.it.

■ It works out cheaper to **buy one of a choice of combined tickets** (€5–€18) for the sights of the Campo dei Miracoli: the Duomo, the Battistero, the Camposanto cemetery and the museums. Leaning Tower guided tours are booked online (€17) or at the tourist office in the Piazza del Duomo (€15).

Getting there The easiest way to reach Pisa from Florence is by **train**. There are two or three trains an hour and the journey takes approximately one hour.

Walks

1 SAN MINIATO

Walk

Among Florence's many charms is its proximity to the Tuscan countryside. This walk starts from the Ponte Vecchio and takes you into the chain of hills that frame the southern perimeter of the city beyond the Oltrarno, with unforgettable views not only of Florence but also of the surrounding rural landscape.

DISTANCE 4.5km (3 miles) **TIME** 2.5 hours (including visits)
START/END POINT Ponte Vecchio ✚ 199 E4
WHEN TO GO? The walk is long and hilly and therefore best avoided in the heat of the midday sun. Take a sun hat, your camera and plenty of water.

1–2

Begin on the southern bank of the River Arno, with the **Ponte Vecchio** (➤ 122–125) immediately behind you. Walk straight ahead up Via de' Guicciardini. The elevated **Corridoio Vasariano** (➤ 54), with its distinctive circular windows called *occuli* (eyes), will be on your left-hand side. Turn left into **Piazza di Santa Felicita** (➤ 152). Santa Felicita is believed to stand on the site of a late Roman church. In the square, a fountain combines a 16th-century bronze Bacchus with a Roman marble sarcophagus.

2–3

Take the right-hand fork out of the piazza, signed to Costa di San Giorgio. This narrow lane winds steeply uphill, quickly leaving the city behind. The house at No 19 was once Galileo's home.

Soon the small houses give way to large villas and beautiful gardens hidden behind forbidding high stone walls on either side of the lane. The road flattens out at Porta San Giorgio, the city's oldest surviving gate. Built in 1260, it is decorated with frescoes and carvings of St George and the dragon. Go through the gate and to your immediate right is the Forte di Belvedere. The Medici family added this once-impregnable fortress to the city defences in 1590, with just one means of access – through a secret door in their palace gardens. Its ramparts command

Forte di Belvedere and the walls, added by the Medici family to protect the city

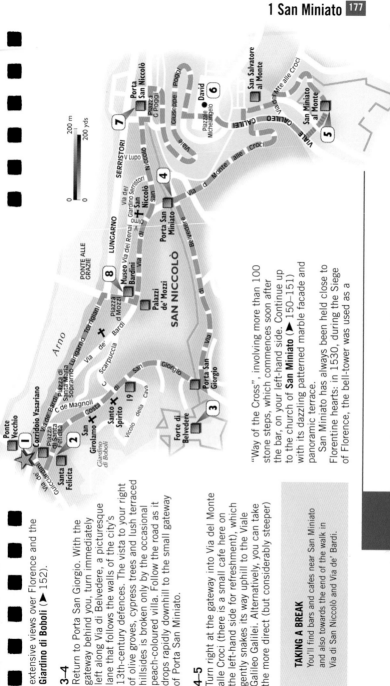

extensive views over Florence and the **Giardino di Boboli** (➤ 152).

3–4
Return to Porta San Giorgio. With the gateway behind you, turn immediately left along Via di Belvedere, a picturesque lane that follows the walls of the city's 13th-century defences. The vista to your right of olive groves, cypress trees and lush terraced hillsides is broken only by the occasional peach-coloured villa. Follow the road as it drops rapidly downhill to the small gateway of Porta San Miniato.

4–5
Turn right at the gateway into Via del Monte alle Croci (there is a small cafe here on the left-hand side for refreshment), which gently snakes its way uphill to the Viale Galileo Galilei. Alternatively, you can take the more direct (but considerably steeper)

"Way of the Cross", involving more than 100 stone steps, which commences soon after the bar, on your left-hand side. Continue up to the church of **San Miniato** (➤ 150–151) with its dazzling patterned marble facade and panoramic terrace.

San Miniato has always been held close to Florentine hearts: in 1530, during the Siege of Florence, the bell-tower was used as a

TAKING A BREAK
You'll find bars and cafes near San Miniato and also towards the end of the walk in Via di San Niccolò and Via de' Bardi.

Michelangelo's most celebrated sculptures and packed with souvenir stalls, the square is always abuzz with visitors, here to enjoy the exceptional views over the terracotta roofs of Florence to the hilly countryside beyond.

6–7

Several stairways descend from Piazzale Michelangelo. Take the flight that leaves the square centre-left, and zigzag your way down towards the Arno on the footpath through acacia groves to Porta San Niccolò, the imposing 14th-century gateway in the city wall at the bottom.

7–8

Turn left along Via di San Niccolò. Majestic buildings line the street, among them the 13th-century Palazzo Mozzi in Piazza de' Mozzi and Museo Bardini opposite (open Sat–Mon 11–5). The latter, the home of the 19th-century antiquarian and collector Stefano Bardini, is built almost entirely from medieval and Renaissance masonry.

8–9

From Piazza de' Mozzi, head towards the Arno and make your way back to the Ponte Vecchio along the riverbank.

Via di San Salvatore, a gently shaded walkway

5–6

Leave San Miniato by an archway in the buildings to the west (beside the monks' shop) and start your gradual descent back to the city. Before long you will pass the apricot-coloured church of San Salvatore al

Monte, a charming Franciscan church with sober *pietra forte* decoration and early panel paintings dedicated to martyrs Cosmas and Damian, twin-brother physicians who refused to charge any fee for their services.

Continue downhill to Piazzale Michelangelo, laid out in 1869 by Giuseppe Poggi (who also converted the fortified area around the church into a grand cascade of terraces and stairways). Decorated with reproductions of

watchtower. It was installed with cannon to shoot at the Medici troops and wrapped in mattresses to absorb the impact of enemy fire. In 1600 it was used as a hospital for plague victims and, later, as a hospice for the poor. The cemetery contains a splendid array of funerary monuments, including impressive family tombs the size of miniature houses and the grave of Carlo Collodi, creator of *Pinocchio*.

2 FIESOLE
Walk

This walk around the ancient hilltop town of Fiesole offers a taste of the lush, rolling countryside surrounding Florence. With its cooling breezes and unforgettable views, it also provides welcome respite from the constant crowds in the city centre.

DISTANCE 3km (2 miles) **TIME** Minimum 2 hours (including visits)
GETTING THERE It is an easy 30-minute bus ride to Piazza Mino da Fiesole. Catch the frequent bus No 7 from Piazza di San Marco
START POINT Piazza Mino da Fiesole
END POINT Piazza di San Domenico

1–2

Start in the main square, Piazza Mino da Fiesole. This hilltop site has been inhabited since the Bronze Age, and around 600BC it was one of the most important Etruscan cities. From the 3rd century BC it became a Roman city, but it began to decline after the Romans founded Florentia in the 1st century BC. The **Duomo**, dedicated to Romulus, the martyred Bishop of Fiesole, dominates the piazza. It was founded in the 11th century and its spartan interior bears much resemblance to San Miniato (▶ 150–151), with a wooden roof, three-tiered structure and columns topped with Roman capitals. After visiting the church, head uphill to the 14th-century **Palazzo Comunale**, a beautiful yellow building with columns, stone crests and an attractive first-floor loggia. Here too is a bronze equestrian statue of King Vittorio Emanuele II and Giuseppe Garibaldi, hero of Italian nationalism.

2–3

Return towards the Duomo and take the first turning to the right, round the back of the church into Via Dupré. At a fork in the road, go through the archway straight ahead of you into the **Zona Archeologica**,

The clock tower rising above the rooftops of Fiesole

an open-air archaeological site set into the hillside containing important Etruscan and Roman remains. Highlights include the Etruscan temple, some partly restored Roman baths and the beautifully preserved Roman theatre, capable of holding 3,000 people. It is still used for ballet, theatre and concert performances during the Estate Fiesolana (Fiesole Summer Festival). Also here is the **Museo Archeologico** with finds from the site.

3–4

On exiting the area, turn left along Via Portigiani past the tourist information office and continue along Via Marini to admire the typically Tuscan landscape stretching into the distance.

4–5

Back-track past the tourist office to the archway. Straight ahead, you will see the entrance to the **Museo Bandini**, worth a visit for its collection of 13th- to 15th-century paintings of the Tuscan School, bequeathed to Fiesole by local aristocrat Angelo Bandini.

5–6

Return to the main square. Turn right out of Via Dupré and follow the main road round to the left along Via Fra' Giovanni Angelico. Bear first right into Via Vecchia Fiesolana, and descend steeply, curving round to the right past the church of San Girolamo. Following a brief stretch with high walls on either side, you will reach the Villa Medici on your left. This impressive cream-coloured mansion with dark green shutters was one of the earliest of the family's country retreats, built in 1461 by Michelozzo for Cosimo il Vecchio de Medici.

6–7

Follow the road as it swerves round to the left beneath the villa. Turn left at the fork in the road down Via Bandini. When you arrive at the intersection with Via San Ansano (a grass track) beside a pretty apricot-coloured church, bear right past olive groves and down a roughly surfaced lane, which twists and turns steeply past numerous attractive villas and gardens. At the bottom you will reach an intersection. Turn left, by more country houses, and continue to the main road.

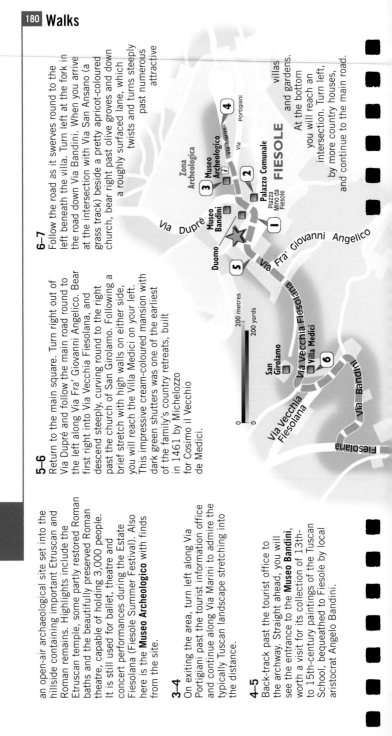

7–8

Turn immediately right (off the main road) and continue a short distance until you reach the **Badia Fiesolana**, a 15th-century church with a pretty Romanesque facade and a magnificent Renaissance interior, decorated with the local grey sandstone called *pietra serena*. Once the residence of the Bishops of Fiesole, it is undoubtedly the most important religious building in the suburbs of Florence, allegedly built where St Romulus was martyred. There are good views of the surrounding countryside.

(although the bell-tower and arcade were added two centuries later). The interior contains several works by Fra Angelico, who was Prior here. A painting attributed to Fra Paolino da Pistoia, depicting Girolamo Savonarola (▶ 70) showing Florence to Christ and the Virgin Mary, is in the *ospiteria* (hostel) next to the church.

The church marks the start of the hamlet of San Domenico with its scattered houses, cafe and pizzeria.

From the bus stop opposite the church, the No 7 bus runs frequently back to the centre of Florence.

The Romanesque facade of the Badia Fiesolana

8–9

Retrace your steps back to the main road. Facing you is the large church of **San Domenico**, built in the early 15th century

TAKING A BREAK

You'll be spoiled for choice of restaurants, cafes and bars in Fiesole. Try **Etrusca** for pizzas or dine alfresco on the panoramic terrace of smart **Ristorante Aurora**.

Opening Times
Tourist Information Office
☒ Via Portigiani 3–5
☎ 055 596 1323
🕒 Mon–Sat 9–5:30, Sun and hols 10–4

Duomo
☒ Piazza della Cattedrale 1
🕒 Daily 7:30–noon, 3–6

Zona Archeologica
☒ Via Portigiani 1 ☎ 055 596 1293
🕒 Apr–Sep Wed–Mon 10–7; Oct and Mar Wed–Mon 10–6; Nov–Feb Thu–Mon 10–4
💰 Expensive (combined ticket with Museo Bandini, Museo Civico and Museo Archeologico)

Museo Bandini
☒ Via Dupré 1 ☎ 055 596 1293
🕒 Hours as for Zona Archeologico

3 EAST OF THE DUOMO

Walk

This circular route takes you away from the frenetic city centre to explore the atmospheric workers' quarter of Florence – an area few tourists penetrate. Its neighbourhood shops, colourful markets and bustling narrow alleys reverberate to the beat of day-to-day Florentine life.

DISTANCE 3km (2 miles) **TIME** 1.5 hours (excluding visits)
START/END POINT Piazza del Duomo ▮ 196 A2
WHEN TO GO? Mornings are best, when the two daily markets are at their liveliest

1–2

Leave Piazza del Duomo along Via dei Servi, the busy street that starts behind the cathedral's apse, to the left of the **Museo dell'Opera del Duomo** (▲ 103), and head in a northeasterly direction. This road was once the old processional route from the Duomo to the church of Santissima Annunziata (▲ 106). At the first intersection (with Via de' Pucci), notice the enormous Palazzo Pucci on your left, the former ancestral home of

Brunelleschi arches – Piazza della Santissima Annunziata

the famous fashion designer Marchese Emilio Pucci (▲ 14–17). Look back periodically for impressive views of the cathedral's dome.

After one more intersection, you'll reach **Piazza della Santissima Annunziata**, an exceptionally fine square, flanked by graceful arcades. On your right, the **Ospedale degli Innocenti** (▲ 107), with its elegant loggia by Brunelleschi, was the first Renaissance building to combine classical proportions with traditional Tuscan Romanesque architecture. But for the traffic racing across the north side of the square, it would still have the feeling of a Renaissance courtyard.

2–3

Follow the flow of the traffic through the archway beside the Ospedale degli Innocenti into Via della Colonna. **The Museo Archeologico** (▲ 106–107) is on your left, set in picturesque gardens.

contains the tombs of the great Renaissance sculptors Mino da Fiesole and Andrea del Verrocchio.

3–4

Take the second turning right into Borgo Pinti, past the church and former convent of Santa Maria Maddalena dei Pazzi at No 58 (now a school) and peer into the charming courtyard garden on the opposite side of the road at No 55.

Turn left at the next intersection into Via de' Pilastri. Straight ahead is the plain, cream-coloured church of Sant'Ambrogio, with its simple brick bell-tower. This neighbourhood church is little known to tourists but

4–5

Cross Piazza di Sant'Ambrogio, and head southwards a short distance down Via de' Macci. The first road on the left leads to the locals' market – **Mercato Sant'Ambrogio** (▶ 81), a smaller version of the city's main cast-iron-and-glass **Mercato Centrale** (▶ 111) – selling clothes, fruit and vegetables, meat, pasta, cheeses, olives, *antipasti* and regional wines.

5–6

Return to Piazza di Sant'Ambrogio. A left turn into Via Pietrapiana leads to Piazza dei Ciompi and a second market – the **Mercato delle Pulci** (flea market), with its

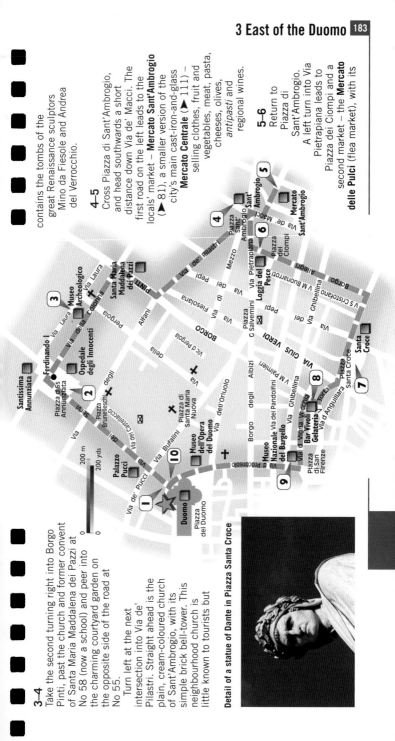

Detail of a statue of Dante in Piazza Santa Croce

TAKING A BREAK

Put together a picnic at Mercato di Sant'Ambrogio, or have a snack at Caffè Cibrèo (➤ 78) on the corner of Via de'Macci.

ramshackle booths of bric-à-brac (➤ 81). Alongside it, you'll find the Loggia del Pesce, built by Giorgio Vasari for the fishmongers of the Mercato Vecchio, but moved here in 1890 when the market was demolished to make way for **Piazza della Repubblica** (➤ 127).

6–7

Head due south from Piazza dei Ciompi along Borgo Allegri towards the campanile of Santa Croce. At the end of the road, turn right along Via di San Giuseppe until **Piazza Santa Croce**, a spacious square graced by the church of Santa Croce (➤ 66–69) and a picturesque row of medieval houses. In Florence's heyday, this piazza was the scene of Medici ceremonies, jousting tournaments, even public executions. It still acts as a pitch for the annual **Gioco di Calcio Storico** (➤ 31), the period costume soccer match that was first played in 1530.

The Santa Croce district is the lowest-lying part of Florence and traditionally the artisans' quarter, for centuries packed with workshops of furniture-makers, weavers and cloth-dyers. However, the flood of 1966 (➤ 32–33) hit this part of the city the hardest. A small wall plaque in the square, set 6m (20 feet) up (on the corner of Via Giuseppe Verdi), shows the level the muddy water reached at its peak and some buildings still have a watermark. Although many small businesses were ruined, the area remains full of small neighbourhood shops and workshops.

Squashes on sale at the Mercato Sant'Ambrogio, smaller than Mercato Centrale, but just as popular

7–8

Leave Piazza di Santa Croce along Via Torta, heading westwards towards the city centre. Notice how this narrow road and its continuations, Via Bentaccordi and Piazza de' Peruzzi, form a curve – they are built along the line of the Roman amphitheatre of Florentia. Turn right off Via Torta up Via Isola delle Stinche to buy an ice-cream at **Bar Vivoli Gelateria** (➤ 73–74).

8–9

The next road to the left – Via della Vigna Vecchia – leads to the **Museo Nazionale del Bargello** (➤ 62–65), the oldest surviving civic building in Florence. Today the fortress-like building houses a priceless collection of Renaissance sculpture and decorative arts.

9–10

When you reach the Bargello, turn right into Via del Proconsolo. As you walk back towards the Duomo, be sure to glance along Borgo degli Albizi (the third road on your right). Lined with grand Renaissance palaces, it is one of the oldest streets in Florence, following the route of the ancient Roman road to Rome. Continue up Via del Proconsolo until you reach your start point in Piazza del Duomo.

Practicalities

BEFORE YOU GO

WHAT YOU NEED

● Required ○ Suggested ▲ Not required	Some countries require a passport to remain valid for a minimum period (usually at least six months) beyond the date of entry – check before booking	UK	Germany	USA	Canada	Australia	Ireland	Netherlands	Spain
Passport/National Identity Card		●	●	●	●	●	●	●	●
Visa (regulations can change – check before booking)		▲	▲	▲	▲	▲	▲	▲	▲
Onward or Round-Trip Ticket		▲	▲	●	●	●	▲	▲	▲
Health Inoculations (tetanus and polio recommended)		▲	▲	▲	▲	▲	▲	▲	▲
Health Documentation (▶ 190, Health)		○	○	○	○	○	○	○	○
Travel Insurance		○	○	○	○	○	○	○	○
Driver's License (national)		●	●	●	●	●	●	●	●
Car Insurance Certificate		●	●	n/a	n/a	n/a	●	●	●
Car Registration Document		●	●	n/a	n/a	n/a	●	●	●

WHEN TO GO

Peak season   Off-season

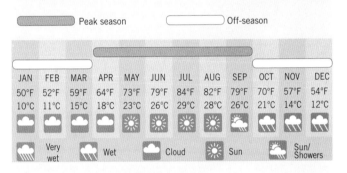

JAN	FEB	MAR	APR	MAY	JUN	JUL	AUG	SEP	OCT	NOV	DEC
50°F	52°F	59°F	64°F	73°F	79°F	84°F	82°F	79°F	70°F	57°F	54°F
10°C	11°C	15°C	18°C	23°C	26°C	29°C	28°C	26°C	21°C	14°C	12°C

Very wet	Wet	Cloud	Sun	Sun/Showers

Temperatures are the **average daily maximum** for each month. The most popular months to visit Florence and Tuscany are May, June and September when there are long, warm days and plenty of sunshine. These are also the busiest months, so be prepared to queue for main attractions. July and August are popular months too, but the city can get extremely hot and sticky. July is the hottest, driest month. Spring and autumn are the best seasons for viewing the colours of the countryside, although autumn is generally the wettest time in Tuscany. When choosing your holiday dates, consider also the fashion shows held in Florence during June and September, and the grape harvest in October, and remember to book up your accommodation plenty of time in advance.

GETTING ADVANCE INFORMATION

■ Florence Tourist Office: www.firenzeturismo.it
■ ENIT: www.enit.it

■ General information: www.fionline.it
www.informacitta.net
■ Museums and art: www.uffizi.firenze.it
www.museionline.it

In the UK
Italian State Tourist Office (ENIT)
1 Princes Street
London W1B 2AY
☎ 020 7408 1254

GETTING THERE

By Air Three main airports serve Florence – Galileo Galilei Airport at Pisa (80km/50 miles west), Guglielmo Marconi Airport at Bologna (105km/65 miles northeast) and Florence's small Amerigo Vespucci Airport (4km/2.5 miles northwest).

Major carriers at Pisa include Alitalia, British Airways, easyJet, Lufthansa and Ryanair. Major carriers at Bologna include Air France, Alitalia, British Airways, KLM, Lufthansa, SAS and TAP Air Portugal. Major carriers at Amerigo Vespucci Airport include Meridiana, Alitalia, SN Brussels, Air France, KLM and Lufthansa. There are few direct intercontinental flights so most visitors from outside Europe need to fly into Milan or Rome (or another major European hub) and then take a connecting flight. Some no-frills European airlines, such as Ryanair, easyJet or Thomson fly to Pisa and offer cheap-rate fares, which are especially good value if you want only a weekend break.

Approximate flying times London (2 hours), Dublin (2 hours), New York (10-plus hours via London, Brussels, Paris or Rome), West Coast USA (14-plus hours via London, Frankfurt or Paris), Vancouver (12-plus hours via Frankfurt or London), Montréal (9 hours via Brussels, London or Paris), Sydney (23-plus hours via Milan).

By Rail Florence's main railway station, Ferrovia Santa Maria Novella, is one of the main arrival points for trains from Europe, with direct rail links with Paris, Frankfurt and Ostend. It is located near the city centre. Italy's state railway (Trenitalia) operates a high-speed train service (Eurostar trains) between major Italian cities.

TIME

Italy operates on Central European Time, one hour ahead of GMT in winter, six hours ahead of New York and nine hours ahead of Los Angeles. Clocks are advanced one hour in April and turned back one hour in October.

CURRENCY AND FOREIGN EXCHANGE

Currency The euro (€) is the official currency in Italy. Coins are issued in denominations of 1, 2, 5, 10, 20 and 50 Euro cents and €1 and €2. Notes are issued in denominations of €5, €10, €20, €50, €100, €200 and €500.

Credit cards Most **credit cards** (carta di credito) are accepted in larger hotels, restaurants and shops, and can also be used in ATM cashpoints.

Exchange Most banks and private exchange offices throughout the city will change cash and travellers' cheques. All transactions are subject to a small commission charge. Remember to take your passport with you. Currency can also be obtained from ATMs with credit or debit cards. You will need a PIN number.

In the US
ENIT
630 Fifth Avenue,
Suite 1565
New York, NY 10111
☎ 212/245-4822/3/4

In Canada
ENIT
175 Bloor Street East
Suite 907 South Tower
M4W 3R8 Toronto
☎ (416) 925-4882

In Australia
Italian Government Travel
Office
Fourth Floor,
46 Market Street
Sydney, NSW 2000
☎ (02) 9262 1666

WHEN YOU ARE THERE

NATIONAL HOLIDAYS

1 Jan	*Capodanno* – New Year's Day
6 Jan	Epiphany
Mar/Apr	*Pasqua* – Easter
Mar/Apr	*Pasquetta* – Easter Monday
25 Apr	Liberation Day
1 May	*Festa del Lavoro* – Labour Day
24 Jun	*San Giovanni* – St John's Day
15 Aug	Assumption of the Virgin Mary
1 Nov	*Tutti Santi* – All Saints' Day
8 Dec	Immaculate Conception
25 Dec	*Natale* – Christmas Day
26 Dec	*Santo Stefano* – St Stephen's Day

ELECTRICITY

Current is 220 volts AC, 50 cycles. Plugs are two- or three-round-pin Continental types; UK and North American visitors will need an adaptor. A transformer is likely to be needed for appliances operating on 110–120 volts.

OPENING HOURS

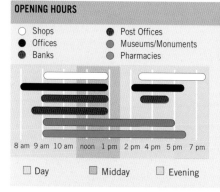

○ Shops
● Offices
● Banks
● Post Offices
● Museums/Monuments
● Pharmacies

8 am 9 am 10 am noon 1 pm 2 pm 4 pm 5 pm 7 pm

☐ Day   ▨ Midday   ☐ Evening

Shops Some shops close on Monday morning in winter and on Saturday afternoon in summer. Summer opening hours are more flexible: some stay open at lunch-time or in the evening. Many shops and markets close for a week or two around 15 August.
Museums Times vary according to the season and many close on Monday. Check individual entries for details.

TIPS/GRATUITIES

Restaurants include a service charge but it is customary to round up the bill. Leave loose change in bars: around €0.05 for drinks at the bar; €0.25 for drinking at a table; or €0.50 at a smart hotel bar. Tipping is necessary elsewhere. As a general guide:

Tour guides	€1–€1.50
Taxis	10 per cent of fare
Porters (per bag)	€0.50–€1.50
Usherettes	€0.50
Lavatory attendants	€0.10–€0.15

FAKE GOODS

In Italy purchases of counterfeited goods are punished by law with fines of up to €10,000 imposed and a policy of zero tolerance has been implemented. Red signs warning you to watch what you buy and beware of fakes are prominently displayed all over central Florence.

TIME DIFFERENCES

GMT	Florence	New York	Germany	Rest of Italy	Australia
12 noon	1pm	7am	1pm	1pm	10pm

STAYING IN TOUCH

Post The main post offices in the centre are at Via Pietrapiana 53 and Via Pellicceria 3. There are also red or blue post boxes, usually set into the wall, on most main streets and at the railway station. Stamps are sold at post offices and tobacconists' shops.

Public telephones Public phones are indicated by a red sign, on the street, in bars and restaurants. Pay phones take coins or a phonecard *(una schede telefoniche)*, available from post offices, tobacconists and bars. Break off the phonecard's corner before use. Cheap rates within Italy and Europe operate Monday to Saturday from 10pm–8am and all day on Sunday.

International Dialling Codes
Dial 00 followed by

UK:	44
USA / Canada:	1
Irish Republic:	353
Australia:	61
Germany:	49

Mobile providers and services Before leaving home check with your network provider that your phone is enabled for use overseas, and how much it will cost. The best way to avoid international roaming charges is to buy a pre-paid Italian SIM card. The main network servers are TIM, Omnitel, Vodafone, Wind and H3G.

WiFi and internet Most high-end hotels offer free wireless broadband connection in the rooms or in a public space. Florence has recently introduced a free service in 12 city centre piazzas, and this project is ongoing. Access is also available at airports, the station and at the cybercafe Internet Train, which has several branches throughout the city.

PERSONAL SAFETY

Petty crime, particularly pickpocketing, is fairly common in Florence. Report any loss or theft to the *vigili urbani* (municipal police – blue uniforms in winter and white in summer). The *carabinieri* are the military police. They dress in red-striped trousers and deal with such offences as theft and speeding. *La polizia* (the state police – blue uniforms with white belts and berets) deal with serious crime.

To help prevent crime:

- Watch out for scruffy, innocent-looking children selling flowers or begging – they may be in gangs.
- Don't carry more cash or valuables than you need; backpacks are a target for expert thieves who gain access from behind without you even noticing.
- Hold bags in front of you on public transport, at markets and in other crowded areas.
- Areas to avoid after dark are Le Cascine, around the station and other dark alleys away from the tourist trail.

Police assistance:
📞 112 from any phone

EMERGENCY 113

📞 **POLICE 112**

FIRE 115

AMBULANCE 118

HEALTH

 Insurance Citizens of EU countries receive free or reduced-cost emergency medical treatment with the European Health Insurance Card, but private medical insurance is still advised and essential for all other visitors.

 Doctors Ask at your hotel for details of English-speaking doctors.
Dental Services Nationals of EU countries can obtain dental treatment at reduced cost, but travel insurance should also cover the cost of dental treatment.

 Weather Minor health worries include too much sun, dehydration or mosquito bites: drink plenty of fluids, and wear sunscreen and a hat in summer (particularly in July and August, which are the hottest months). Insect repellent may be useful if you have to sleep in rooms with windows open in summer.

 Pharmacies Prescription and other medicines are available from a chemist (una farmacia), indicated by a green cross. Their highly qualified staff are able to offer medical advice on minor ailments, provide first-aid and prescribe a wide range of over-the-counter drugs. Hours are usually Mon–Sat 8:30–1 and 4–8, but a rota system ensures there are always some open. Every farmacia displays a list of local chemists providing out of hours cover.

 Safe Water Tap water is safe to drink throughout Italy but most Italians prefer bottled water. Do not drink water that is marked acqua non potabile.

CONCESSIONS

Senior Citizens (over 65) are entitled to free entrance into state museums and galleries.
Students under 18 are entitled to free entrance into state museums. Be sure to carry some form of identification such as a passport.

TRAVELING WITH A DISABILITY

Florence and Tuscany do not cater well for travellers with disabilities, although more museums now have lifts, ramps and modified lavatories, and laws require restaurants, bars and hotels to provide facilities. Some Intercity and Eurostar trains have facilities for wheelchair users. There is a lift at Santa Maria Novella station, but it must be booked 24 hours in advance, and the new intercity trains have special facilities for wheelchairs. Contact the tourist office at 1r Via Cavour for further details (tel: 055 290832).

CHILDREN

Children are welcome in most hotels and restaurants. Many attractions offer reductions. Baby-changing facilities are excellent in newer attractions but limited elsewhere.

RESTROOMS/TOILETS

Most bars, department stores, restaurants and attractions have facilities available to the public. There are public toilets in Piazza San Giovanni.

SMOKING

Smoking is now banned in all enclosed public spaces, including bars, cafes and restaurants.

CONSULATES

UK
055 284133
www.ukinitaly.
fco.gov.uk

USA
055 266951
www.italy.
usembassy.gov

Canada
06 854441
(Rome)

Australia
06 852721
(Rome)

New Zealand
06 853 7501
(Rome)

Useful Words and Phrases

SURVIVAL PHRASES

Yes/no **Sì/non**
Please **Per favore**
Thank you **Grazie**
You're welcome **Di niente/prego**
I'm sorry **Mi dispiace**
Goodbye **Arrivederci**
Good morning **Buongiorno**
Goodnight **Buona sera**
How are you? **Come sta?**
How much? **Quanto costa?**
I would like... **Vorrei...**
Open **Aperto**
Closed **Chiuso**
Today **Oggi**
Tomorrow **Domani**
Monday **Lunedì**
Tuesday **Martedì**
Wednesday **Mercoledì**
Thursday **Giovedì**
Friday **Venerdì**
Saturday **Sabato**
Sunday **Domenica**

DIRECTIONS

I'm lost **Mi sono perso/a**
Where is...? **Dove si trova...?**
  the station **la stazione**
  the telephone **il telefono**
  the bank **la banca**
  the restroom **il gabinetto**
Turn left **Volti a sinistra**
Turn right **Volti a destra**
Go straight **Vada dritto**
At the corner **All'angolo**
The street **la strada**
The building **il palazzo**
The traffic light **il semaforo**
The intersection **l'incrocio**
The signs for... **le indicazione per...**

IF YOU NEED HELP

Help! **Aiuto!**
Could you help me, please?
  Mi potrebbe aiutare?
Do you speak English? **Parla inglese?**
I don't understand **Non capisco**
Please could you call a doctor quickly?
  **Mi chiami presto un medico,
  per favore**

RESTAURANT

I'd like to reserve a table
  Vorrei prenotare un tavolo
A table for two please
  Un tavolo per due, per favore
Could we see the menu, please?
  Ci porta la lista, per favore?
What's this? **Cos' è questo?**
A bottle of/a glass of...
  Un bottiglia di/un bicchiere di...
Could I have the bill? **Ci porta il conto**

ACCOMMODATION

Do you have a single/double room? **Ha
  una camera singola / doppia?**
With/without bath/WC/shower
  Con/senza vasca/gabinetto/doccia
Does that include breakfast?
  E'inclusa la prima colazione?
Does that include dinner?
  E'inclusa la cena?
Do you have room service?
  C'è il servizio in camera?
Could I see the room?
  E' possibile vedere la camera?
I'll take this room **Prendo questa**
Thanks for your hospitality
  Grazie per l'ospitalità

NUMBERS

0	**zero**	13	**tredici**	50	**cinquanta**
1	**uno**	14	**quattordici**	60	**sessanta**
2	**due**	15	**quindici**	70	**settanta**
3	**tre**	16	**sedici**	80	**ottanta**
4	**quattro**	17	**diciassette**	90	**novanta**
5	**cinque**	18	**diciotto**	100	**cento**
6	**sei**	19	**diciannove**		
7	**sette**	20	**venti**	101	**cento uno**
8	**otto**			110	**centodieci**
9	**nove**	21	**ventuno**	120	**centoventi**
10	**dieci**	22	**ventidue**	200	**duecento**
11	**undici**	30	**trenta**	300	**trecento**
12	**dodici**	40	**quaranta**	400	**quattrocento**

500	**cinquecento**		
600	**seicento**		
700	**settecento**		
800	**ottocento**		
900	**novecento**		
1000	**mille**		
2000	**duemila**		
		10,000	**diecimila**

MENU

acciuga anchovy

acqua water

affettati sliced cured meats

affumicato smoked

aglio garlic

agnello lamb

anatra duck

antipasti hors d'oeurves

arista roast pork

arrosto roast

asparagi asparagus

birra beer

bistecca steak

bollito boiled meat

braciola minute steak

brasato braised

brodo broth

bruschetta toasted bread with garlic or tomato topping

budino pudding

burro butter

cacciagione game

cacciatore, alla rich tomato sauce with mushrooms

caffè corretto/ macchiato coffee with liqueur/spirit, or with a drop of milk

caffè freddo iced coffee

caffè lungo weak coffee

caffellatte milky coffee

caffè ristretto strong coffee

calamaro squid

cappero caper

carciofo artichoke

carota carrot

carne meat

carpa carp

casalingo home-made

cassata Sicilian fruit ice-cream

cavolfiore cauliflower

cavolo cabbage

ceci chickpeas

cervello brains

cervo venison

cetriolino gherkin

cetriolo cucumber

cicoria chicory

cinghiale boar

cioccolata chocolate

cipolla onion

coda di bue oxtail

coniglio rabbit

contorni vegetables

coperto cover charge

coscia leg of meat

cotoletta cutlets

cozze mussels

crema custard

crostini canapé with savoury toppings or croutons

crudo raw

digestivo after– dinner liqueur

dolci cakes/ desserts

erbe aromatiche herbs

fagioli beans

fagiolini green beans

fegato liver

faraona guinea fowl

facito stuffed

fegato liver

finocchio fennel

formaggio cheese

forno, al baked

frittata omelette

fritto fried

frizzante fizzy

frulatto whisked

frutti di mare seafood

frutta fruit

funghi mushrooms

gamberetto shrimp

gelato ice-cream

ghiaccio ice

gnocchi potato dumplings

granchio crab

gran(o)turco corn

griglia, alla broiled

imbottito stuffed

insalata salad

IVA Value Added Tax (VAT)

latte milk

lepre hare

lumache snails

manzo beef

merluzzo cod

miele honey

minestra soup

molluschi shellfish

olio oil

oliva olive

ostrica oyster

pancetta bacon

pane bread

panna cream

parmigiano parmesan

passata sieved or creamed

pastasciutta dried pasta with sauce

pasta sfoglia puff pastry

patate fritte chips

pecora mutton

pecorino sheep's milk cheese

peperoncino chilli

peperone red/ green pepper

pesce fish

petto breast

piccione pigeon

piselli peas

pollame fowl

pollo chicken

polpetta meatball

porto port wine

prezzemolo parsley

primo piatto first course

prosciutto cured ham

ragù meat sauce

ripieno stuffed

riso rice

salsa sauce

salsiccia sausage

saltimbocca veal with prosciutto and sage

secco dry

secondo piatto main course

senape mustard

servizio com- preso service charge included

sogliola sole

spuntini snacks

succa di frutta fruit juice

sugo sauce

tonno tuna

uova strapazzate scrambled eggs

uovo affrogato/ in carnica poached egg

uovo al tegamo/ fritto fried egg

uovo alla coque soft boiled egg

uovo alla sodo hard boiled egg

vino bianco white wine

vino rosso red wine

vino rosato rosé wine

verdure vegetables

vitello veal

zucchero sugar

zuppa soup

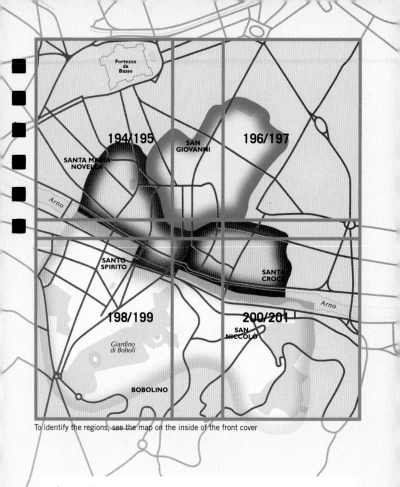

Fortezza
da
Basso

194/195

SAN
GIOVANNI

196/197

SANTA MARIA
NOVELLA

Arno

SANTO
SPIRITO

SANTA
CROCE

Arno

198/199

200/201

SAN
NICCOLO

Giardino
di Boboli

BOBOLINO

To identify the regions, see the map on the inside of the front cover

Streetplan

——— Main road	▨ Important building
——— Other road	▨ Park
——— Minor road	▤ Featured place of interest
——— Narrow road/path	𝑖 Tourist information
——— Railway	● Monument
——— Wall	† Church
	✉ Post Office

194–201 0 ——————— 200 metres
         0 ——————— 200 yards

Streetplan

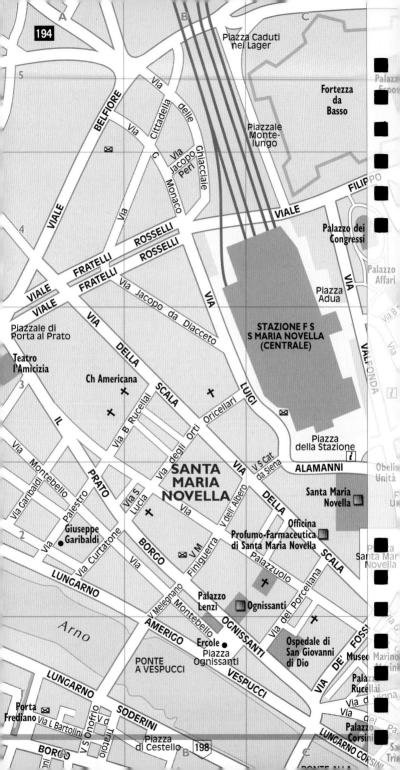

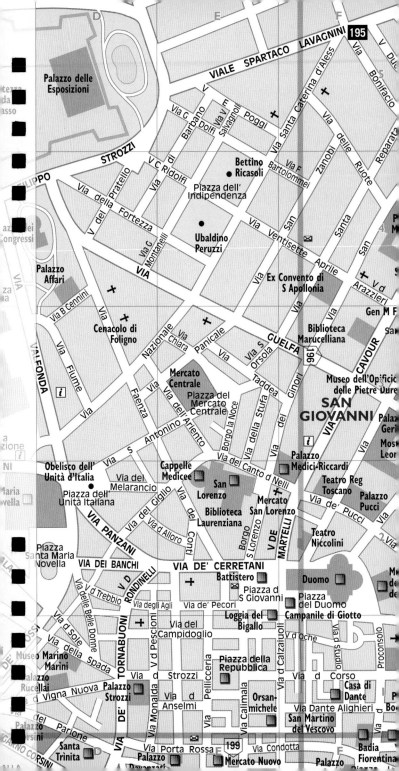

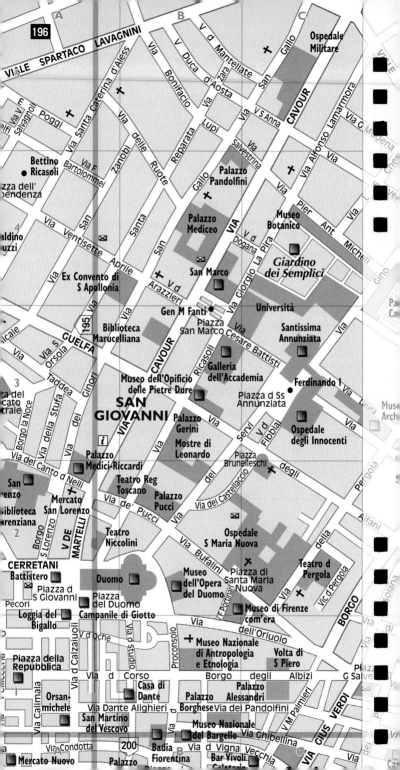

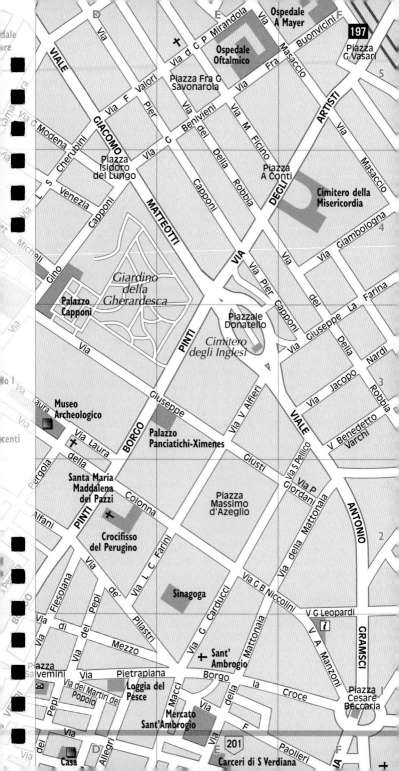

Ospedale A Mayer

Piazza G Vasari

Ospedale Oftalmico

Piazza Fra G Savonarola

VIALE

Via F Valori

GIACOMO

Via C Modena

Cherubini

S Venezia

Piazza Isidoro del Lungo

Capponi

Pier

Gino

MATTEOTTI

Via dei Benivieni

G

Capponi

Della Robbia

Via M Ficino

Piazza A Conti

DEGLI

ARTISTI

Masaccio

Via

Buonvicini

Fra Masaccio

Cimitero della Misericordia

Via Giambologna

VIA

Palazzo Capponi

Giardino della Gherardesca

PINTI

Piazzale Donatello

Cimitero degli Inglesi

Via Pier Capponi

Via dei Giuseppe La Farina

Della

Nardi

Via Jacopo

Robbia

Museo Archeologico

BORGO

Giuseppe

Via Laura

Via della

pergola

Palazzo Panciatichi-Ximenes

Via V Alfieri

VIALE

Via S Spellio

V Benedetto Varchi

Santa Maria Maddalena dei Pazzi

PINTI

Alfani

Colonna

Giusti

Piazza Massimo d'Azeglio

Via P Giordani

Via della Mattonaia

ANTONIO

Crocifisso del Perugino

Via

Fiesolana

Via dei Pepi

Pilastri

Via L C Farini

Via G B Niccolini

Sinagoga

Via G Carducci

Mattonaia

V G Leopardi

V A Manzoni

GRAMSCI

Via di

Mezzo

Piazza Salvemini

Via dei Martiri del Popolo

Via

Pietrapiana

Sant' Ambrogio

Borgo

la

Croce

Piazza Cesare Beccaria

Pepi

Loggia del Pesce

Macci

Via

Mercato Sant'Ambrogio

Via

F

Via dei Allegri

Casa

D

E

201

Carceri di S Verdiana

Paolieri

F

A

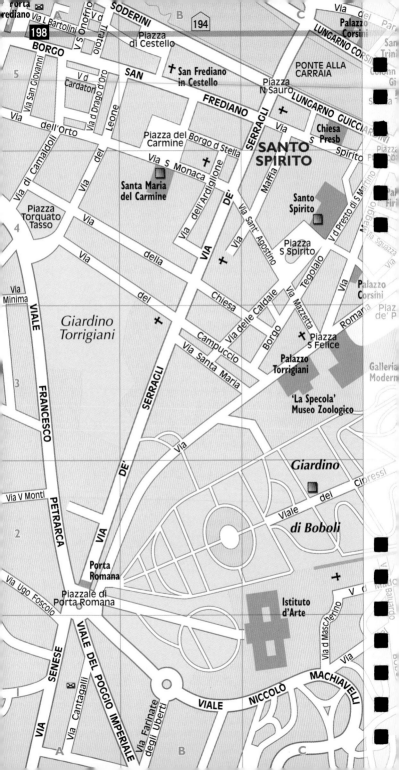

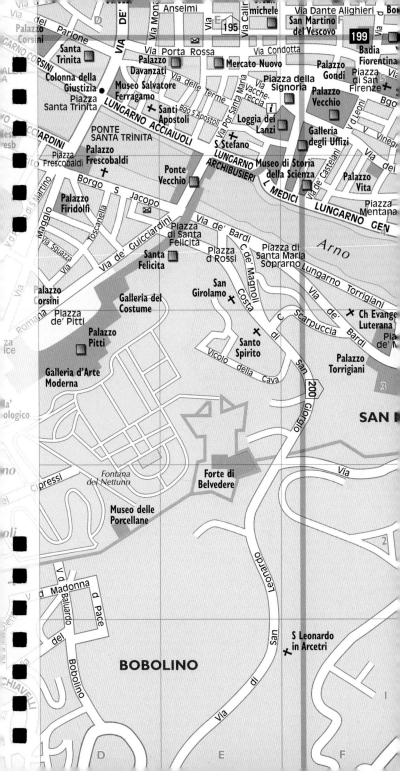

Via Anselmi · michele · Via Dante Alighieri · Bo

Palazzo Corsini

Via del Parione

San Martino del Vescovo

199

VIA DE'

Via Monti

Via E

Via Calir

195

Via Dante Alighieri

Santa Trinita

Via Porta Rossa

Via Condotta

Badia Fiorentina

Piazza di San Firenze

Palazzo Davanzati

Mercato Nuovo

Palazzo Gondi

Colonna della Giustizia

Piazza Santa Trinita

Via delle Terme

Piazza della Signoria

Palazzo Vecchio

Museo Salvatore Ferragamo

Santi Apostoli

Via Por Santa Maria

Via Vacchereccia

i

Galleria degli Uffizi

LUNGARNO ACCIAIUOLI

Bgo S Apostoli

Loggia dei Lanzi

PONTE SANTA TRINITA

S. Stefano

LUNGARNO ARCHIBUSIERI

Museo di Storia della Scienza

Via de' Castellani

Palazzo Vita

Piazza Frescobaldi

Palazzo Frescobaldi

Ponte Vecchio

L. MEDICI

LUNGARNO GEN

Piazza Mentana

Palazzo Firidolfi

Borgo S. Jacopo

Via Toscanella

Piazza di Santa Felicita

Via de' Bardi

Arno

Via Maggio

Via de' Guicciardini

Santa Felicita

Piazza d'Rossi

Piazza di Santa Maria Soprarno

Lungarno Torrigiani

Palazzo Corsini

Galleria del Costume

San Girolamo

C de' Magnoli

Costa

Via de' Bardi

Ch Evange Luterana

Piazza de' M

Piazza de' Pitti

Palazzo Pitti

Vicolo della Cava

Santo Spirito

Scarpuccia

Palazzo Torrigiani

Galleria d'Arte Moderna

Via San Giorgio

200

SAN

Fontana del Nettuno

Forte di Belvedere

Via

Museo delle Porcellane

Via Leonardo

2

V d Madonna

d Pace

del Baluardo

S Leonardo in Arcetri

Via di San

BOBOLINO

Via Bobolino

D

E

F

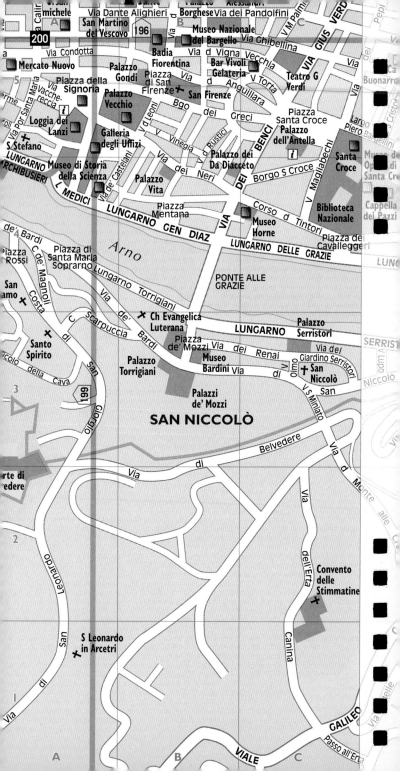

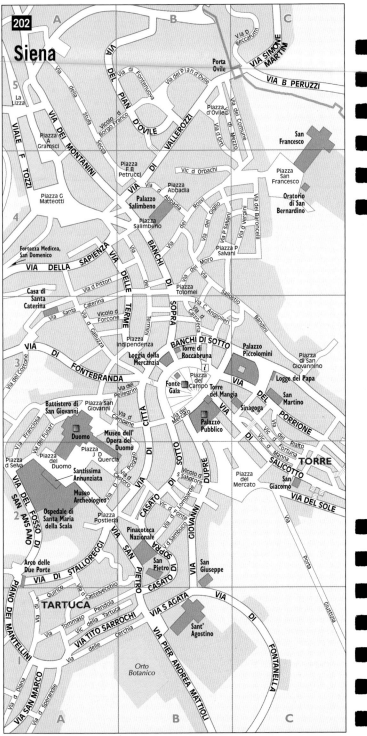

202

Siena

Acknowledgements

The Automobile Association would like to thank the following photographers, companies and picture libraries for their assistance in the preparation of this book.

Abbreviations for the picture credits are as follows – (t) top; (b) bottom; (c) centre; (l) left; (r) right; (AA) AA World Travel Library.

2(i) AA/C Sawyer; 2(ii) AA/T Harris; 2(iii) AA/S McBride; 2(iv) AA/K Paterson; 2v AA/K Paterson; 3(i) © Getty Images/Dorling Kindersley/John Heseltine; 3(ii) AA/T Souter; 3(iii) AA/C Sawyer; 5l AA/C Sawyer; 5bl AA/M Jourdan; 5br AA/S McBride; 6 AA; 7t AA/C Sawyer; 7b AA; 8 Lorenzo de Medici (1449–92) "The Magnificent" (oil on panel), Vasari, Giorgio (1511–74)/Galleria degli Uffizi, Florence, Italy,/The Bridgeman Art Library, 9 AA/C Sawyer; 10 AA/C Sawyer; 10/1 AA/C Sawyer; 11 AA/W Voysey; 13 AA/S McBride; 14 © Ted Spiegel/CORBIS, 15 Rex Features; 16 © David Lees/CORBIS, 17 AA/S McBride; 18 Alinari Archives, Florence/ Reproduced with the permission of Ministero per i Beni e le Attività Culturali; 19 The Trinity, 1427–28 (fresco) (see also 173689-91, 200125-200130), Masaccio, Tommaso (1401–28)/Santa Maria Novella, Florence, Italy,/The Bridgeman Art Library; 20/1bg AA/S McBride; 21tl AA/S McBride; 21tr AA/S McBride; 21bl AA/C Sawyer; 21br Mary Magdalene, c.1455 (polychrome & gilded wood), Donatello, (c.1386–1466) / Museo dell'Opera del Duomo, Florence, Italy,/The Bridgeman Art Library; 22/3 AA/K Paterson; 24 AA/W Voysey; 25l AA/T Harris; 25r AA/W Voysey; 26/7 Alinari Archives, Florence/Reproduced with the permission of Opera di Santa Maria del Fiore; 27 AA/S McBride 28t AA/T Harris; 28b AA; 29 AA; 30/1 AA/S McBride; 32 Fratelli Alinari Museum of the History of Photography-Aranguren Collection, Florence, 33 RCS/Alinari Archives Management, Florence, 34 AA/S McBride; 35l AA/T Harris; 35bl AA/M Jourdan; 35br AA/A Mockford & N Bonetti; 47l AA/S McBride; 47bl Alinari Archives, Florence/Reproduced with the permission of Ministero per i Beni e le Attività Culturali; 47br AA/C Sawyer; 48 AA/S McBride; 49 AA/S McBride; 50t AA/S McBride; 50b AA/S McBride; 51t AA/S McBride; 51b AA/S McBride; 52/3 AA; 54/5 AA/S McBride; 55 AA/T Harris; 56 Alinari Archives, Florence/ Reproduced with the permission of Ministero per i Beni e le Attività Culturali; 57 Alinari Archives, Florence/ Reproduced with the permission of Ministero per i Beni e le Attività Culturali; 58 AA/S McBride; 59t Alinari Archives, Florence/Reproduced with the permission of Ministero per i Beni e le Attività Culturali; 59b AA/T Harris; 60 AA/C Sawyer; 61 © FirstShot/Alamy; 62 © Arte & Immagini srl/CORBIS; 63 AA/S McBride; 64 AA/S McBride; 65 AA/S McBride; 66 © Hubert Stadler/CORBIS; 67 AA/S McBride; 68 AA/S McBride; 68/9 AA/C Sawyer; 70 AA/C Sawyer; 71 AA/C Sawyer; 72t AA/C Sawyer; 72b AA/S McBride; 73 AA/C Sawyer; 74 AA/S McBride; 75 AA/T Harris; 83l AA/K Paterson; 83bl AA/S McBride; 83br AA/T Harris; 85t AA/S McBride; 85b AA/S McBride; 86t AA/S McBride; 86b AA/C Sawyer; 87 AA/S McBride; 88/9 AA/K Paterson; 90 AA/S McBride; 91 AA/S McBride; 92 AA/S McBride; 93t AA/S McBride; 93b AA/S McBride; 94 AA/S McBride; 95 AA/T Harris; 96 AA/T Harris; 97 AA/T Harris; 98 AA/S McBride; 99 AA/S McBride; 100 AA/S McBride; 101 AA/S McBride; 102 AA/J Edmanson; 103 AA/S McBride; 104 AA/S McBride; 105 Tile with a Sunflower Design (pietra dura), /Museo Opificio delle Pietre Dure, Florence, Italy,/The Bridgeman Art Library; 106 AA/C Sawyer; 107 AA/T Harris; 113l AA/K Paterson; 113bl AA/C Sawyer; 113br AA/S McBride; 114t AA/C Sawyer; 114b AA/C Sawyer; 116 AA/S McBride; 117t AA/T Harris; 117b AA/S McBride; 118/9 AA/S McBride; 120 AA/K Paterson; 121 AA/S McBride; 122/3 AA; 123 AA/C Sawyer; 124t AA/T Harris; 124b AA/T Harris; 125 AA/S McBride; 126 AA/T Harris; 127 © Andy Myatt/ Alamy; 128 AA/T Harris; 129 AA/S McBride; 137l © Getty Images/Dorling Kindersley/John Heseltine; 137bl © Getty Images/Dorling Kindersley/Kim Sayer; 137br © Getty Images /Dorling Kindersley/Kim Sayer; 138/9 AA/K Paterson; 140 AA/S McBride; 141t AA/S McBride; 141b AA/S McBride; 142 AA/S McBride; 143 AA/R Ireland; 144/5 AA/S McBride; 145 AA/S McBride; 146 AA/S McBride; 146/7 AA/S McBride; 149 AA/C Sawyer; 150t AA/C Sawyer; 150b AA/B Smith; 151 AA/C Sawyer; 152 AA/S McBride; 153 Fototeca ENIT; 157l AA/T Souter; 157tl AA/K Paterson; 157tr AA/C Sawyer; 158/9 AA/C Sawyer; 160/1 AA/S McBride; 162 AA/C Sawyer; 163 AA/T Harris; 164 © Ted Spiegel/CORBIS;166 AA/S McBride; 167 AA/K Paterson; 168 AA/K Paterson; 169 AA/T Harris; 170t AA/R Ireland; 170b AA/K Paterson; 171 AA/C Sawyer; 172/3t AA/C Sawyer; 173 AA/T Harris; 174 AA/T Harris; 175l AA/C Sawyer; 175bl AA/S McBride; 175br AA/A Mockford & N Bonetti; 176 AA/S McBride; 178 AA/ S McBride; 179 AA/T Harris; 181 AA/K Paterson; 182 AA/T Harris; 183 AA/C Sawyer; 184 AA/C Sawyer; 185l AA/C Sawyer

Every effort has been made to trace the copyright holders, and we apologise in advance for any accidental errors. We would be happy to apply the corrections in the following edition of this publication.

SPIRALGUIDES

Questionnaire

Dear Traveler

Your comments, opinions and recommendations are very important to us. So please help us to improve our travel guides by taking a few minutes to complete this simple questionnaire.

Send to: **Spiral Guides, MailStop 64, 1000 AAA Drive, Heathrow, FL 32746–5063**

Your recommendations...

We always encourage readers' recommendations for restaurants, nightlife or shopping – if your recommendation is added to the next edition of the guide, we will send you a FREE AAA Spiral Guide of your choice. Please state below the establishment name, location and your reasons for recommending it.

_____

_____

_____

_____

_____

Please send me AAA Spiral _____
(see list of titles inside the back cover)

About this guide...

Which title did you buy?

_____ **AAA Spiral**

Where did you buy it? _____

When? m m / y y

Why did you choose a AAA Spiral Guide? _____

_____

_____

_____

Did this guide meet your expectations?

Exceeded ☐   Met all ☐   Met most ☐   Fell below ☐

Please give your reasons _____

_____

_____

_____

continued on next page...

Were there any aspects of this guide that you particularly liked?

Is there anything we could have done better?

About you...

Name (Mr/Mrs/Ms)

Address

Zip

Daytime tel nos.

Which age group are you in?

Under 25 ☐   25–34 ☐   35–44 ☐   45–54 ☐   55–64 ☐   65+ ☐

How many trips do you make a year?

Less than one ☐   One ☐   Two ☐   Three or more ☐

Are you a AAA member? Yes ☐   No ☐

Name of AAA club

About your trip...

When did you book? m m / y y   When did you travel? m m / y y

How long did you stay?

Was it for business or leisure?

Did you buy any other travel guides for your trip?   Yes ☐   No ☐

If yes, which ones?

Thank you for taking the time to complete this questionnaire.